Wed. Final

Monday - 2 copies of 9 measures

Piano   score

meter
terms
tempo
time beating
accent
expression

Chap. 18   examples   p. 226

The Modern Conductor

The Modern Conductor

second edition

A college text on conducting
based on the principles of
DR. NICOLAI MALKO
as set forth in his
The Conductor and His Baton
WILHELM HANSEN MUSIK-FORLAG, COPENHAGEN

Elizabeth A. H. Green

Professor of Music
The University of Michigan
Ann Arbor

PRENTICE-HALL, INC., Englewood Cliffs, New Jersey

Printed in the United States of America

13–590190–1

Library of Congress Catalog Card Number: 69–11341

Current printing (last digit) :

10 9 8 7 6 5 4 3 2

PRENTICE-HALL INTERNATIONAL, INC., London
PRENTICE-HALL OF AUSTRALIA, PTY. LTD., Sydney
PRENTICE-HALL OF CANADA, LTD., Toronto
PRENTICE-HALL OF INDIA PRIVATE LTD., New Delhi
PRENTICE-HALL OF JAPAN, INC., Tokyo

The Art
of Conducting

by EUGENE ORMANDY

Music Director
of the
Philadelphia Orchestra

The art of conducting, one of the most complex and demanding activities in the realm of music, comprises both the visual public performance and the constant application of technique. Although they are inseparable in performance, they can be analyzed in the light of the unique problems which each presents. Similarly, the conductor himself functions on three levels, each dependent upon the other, all culminating in the performance itself.

Personal Study. On the first level, his period of study, the conductor prepares himself both technically and artistically. On this level he must be musician, historian, stylist, orchestrator, and listener. He must study the score so that he "hears" it in his mind. As he does this he evaluates the music and makes a beginning toward balancing the many strands of musical line. He must understand the historical context in which a particular work is conceived, and bring to bear upon the growing interpretive edifice a thorough knowledge of the stylistic requirements inherent in the work. To study such a masterwork as Beethoven's *Eroica* Symphony without some knowledge of the composer's response to the ideals of the French Revolution and Napoleon's unique political position in 1806 is to study music in a vacuum. Needless to say, it was not

Reprinted from *Encyclopedia International* by permission of the publishers, Grolier Incorporated, New York.

created in a vacuum. Among the elements of stylistic validity are tempi and dynamics. A Mozart allegro differs by far from a Tchaikovsky allegro. Similarly, a forte in Haydn is an entirely different matter from a Wagner forte.

A thorough knowledge of the orchestral colors and timbres enables the studying conductor to "hear" the orchestral sound while he studies. When conducting older composers he must sometimes compensate for the technical inadequacies of the times by delicately rewriting certain passages in terms of today's more complete orchestras and more highly skilled players. Present-day performances of such works as the Fifth Symphony of Beethoven, the Great C Major Symphony of Schubert, the symphonies of Schumann, to mention but a few, are rarely given without many instrumental changes. Even so "pure" a conductor as Toscanini did not deny the composer the benefit of today's heightened instrumental resources.

Finally, while he studies, the conductor must "listen" objectively to the work, pacing its progress, spacing its climaxes, deriving a general aural concept of the musical architecture, and evaluating its merit as it will be heard by the public. He must recall Richard Strauss's dictum: "Remember that you are making music not for your own pleasure but for the joy of your listeners."

Rehearsal. The second level upon which the conductor functions is the rehearsal, in which he prepares the orchestra both technically and artistically. It is on this level that he acts as a guide to the orchestra, building up in their minds a concept of the work parallel to his own, for the eventual public performance requires an enlightened and sensitive orchestra playing not "under" a conductor, but rather "with" him.

During the rehearsals he must clarify all problems of metrics and tempi, elucidating his own pacing of the work. He must temper all dynamic markings so that the instrumental "sound" is balanced in all its components. The older composers always wrote the same dynamics vertically for each simultaneous part, straight down the page in their scores. It was only composer-conductors like Mahler or Wagner, who realized the pitfalls of dynamics incautiously marked.

As he rehearses, the conductor, surrounded by the physical sound of the work, checks his own concept of the music, comparing it with the actual music. In those particular instances where the two do not fit, he must alter one or the other. It is essential that the two, the concept and the actuality, run amicably along. In addition, there are instances, such as the lengthy oboe solo in Strauss's *Don Juan*, where the prudent conductor who is fortunate enough to possess a highly sensitive oboe player permits him to "have his head," acting almost as an accompanist rather than a leader.

Performance. It is in performance that the conductor operates upon the highest and most demanding level. Here the work is finished technically; the orchestra is fully prepared for all of its demands; the conductor, his study and preparation behind him, now immerses himself in the music, identifying himself with it both emotionally and mentally. But it is at this crucial time that the most difficult function of the conductor comes into full play. He must, while identifying himself with the music, keep a constant watch upon the progress of the work, allowing a portion of his analytical mind to constantly evaluate the sound and pace of the performance. He must be prepared to instantaneously make any adjustments, large or small, in the actual performance required for the fullest realization of his inner concept. Many factors make this necessary: a different hall, a player's momentary inattention, the effect of several thousand persons upon the acoustics, even the understandable enthusiasm of performance which might affect the tempo. At such a moment the conductor meets his greatest challenge, for the progress of the work must not suffer in the slightest; there must be no detectable "hitch." At such moments the experience of a conductor tells, for the young conductor, new to such emergencies, tends to do one thing at a time. Music does not permit this, for it flows in time, and all adjustments must be superimposed upon the uninterrupted continuum.

In the extent to which he succeeds on any or all of these levels lies the measure of the conductor's merit, both as a musician and as an artist. In his study he can separate the art from the technique, but in performance he must strive fully and constantly for a total artistic experience. Otherwise he can never fulfill his high calling: creating the reality of the work itself.

Preface

The chief purpose of this work is to provide as complete and helpful a volume as possible for the student whose goal is to become a conductor.

The book contains all of the information *necessary* to a student of conducting, and is designed to be used in conjunction with the repertoire preferred by the individual teacher. Section I, "The Manual Technique," may be paralleled with material from Section II, "Score Study." The teacher himself is the best judge of what his students need and when. The book is thoroughly cross-referenced so that chapters are not dependent upon each other as to sequential order.

A workbook is available (*The Modern Conductor, Workbook, 1964*). It is comprised of short excerpts from the symphonic repertoire, to which it applies the techniques of the text. All are full scores and playable.

The Reference Readings at the ends of the chapters serve to expand the student's horizon whether they be read as part of the course or used for further development after graduation. These have been up-dated in this edition.

The edition has profited from the ten years of experience it has provided during its service in university classes in the United States and Canada. Many fine suggestions for its betterment have been incorporated —we hope to the benefit of all concerned.

In these institutions of higher learning, classes have been growing larger and larger. Conducting classes that formerly enrolled fifteen or twenty now find thirty to forty eager students asking for attention. Time, for students and teachers alike, is more than ever at a premium. Many things formerly dealt with in class lectures now have to be read at home by the students in order to free the recitation periods for the actual process of conducting, the practice of the art.

The technical material and physical exercises herein—as with the first edition—are those organized and taught by Nicolai Malko before his death in 1961. Malko had spent a lifetime conducting the great orchestras of Europe and Russia, North and South America, Israel and Japan. He was knighted by the King of Denmark for his contributions to the musical life of that country. He was the Musical Director and resident conductor of the Sydney, Australia, Symphony Orchestra at the time of his death in 1961.

Malko's great methods of teaching were developed when he "had to become conscious of technical means in order to teach." There are people today who believe that the accomplishment that will give him immortality in the history of music will be his research into the manual technique of the conductor and the knowledge he left us concerning the readability of the conductor's gestures.

Malko used to say, "Every precise and easily-understood gesture is clear speaking, but every unnecessary motion is idle chatter." Through his work we now *know* what clear speaking is.

The musician's hands, with or without the baton, are his means of eliciting musical expression from his instrument, whether that instrument be a piano, a violin, or a symphony orchestra. As such, they need "études" for the development of a genuinely skillful technique. *The Modern Conductor* provides those études.

Ivan Galamian, the world-renowned violin teacher, defines technique as "the immediate and precise response of the hands to the directives sent out by the mind." It is true: the conductor's mind must be trained to (as the text says) "work like lightning and a thousand times more continuously." To train the mind during the practice sessions, it must be given "problems to solve." Such problems to challenge the mind and hands are given in the *Exercises for Practice.*

The student should emerge from his course in conducting with a quickened desire to make *music,* with adequate technical equipment to do so, with an imagination that has been challenged musically to its utmost, and with an understanding that when monotony sets in music has arrived at its state of rigor mortis.

Sincere acknowledgement and appreciation are extended to the following:

To Mr. Charles Blackman for the use of the quotation from his book *Behind the Baton;* to the many publishers whose credit lines appear with the quoted musical examples; and to conductor Eugene Ormandy and the Grolier Society for "The Art of Conducting," which introduces the reader to this second edition. I would also like to thank my production editor, Mrs. Raeia Maes of Prentice-Hall, for her invaluable assistance.

Finally, a bravo to the many students who have, with their interest, enthusiasm, and intelligent criticism, helped this work along. And a memorial word of gratitude to Nicolai Malko whose pupils all over the world owe so much to his patience and skill.

Elizabeth A. H. Green

Contents

stepwise approach to the score. Recognizing the
danger signals. Rhythmic difficulties. Problems in
intonation. Ensemble factors. Preparing the conducting. Preparing the players. Reading the stick
for good ensemble. Tuning. Mechanics of rehearsing.

APPENDIXES

The Modern Conductor

Find the melody in every measure.

Richard Wagner

The primary function of the conductor Is communication.

Charles Blackman

So You Want
To Be a Conductor ?

To stand in front of an orchestra, band, or chorus and beat time does not make one a conductor.

But to bring forth thrilling music from a group of singers or players, to inspire them (through one's own personal magnetism) to excel, to train them (through one's own musicianship) to become musicians themselves, personally to feel the power of music so deeply that the audience is lifted to new heights emotionally—or gently persuaded, through music, to forget momentarily the dust of earth and to spend a little time in another world—yes, *this* can be called conducting.

A fine conductor is, first of all, a fine musician. He must be a sincere and inspiring leader. He must have integrity where the music is concerned. He knows his score thoroughly and can convey its meaning to the players through superbly trained hands. He has developed his sense of pitch not only to be able to sing any part of the score, but to be able to hear it in the mind (the inner ear) so loudly that when the actual rendition does not come up to the standard fixed in the musical imagination he will set about attaining that ideal during the rehearsal. He *knows* theory, harmony, counterpoint, musical history, form and analysis. He has reached a professional performance level himself on some one instrument (or with his voice), and he is eternally interested to learn more and more about the problems of each instrument of his ensemble. He has, somewhere along the way, taken a thorough course in orchestration; and all transpositions have become second nature.

The best conductors are innately endowed with musicality—a term that need not be defined because those who have it know what it means and those who do not will never understand it through definition. Finally, any conductor worth his salt must have a mind trained to work as fast as lightning and a thousand times more continuously.

The art of conducting is the highest, most complete synthesis of all facets of the musical activity, and it should be so regarded by anyone dedicating himself to the profession of the baton.

Preliminary Observations

The student of conducting should remember that, whether he is practicing exercises for skill with his hands and baton, or whether he is studying repertoire, *he should constantly carry in his mind a musical sound*. The practicing musician is a merchant in sound. It is his stock in trade. It must be desirable in its own right and pleasing to the audience. Like any other marketable commodity, it must fill a need. The final judge of any musical endeavor is the human ear.

Early in his career, the student will learn that there is *never* enough rehearsal time. It is a most precious commodity and must not be wasted. *The goal for each rehearsal should be set in the conductor's mind before he steps on the podium.* He should have thought through what he wishes to accomplish, and then he should proceed to do it confidently and enthusiastically. Things will not always go as he has planned, but he will not be so inclined to waste his opportunities *if* he has planned.

In the school-music field, a pleasing personality is a great help. In the professional field it will also help provided the young conductor is modest, sincere, and knows his business. If he respects the musicians of the orchestra, he will start out with at least a chance of winning their respect in return.

No conductor can disassociate himself completely from the teaching facet of his trade. Knowing how to teach, how to suggest changes, without prejudicing the members of the ensemble, is a valuable asset.

A conductor does not "conduct" every note of the score-page, even though he must *know* every note. Learning what to conduct is a process of continuous growth. Gradually the score will tell him, beforehand, that this or that is going to cause trouble. Such things as the very first sound at the beginning of the composition, the indicating of cues when the players are depending upon the conductor for them, the cymbal crashes (Heaven help the conductor who forgets to show them!), sudden pianos (*piano subito*), dangerous cut-offs and subsequent entrances, difficult tutti chords that come on irregular beats—for these and similar hazards the conductor *must* be there when he is needed.

As the conductor works with his own organization he will come to know his players individually as musicians. He will find that this one needs to be reminded (by the conductor's gestures) of certain things that transpired during the rehearsal; that that one must be kept under control dynamically;

that this wind-melody-line must be encouraged to project; that the strings will not use the necessary sweep of bow-stroke in certain passages unless the conductor's gestures show that sweep; and that the pianissimo will always be too loud if the conductor does not control his own hands with infinite care. All of this knowledge comes with experience. But during the conductor's student days, he must build the *skill in his gestures* that will give him the control and the interpretative technique he will need as he gains experience.

Above all else every conductor must remember that he is there for the purpose of making music. He makes this music through the medium of his ensemble, the human beings in it. He himself must be inspired by the music; but he must also be able to translate that inspiration into readable signs for the musicians in front of him. He should be dynamically conscious, should have a vital sound-concept of the grandeur of a double-forte or the intensity of the most breath-taking of triple pianos. Every phrase should glow and diminish as the music requires. His gestures should show these things. He must be vital and excited when the music is vital and exciting. He must be able to change instantly to utter calm when the music demands it. Always it is the music and the musical sound that must assume pre-eminence over everything else. After all, that is what made Toscanini Toscanini.

EXERCISES FOR PRACTICE

1. Take with you to a piano any full score. Establish the key of the composition. Then proceed to sing each part, horizontally, skipping octaves as necessary to keep it within your range. Check your pitch often against the piano. If you find that mistakes are creeping in, then sing softly all notes that are skipped between the terminal ends of the intervals. Be sure that you sing them in the given key.

2. Drill your sense of "inner hearing" by playing any note on the piano and then, *without singing that note, imagine* the sound of the next higher half-step and sing *that* pitch. Do the same with the lower half-step; then with whole tones. When the *correct pitch forms in the imagination,* it will come out of your throat. Your vocal chords can produce only what you imagine, nothing else.

3. Further drill your musical imagination by memorizing several lines of one part and then writing them from memory.

RECOMMENDED REFERENCE READINGS (SEE APPENDIX G)

Blackman, Charles, *Behind the Baton*, The first three chapters, pp 17–40. Very readable. The why and wherefore of conducting. The book includes a section written by professional orchestral players.

Davison, Archibald T., *Choral Conducting*, Chapter 1, pp 3–10. A fine set of ideals for the choral conductor.

Munch, Charles, *I Am a Conductor*, Chapter 1, "Prelude on Several Themes." This book tells what it means to be a conductor, professionally.

The
Manual
Technique

2

The Baton

The baton is the conductor's *technical* instrument as distinguished from his *sounding* instrument, the orchestra, chorus, or band.

The technique of conducting is based on the gestures made by the hands and/or baton. The manual technique should be mastered both with and without the baton. Whether or not to use the stick should be the inspiration of the moment, not the result of insecurity in one form or other of the conductorial gestures.

The baton in its present form is the end result of hundreds of years of experimentation in the leading of massed musical performances. The earliest conducting was done with gestures of the hands alone, describing melodic contour, pitches, lengths of notes and phrases. Passing through stages where the leader sat at the organ or piano (often with his figured bass part) and made signs now and then to the singers and players, progressing through the thumping-out of an audible beat, to the silent waving of the concert-master's bow, and finally resulting in the use of the baton and patterned rhythmic designs, conducting has grown into the most refined sign-language we know today. The conductor's slightest gesture has an impact on players that have been trained to watch. And the baton has emerged (especially for the instrumental ensembles) as the *most efficient means of conveying a precise message to the players, if its technique has been mastered*. The tip of the stick gives the clearest possible definition of the exact instant of the beat (the rhythmic pulse called the *takt*), and the cleanest outline of the beat-pattern as such. A skilled baton technique is a great time saver in rehearsals.

When the baton is used, it is of utmost importance that it be held so that the tip is clearly visible to all members of the performing group. There is a current tendency to grasp it so that it points toward the left too much. This handicaps the players on the conductor's right.

It has been said that the conductor and the orchestra meet at the tip of the stick. Therefore the conductor should project his commands to the very point of the baton. This is done through the medium of a flexible wrist. The wrist should respond to the arm with a natural flexibility, and the tip of the baton to the wrist and hand.

Gestures initiated from the elbow and accompanied by an *in*flexible wrist are less musical in appearance. Such gestures are usually larger than necessary and more unwieldy, and the resulting tone from the players is inclined to sound somewhat harsher.

The Exercises for Practice at the end of the chapters should be used after the manner of etudes. They will gradually develop the necessary flexibility if conscientiously practiced. As for practice, no instrument—not even the baton—was ever mastered without it.

Ease with the Baton

The manner in which the baton is held has a great deal to do with the subsequent development of a facile and comfortable technique.

In our era, there has emerged a certain *basic grip* of the hand on the stick which is rather generally accepted, professionally. Pictures of many internationally known conductors show variations of this basic grip in use in their conducting; for example: Carl Ancerl, Sir Thomas Beecham, Wilhelm Furtwängler, Nicolai Malko, Pierre Monteux, Charles Munch, Paul Paray, Herbert von Karajan, Bruno Walter, and George Szell.

The *basic grip* is a fundamental way of holding the baton. As such it should be made the point of departure. This grip, however, is not an eternal attribute. It is often varied slightly during performance in order to show some particular quality dictated by the music itself. Such variations are seen when a number of pictures of any one conductor are studied. The conductor's left hand will usually furnish a clue as to why the change in the basic grip has taken place.

There are several good ways to hold the stick. What must be avoided are the bad ways that render the baton ineffective in its presentations to the players.

We shall examine the positive facets of a good baton hand first, and then take up the negative aspects of the poor grip, together with the reasons why certain things ought to be avoided.

To set the basic grip, the following points should be given careful attention:

1. The stick is held, fundamentally, between the tip of the thumb and the *side* of the index finger. The stick contacts the finger somewhere between the

middle joint of the finger and the nail. Just where the contact is made depends upon the relative length of the individual's thumb and finger. It varies among the great conductors. Experimentation will result in the proper and comfortable adjustment. (Figure 1.)

2. The heel of the stick rests in the palm of the hand, between the center of the palm and the base of the thumb. (Figure 2.) *The ring finger touches the base of the stick lightly and the little finger is curved.* (Figures 3, 4, and 5.)

3. The thumb should preserve a *slight* outward curve (away from the stick) at its knuckle. (Figures 1 and 3.) This relaxes a big muscle in the wrist and lays the foundation for wrist flexibility.

4. For the initial efforts at time-beating with the baton, the palm of the hand should face the floor. (Figure 4.) This permits the hand to move freely in the wrist joint in its most natural manner (i.e., up and down). In performing the time-beating patterns, the student should feel as if he is tapping each beat with the *tip* of the stick.

5. For best results, the tip of the baton should point forward (not toward the left) so that it is easily seen by all members of the ensemble. (Figures 4 and 5.)

The foregoing paragraphs deal with the basic grip. Most conductors, however, have also a second type of grip, the "light" grip. It is shown in Figures 2 and 6. It is fine for the delicate passages in the music, but lacks intensity in the fortes. Therefore both grips should be practiced, as well as the easy sliding of the fingers from one to the other.

Let us now take a look at the things to be avoided.

1. When the first finger rests on top of the stick (Figure 7), a certain stiffness is inclined to transfer itself to the wrist. Often such a placing of the finger will result in a very low wrist that is also completely inflexible. Thereafter, the beat-point, instead of being projected to the tip of the stick actually lies under the wrist itself. In passing, notice the stiffness of the ring and little fingers in Figure 7.

2. When the heel of the stick does not contact the palm of the hand, but is allowed to "float," the tip of the stick becomes too free in its action and loses precision. (Figure 8.)

3. One should guard against letting the heel of the baton slide to a position under the little finger. (Figure 10.) Such a position causes the stick to point far left and presents it, broadside, to the players in the center of the orchestra, when the hand is in its normally flexible position with the palm toward the floor. Moreover, this position often permits the heel of the stick to protrude beyond the palm of the hand (Figure 11) thus resulting in "two conductors." When the tip is downward to the left, the heel is upward to the right. Ragged ensemble is caused by the conductor himself, in this case, but the players are blamed. Figure 12 shows this grip with the thumb upward

Figure 1

Figure 2

Figure 3

Figure 4

Figure 5

Figure 6

Figure 7

Figure 8

Figure 9

Figure 10

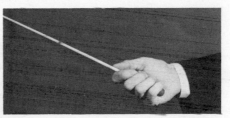

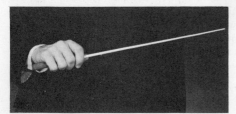

Figure 11

Figure 12

11

and the palm facing left. This will correct the angle of the stick, so that all can see it, but now the wrist cannot bend in its natural direction and cannot effectively deliver the conductor's intentions to the tip of the stick.

4. Lack of curve in the thumb tends to transfer tension to the muscles in the wrist, especially when a stiff, straight thumb applies pressure to the stick. With a curve, the thumb throws no tension into the wrist, regardless of the amount of pressure it exerts. A relaxed muscle is a curved muscle. Straight muscles presuppose tension. Rigid muscles tire very quickly.

The Straight-line Motion in the Baton

The *natural* motions of the arm are all circular in character. Any bending of the elbow causes the fingers to describe a section of a circle. In spite of this, the baton should not be allowed to describe circles around the conductor's body nor should it make arc-like vertical lines in its up-and-down motion, swinging back over the conductor's shoulder or dropping below his music stand. The straight-line motion in the baton depends upon the tempering of the natural, circular motions of the arm. Flexibility in the wrist provides this tempering. The basic "etudes" for this facet of the technique are given at the end of this chapter. They should be practiced regularly throughout the course of study.

EXERCISES FOR PRACTICE: BUILDING WRIST
FLEXIBILITY AND THE STRAIGHT-LINE MOTION IN THE BATON

1. Stand facing a wall and rather close to it. Place the back of the right hand on the wall, fingers hanging downward, Gradually raise the arm to eyebrow level, maintaining the hanging position of the hand and its contact with the wall. At the top of the stroke, flip the hand so that the palm contacts the wall, fingers pointing upward, and bring it back down to waist level, contacting the wall all the way. Practice such an exercise with each hand alone and then with both hands simultaneously. Gradually the hands and arms will acquire the feel of the vertical straight-line motion and wrist flexibility will have begun its development.

2. When the preceding exercise is easy, repeat it with the hands about two inches from the wall, maintaining the straight-line motion throughout.

3. Take the baton in hand using the basic grip. Stand about twenty inches from the wall. Make the vertical motions given above, keeping the tip of the stick equidistant from the wall throughout. Arm moves up and down, wrist bends as necessary. Keep the shoulders relaxed. Do not shrug.

4. Laying aside the baton, stand once more close to the wall. Place the hands in a horizontal position in front of the diaphragm, palms toward the body, right-hand fingertips opposite left wrist. Run the hands outward, right hand to the right, left hand to the left, as far as you comfortably can. Keep the fingers pointing toward each other all the way and the backs of the hands about two inches from the wall.

At the terminal ends of this outward motion, turn the hands so that the palms face the wall and bring the hands back to their position in front of the diaphragm. The fingertips should point *outward* as nearly as possible during this entire return motion. The motion is completed when the wrists cross in front of the body. The hands are then flipped into the original position and the motion repeated from the beginning.

NOTE: The three exercises given above should be practiced daily for a few minutes until mastery of the straight-line motion is achieved. Later these exercises form the basis for a unit on the development of *independence* of action in the two hands. *Take this point seriously.* The foundation must be laid.

5. Practice holding the baton with the basic grip while you are reading a book, or studying. This will help the hand to acquire a feeling of ease and familiarity with the stick. Be sure that you check accurately on the directions as given in the text. It is a waste of time to form an incorrect habit.

6. Practice flicking imaginary drops of water from the tip of the stick. This produces a "crack-the-whip" motion in the wrist which is valuable in showing a clean-cut definition of the beat-point—the size of the flick being tempered down. This motion also is used later on in the performance of the staccato gesture.

7. Study the time-beating patterns for three and four beats per measure. (Figures 19, 20.) Perform them with an easy, natural and free swing in the arm. Check on the appearance of your time-beating by looking in a mirror while you practice. Can the players on your right see the tip of your stick? Does the wrist flex so that the beat-point is clearly defined on each beat? Is the wrist too flexible so that the hand appears floppy? Does the tip of the baton describe a good arc between the beat-points? Judge yourself candidly and practice for perfection.

RECOMMENDED REFERENCE READINGS (SEE APPENDIX G)

Krueger, Karl, *The Way of the Conductor*, Chapter III, pp 25–36, "The Conductor."
Schonberg, Harold C., *The Great Conductors*. This book gives a history of the art of conducting.

3

Time-Beating :
Traditional Patterns
(The Basic Instruction)

Time-beating is chiefly the business of the baton, i.e., of the right hand. Students who are naturally left-handed should be urged to do their time-beating with the right hand, regardless. When time-beating is done with the left hand, all horizontal beats are reversed as to direction: thus the second beat, in 4/4 time for example, would go to the right and the third beat to the left. Naturally, this appears "backward" to the players. Since both hands have to be used eventually, and used independently, it is best, right from the start, to place the time-beating in the right hand.

To give the left-handed student courage, let it be noted here and now that there are famous professional conductors who handle the baton in the normal right-handed manner (and violinists who handle instrument and bow in the normal way) even though they themselves are naturally left-handed. As long as both hands have to be used, independently of each other, it makes little difference which hand does what as far as the ultimate technique is concerned. The "unnatural" hand will have to be developed anyway. It is merely a matter of training and self-discipline.

By following the exercises given herein, left-handed students, as they have progressed through the course have become very successful in right-handed time-beating.

The young conductor will find that his first two problems are starting the sound and stopping the sound. Courage is needed for the former and precision without accent for the latter.

The term "impulse of will" is now introduced. The conductor must *will* certain things to happen. If he can will his hand to make the right gesture, the orchestra will read it correctly. Once his gestures are habitual in describing anything the composer writes, this "impulse of will" transfers his musical ideas in a positive manner to the musicians themselves.

Starting the Sound: The Preparatory Beat

At the beginning of any piece, before the first note is played, the conductor has to signal to his group his forthcoming intentions regarding speed, dynamic and style. This he does in what is called the preparatory beat.

The speed with which this beat is executed shows the coming tempo. It must, therefore, be absolutely accurate rhythmically. The conductor raises his hands for calling the orchestra (and the audience) to attention. Then, before the actual playing of the first note, the baton (or both hands) swings into the preparatory beat (a single beat) which leads directly into the first playing beat. When the baton *starts to move* (in the preparatory gesture), the rhythm of the piece begins. This means, then, that *the preparatory beat must take the time of exactly one beat of the time-beating gestures to follow.*

The size of the preparatory beat usually gears itself to the loudness of the coming dynamic. In general, the larger the preparatory beat, the bigger the sound to follow.

The style of the preparatory beat (legato, staccato, tenuto, light, heavy, sustained, ponderous) should set the mood of the music.

The slant of the preparatory beat should be slightly *upward. Too much downward curve in the preparatory beat can be mistaken by some of the players as a command to play—with unhappy results.* For the exceptions see page 76.

The preparatory beat has the connotation, "Ready!" The following beat should say, in no uncertain terms, "Play!" The beat that gives the command to play should have the downward trajectory.

The preparatory beat may take one of several directions. Samples are shown by the broken lines in Figures 13 and 14.

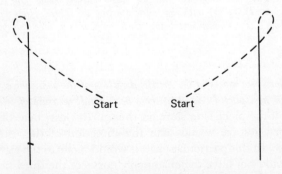

Figure 13. The preparatory gesture for starting on the first beat of the measure.

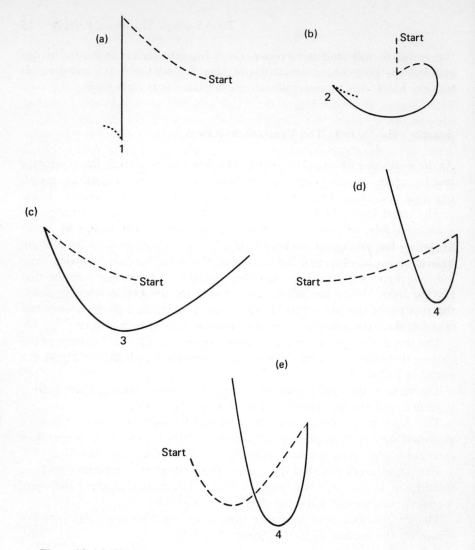

Figure 14. (a) *The preparatory beat with the music starting on the One;* (b) *with the music starting on Two;* (c) *with the music starting on Three;* (d) *with the music starting on Four;* (e) *common error, too much drop in the preparatory beat, causes accidents.*

The preparatory beat moves in the specific direction of the beat which would normally have preceded the first played beat, had there been a full measure of silent beats given. For example, if the piece is to start on the fourth (last) beat of the measure, the preparatory gesture would take the direction of the usual third beat of that measure. In this particular case, it would move to the right and slightly upward. It would not have the customary curve of the third beat, this being replaced with the upward trajectory. See Figure 14.

It is well for the student to practice thinking his rhythm for several measures *before he lifts his hands* to call the orchestra to attention. It is not good to hold the hands ready to start for too long a period before beginning to move. This becomes disconcerting to the winds who have undoubtedly prepared their breath to begin. See that the hands stand still during the "Ready" position. The instant they begin to move, the rhythm of the piece has started.*

Young conductors are often prone to making a long, slow preparatory beat followed by the real tempo of the music. This results in a ragged execution of the music by the ensemble during the first measure or two. *The preparatory beat must be rhythmic.*

Stopping the Sound:
The Gesture for Cutting Off the Sound

Having produced a good "attack" by a proper use of the preparatory beat, the next problem is to be efficient in showing the "release," the cutting off of the sound. The gesture for cutting off is pertinent to phrase endings fol-

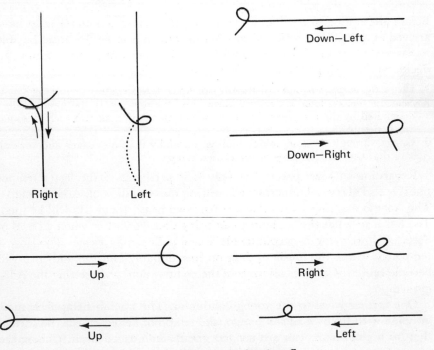

Figure 15. The gesture of cutting-off.

* The novice conductor should form the habit of glancing around quickly at his musicians when he raises his hands to the "Ready" position to make sure that they, too, are prepared to start. His tempo should already be clearly in mind.

lowed by rests, to long tutti notes such as certain fermatas, to complete endings at double bars, and in choral music most importantly to showing the exact articulation of dangerous final consonants.

The cut-off gesture is performed by a looping motion which may take any of the four directions: right, left, up or down. *In choosing the direction for the cut-off, the essential thing is to arrive, at the completion of the motion, at such a position in space that the baton is ready to proceed easily into the next gesture, whatever it may be.* See Figure 15.

Practice the given cut-off shapes with the baton, with the hand alone, with the left hand, and with both hands moving in contrary directions.

Too sharp or too sudden a gesture of cutting off can result in an extra-sudden release of breath from the singers or wind-instrument players and a sudden jerk of the bow among the string players, thus causing an unpleasant accent at the very instant of the cut-off. Listen carefully to your group as you cut off the sound.

Choosing the Tempo

Before attempting to conduct a live group, the young conductor must have arrived at a definite decision as to what his tempo is to be. He must be able to carry that feeling for tempo with him as he approaches the podium. To decide upon a tempo the process is usually as follows:

1. Check the composer's indication: Allegro, Adagio, Moderato.
2. Sing the melody line. Try several variations of tempo within the broad outline designated by the composer. Certainly one of them will make the melody sound "as it should."
3. Glance through the composition, noting especially the faster notes and making sure that they are playable at the chosen tempo.

Regarding this last point: Not only is it pertinent to the faster tempos but it is also of special importance in setting the very difficult Adagio tempo. The Adagio marking means that the "divided beat" (page 31) will be used. Too fast a speed at the beginning can bring disaster with it when a series of notes of short value is encountered; a real gallop may ensue. Too slow a tempo will cause the music to drag on interminably and the audience will become restless. Consider all parts of the composition when setting the Adagio tempo.

One further word to the young conductor. The human being feels most at home with his own *natural* tempo, the tempo of his heartbeat. Be careful that, as a conductor, you are not too greatly influenced by it. Choose the tempo *demanded by the music itself.* The convincing sound of the melody with its figurations and counterpoints should be your cue. Consider also the dynamic in choosing the tempo and let the general style of the piece (heavy, light) aid in the choice.

The Time-Beating Gestures

Three things are important in time-beating: (1) a good sense of rhythm, (2) muscular relaxation that permits the free swinging of the baton arm, and (3) a readable pattern in shaping the beats.

In the initial stages, one should allow his natural sense of rhythm to take over, not trying too hard to be overly technical. For the purposes of our discussion, however, certain things must be mentioned in order that the writing may progress with clarity. For this reason, the following analysis of a time-beating gesture is made at this time, chiefly to set up a usable terminology.

Every time-beating gesture has three parts: the preparation (the motion leading into the beat-point), the beat-point itself (the *ictus*), and the rebound or reflex after the tip of the stick has tapped the beat-point.

THE PREPARATION

Just as the preparatory beat at the beginning of a composition should warn the musicians of what is to follow, so the preparatory part of any time-beating gesture should become a *declaration of intent* on the part of the conductor. This will not have great significance for the student at this time, but as his time-beating becomes habitual and the interpretative or expressive gestures are introduced, the declaration of intent will assume an important place in his work.

THE ICTUS

In beating time it is of great importance that the exact instant of the beat-point be clearly recognizable. This indication of the precise instant of the rhythmic pulse is termed the *ictus* of the beat. The steady reiteration of beat-points we shall call the *takt*.

The precise definition of the ictus by the baton is shown by a very small flicking motion at the lowest point of each beat—the motion suggested in Exercise 6 of the preceding chapter. The motion between ictus points should be well curved. A very slight flick is sufficient for the definition of the ictus. We use also a legato type of beat that does not indicate the beat-point quite so sharply, but smooths it out into a gentle curve (see Figures 19, 19(a); 20, 20(a), pages 26–27.

In time-beating the tip of the baton should have the feel of tapping the beat and then of bouncing away, much as if the ictus were the impulse that the fingers give to a ball in bouncing it; the rebound of the tip, immediately after the ictus, would correspond, then, to the upward flick of the hand after its contact with the ball. After this recoil, the arm and hand swing in an arc-like pattern toward the next ictus point. The student can best clarify this point by glancing again at the diagrams of the beat-patterns for three and four beats per measure. These are found on page 26. Notice the well-curved arc joining one ictus to the next.

THE REFLEX OR REBOUND

The first beat of every measure is the vertical, downward motion directly in front of the conductor, the "down" beat. The exceedingly important rule for the reflex after the down beat is as follows: *for clarity, the rebound must never be more than half the height of this initial down beat*, except in time-beating of 1-to-the-bar. This point is one of the basic features that distinguish a genuine conducting technique from "cheer-leading" tactics. Guard intelligently the height of the rebound after the down beat. It is probably the most important single factor of all in producing true clarity in the time-beating patterns. Practice in front of a mirror.

The vertical motions set the rhythm while the horizontal line becomes the line of sustaining.

Large gestures are pertinent to the slower tempos and the louder dynamics. The faster tempos require smaller gestures. When the gestures become too large they tend to slow down the tempo. Soft passages are usually conducted with small gestures.

CAUTION: Do not reach toward your performers. Stand up straight. Leaning toward the players presents an ungainly appearance to the audience. Feel that you are balanced on the balls of the feet, not the heels.

The Time-Beating Patterns (Traditional)

NOTE: For future ease in searching out needed information, the time-beating gestures are given here in logical sequence according to the number of beats per measure. However, it is strongly recommended that time-beating in THREE and FOUR be studied before going into ONE and TWO. Regarding the diagrams: The preparatory beat at the beginning is shown in broken lines; the main part of the beat itself in solid lines; the rebound or reflex in dotted lines. A free-swinging motion of the arm plus a good natural sense of rhythm will produce all parts of the beat automatically, but the rebound after the down beat should not be allowed to move too high. Control should be superimposed on that reflex right from the start. This is the *beginning* of technical control. Avoid a wholly perpendicular style of conducting. Pay attention to the horizontal line, the line of breadth. It depicts the flow of the music. Loosen up the elbow and let the arm move freely as it swings to the right.

TIME-BEATING IN ONE (DOWN)

The motion of time-beating in 1-to-the-bar is straight down. The distinctive feature of this beat is that *its reflex springs back* immediately *to the starting point*. This is the *only* time-beating pattern where this should occur. See Figure 16 and Example 1.

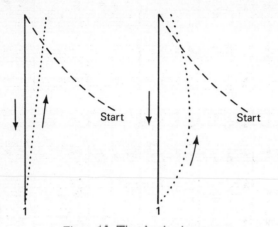

Figure 16. Time-beating in ONE.

1. Franz Joseph Haydn, *Symphony No. 94* (*"Surprise"*) *in G Major*. Third movement, beginning.

(*Continued*)

The conducting of such opening phrases, starting after the beat instead of on the beat, is fully discussed on p. 78.

Note: Minuets in the Haydn symphonies are usually in THREE. However, this one lends itself nicely to time-beating in ONE.

In time-beating of one beat per measure, many young conductors have a tendency to pause momentarily with the stick at the ictus point. This gives the illusion of a rhythmic two-beat pulse, the beat itself moving downward on One while its rebound comes exactly on the "And" of the beat. Since time-beating in ONE, more often than not, concerns itself with triple-meter (3/4, 3/8) in Presto, such an error in the performance of the time-beating can be disastrous. *The single feature which distinguishes time-beating in* ONE *from other types of time-beating is the immediate full-length rebound to the starting point.*

For a more legato character, the rebound in ONE is sometimes curved as shown in Figure 16(b). This curve may go to the right, the left, outward, or inward toward the conductor.

TIME-BEATING IN TWO (DOWN-UP)

For two beats per measure see Figure 17 on the next page.

Very seldom does one see a conductor in school music festival competition use any other style of TWO. This is a most legitimate and acceptable shape for the 2-beats-per-measure, but it has one danger-point. The hazardous factor is that the rebound of One, which swings to the right of the ictus, often rises too high. Beat Two, thereupon, becomes indistinguishable from the down beat, especially for the players sitting at the far right and far left of the conductor. In this type of TWO the upswing to the right should ascend only half as high as the peak of the initial One.

The forms of TWO, shown in Figure 18, are also traditional.

The two-beat patterns are pertinent to music in 2/4 meter, cut time (¢), and the faster 4/8, 5/8, 6/8, and 7/8 rhythms.* One caution is necessary here, however. In music of the earliest classic periods the cut-time signature often appears in Andante and Adagio movements. In such cases it means, very simply, two major pulses per measure. The four-beat pattern, or the divided TWO (Figure 27), would be used, in keeping with the slow character of the music. In modern scores, the cut-time marking means a faster tempo with only *two* beats per measure.

TIME-BEATING IN THREE (DOWN-RIGHT-UP)

This pattern is so standard that it needs no explanation other than to call attention to the fact that the *second beat* of the measure moves to the *right*. See Figure 19, and Example 3, page 26.

There exists, in the French school of conducting, a type of THREE pattern where the second beat moves to the left. When one sees it today, it is usually in the opera pit, and upon special occasions as given on page 44.

The THREE pattern is used in the slower 3/4 time signatures, often in the 9/8, and in the Adagio 3/8 meters when subdivision of the beat is not found to be necessary.

---

* In 5/8 and 7/8, beaten in two beats per measure, one beat is of longer duration (by one eighth note) than the other beat. See page 47, Figure 30.

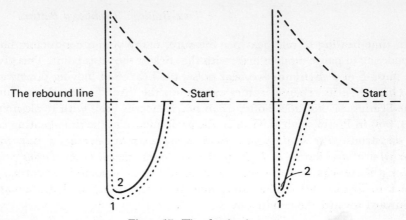

Figure 17. Time-beating in TWO.

2. Haydn, *Symphony No. 94* (*"Surprise"*) *in G Major*. Finale, beginning.

Full score uses: 2 Flutes, 2 Oboes, 2 Horns, 2 Trumpets, Timpani, Strings (all tacet at the beginning.)

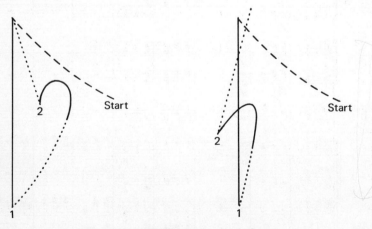

Figure 18. Variations in the shape of TWO.

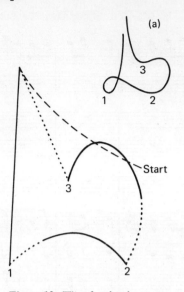

Figure 19. Time-beating in THREE.

3. Haydn, *Symphony No. 101* (*"The Clock"*) *in D Major.* Third movement, beginning.

4. Peter Ilyitch Tchaikowski, March from the *Nutcracker Suite*, beginning (condensed and transposed to C Score).

TIME-BEATING IN FOUR (DOWN-LEFT-RIGHT-UP)

Here again we have a very standard pattern that needs no explanation. Beginning with four beats per measure, the second beat moves to the *left*. See Figure 20, and Example 4.

Figure 20. Time-beating in FOUR.

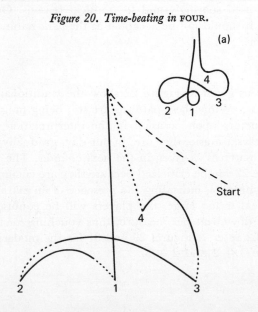

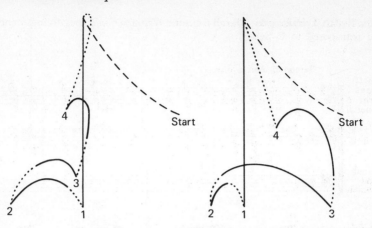

Figure 21. Unbalanced patterns in FOUR.

One word of caution should accompany the time-beating in FOUR. Students are sometimes given to performing this gesture in a lopsided manner as shown in Figure 21.

When the second and third beats of the four are not equally balanced on either side of the vertical line of the down beat, then the four-beat pattern looks a little out of kilter and sometimes even produces a slight rhythmic inaccuracy on the part of the players. It is important to see that the *third beat crosses over to the right of the vertical line of One.* The pattern should appear *balanced.*

We are dealing now with *fundamentals.* The shape being criticized here has its place when used sparingly and for musical reasons. Our point at the moment is that it should not be accepted as the *basic* habit. More of this in the next chapter.

TIME-BEATING IN FIVE

The patterns as given in Figure 22 show the traditional shapes for five beats per measure. While these patterns are still being taught and are used by name conductors upon occasion in the interpretation of Tchaikovski and pre-Tchaikovski music, they are, in our day, gradually being replaced by the modern patterns as given in the next chapter. The patterns as presented in Figure 22 can be criticized because they are encumbered with two downbeats per measure, indicating the presence of an extra bar-line. If the second down-beat is too large, the players will be confused. A true FIVE shows only one downbeat per measure, thus vouching for the unity of the measure. (See Chapter 4, Figures 29 and 31 for the modern FIVES.) Traditional FIVES are 3 + 2 and 2 + 3.

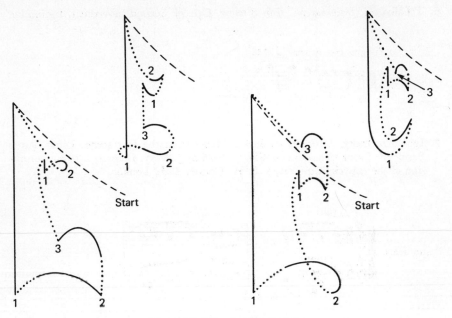

Figure 22. Time-beating in FIVE.

In the execution of these patterns, attention should be paid to the smallness of the gestures used for the second half of each measure—the "plus" part. The gesture for One of the measure should be the large One, while the gesture for One of the "plus" part should be a very small One.

Which pattern is to be used depends entirely upon the composer's written stress or phrasing within the measure. Sometimes one pattern is followed by the other in the very next bar. Typical measures in FIVE are shown below as follows: Example 5: 3 + 2; Example 6: 2 + 3; Example 7: one following the other in consecutive measures.

5. Samuel Barber, *Medea's Meditation and Dance of Vengeance*, Op. 23A (measure 104.)
© 1956 by G Schirmer, Inc. Used by permission.

6. Tchaikovski, *Symphony No. 6 in B minor*, Op. 74. Second movement, beginning.

7. Igor Stravinsky, *L'Histoire du Soldat*. Music from the first scene: Little Tunes Beside the Brook (measures 64–65). © 1924 by J. & W. Chester, Ltd. By permission of the copyright owners, J. & W. Chester Ltd., London.

The conductor should use the correct beat-pattern in each measure, varying the pattern to fit the phrasal emphasis.

Let us reiterate: *the second group of beats in each measure should be smaller and higher in space than the first group, when using these traditional patterns.*

The forms of FIVE, as given in Figure 22, more accurately describe music where three-beat and two-beat measures (or vice versa) alternate than they do the true five-beat measures quoted in Examples 5-7. Example 8 shows the second type of notation.*

8. Stravinsky, *The Rite of Spring*. Evocation of the Ancestors (measures 28–31). © 1921 by Edition Russe de Musique. Copyright assigned to Boosey & Hawkes 1947. Reprinted by permission of Boosey & Hawkes.

* This example serves two purposes: first, to exemplify the type of writing with a five-beat feeling which requires two downbeats within the FIVE structure (one at the beginning of each bar); second, the fast tempo marking which condenses the time-beating into one beat per measure, the value of the quarter note remaining constant throughout.

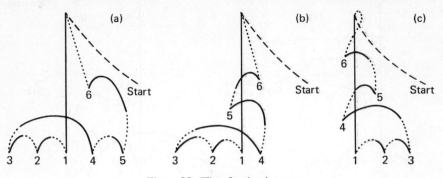

Figure 23. Time-beating in SIX.

TIME-BEATING IN SIX

Three forms of time-beating in SIX are in use today. All are traditional. See Figure 23.

Sometimes the choice of which to use depends upon where the musical interest is located in the ensemble—to the right or to the left of the conductor. Figure 23 (b) would be chosen if the conductor wished to address himself particularly to the musicians seated to his left; Figure 23 (c) for those on his right.

In passing, let us mention that the *modern* FIVES spring from a curtailment of one of the beats of the SIX pattern given under (a) above. Usually either the third or the fifth beat is deleted. See Figure 29 on page 46.

THE "DIVIDED-BEAT" PATTERNS

When it is necessary to show the "And" beats of the measure, we call the pattern a *divided-beat* pattern. In the slow-moving Adagio, which may well incorporate thirty-second notes into its scheme of notation, the "And" beats have to be delineated by the conductor for the sake of good ensemble. To show the "Ands," the conductor simply adds to each principal beat a second smaller beat, moving in the same direction as the main gesture. Notice, however, that the "And" following One goes in a direction opposite to the next main gesture. See Figure 24.

The divided beat is almost always used in Adagio movements. An excellent example for the use of this type of time-beating is to be found in Example 86 on page 144.

Let us pause a moment to compare the true SIX as given in Figure 23(a) with the DIVIDED-THREE shown in Figure 24. The true SIX splits the measure into *two groupings of three beats* (notes) *each*. The DIVIDED-THREE makes *three*

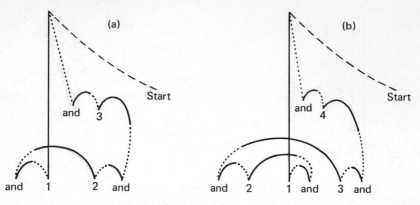

Figure 24. Showing the "And" beat.

groupings of two beats (notes) *each.* It is the differentiation of accent within the measure that dictates the choice of pattern to be used.

Example 9 depicts visibly the two types of accentuation. (This movement, however, is beaten in TWO, due to its fast tempo.) Rhythm only quoted here.

9. Tchaikovski, *Symphony No. 5 in E minor*, Op. 64. First movement (measures 97–100).

Allegro con anima (♩.=104)

TIME-BEATING IN NINE AND TWELVE

When nine and twelve beats are to be shown, the basic THREE and FOUR patterns are used with the addition of *two* small pulses following each of the principal beats. The basic THREE is divided into NINE in Figure 25 (a) while Figure 25 (b) shows the basic FOUR divided into TWELVE. Again the series of small beats following the first beat of the measure proceeds in a direction *opposite* to the next main gesture. The reason for this is that readability of the stick is sacrificed when too many beats advance in one direction. A player, glancing up suddenly, cannot tell which beat is being delineated at the

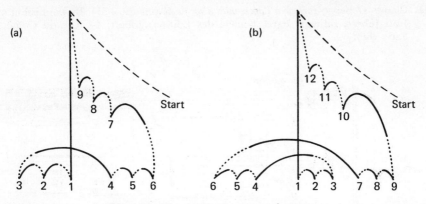

Figure 25. Time-beating in NINE and TWELVE.

moment. Therefore, it is an unwritten law that *not more than three beats should be given in* one *direction*. The added beats should be kept small so that they cannot be confused with the larger principal gesture.

In Moderato and faster tempos, the 12/8 is usually beaten in FOUR. It occurs much more often in this form in the repertoire than it does in the very slow Adagio tempo where the full twelve beats must be shown by the stick. The same thing is largely true of the 9/8—it is more often in THREE than in NINE. The speed indicated by the tempo marking, plus the number of notes crowded into certain beats, is the conductor's cue as to which type of time-beating will best interpret the music to the players. Example 10 shows the full NINE and Example 11 the full TWELVE.

10. Serge Prokofiev, *Symphony No. 5*, Op. 100. Third movement (measure 128). © Copyright 1946 by MCA MUSIC, a division of MCA Inc., New York, New York. Reprinted by permission. All rights reserved.

11. Claude Debussy, *Prélude à l'après-midi d'un faune* (measure 31). By permission of Jean Jobert, Editeur, Paris. Société des Editions Jobert, 44 Rue du Colisée, Paris (8e).

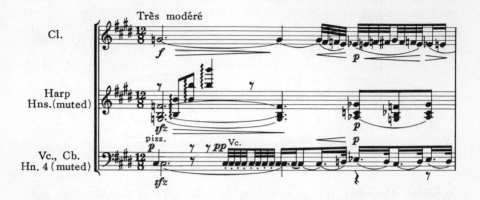

EXERCISES FOR PRACTICE: FACILITY IN TIME-BEATING

1. Practice each of the assigned time-beating patterns until its reiteration has become easy and natural. Look at your motions in the mirror. While the right hand (the baton) is engaged in the time-beating, pay some attention to the left hand. See that it is hanging quietly at the side in a relaxed manner, not jerking sympathetically with the right hand. Then reverse the process, putting the time-beating into the left hand with the right arm hanging freely relaxed. (The purpose of this procedure is to start, right from the outset, to train the two hands in independence.) In placing the time beating in the left hand, the *horizontal* lines are reversed as to direction: The second beat in FOUR would go to the right, the third beat to the left. Apply similar corrections to the other beat patterns.

2. Practice each pattern using several different speeds and setting each new tempo in turn by a rhythmically precise preparatory beat. Then add to this the use of gestures of different sizes. Take a Moderato tempo, time-beating in Four. Begin with very small gestures in the tip of the stick. Use only the wrist for these and keep them about one inch in size. Gradually enlarge them, adding arm to the gestures, until they cover a two-foot square. Pay attention to keeping the takt regular throughout. After reaching the maximum size, gradually close down again until the one-inch gestures are resumed.

NOTE: The beats themselves are not conquered until the student can move easily and smoothly from one type of time-beating to another without hesitation or interruption. Therefore the following series is devised to give drill in this phase of the time-beating. If musical examples are given instead of the form taken here, then the student learns *only* one example—only the one use for the pattern. But by presenting the material in the form chosen here, each exercise will be found to be applicable in many places and for many types of notation. This is exemplified in the musical excerpts of Exercise 3 (a), below. The student, if he wishes, may write examples to go with the other exercises. In any case, he should think a musical sound or phrase for each exercise as he practices it.

3. When the beats are conquered individually as such, then try the following exercises, repeating each many times consecutively with no break between and until the change from one pattern to the next becomes easy and habitual. See that the speed of the takt is a constant throughout at this time. All beats, for the moment, are evenly spaced, regardless of what may be their relationship later on in the repertoire.

    a. Two measures in TWO and one measure in THREE. (Notice that each of the following notations will require *this same type of time-beating*.)

    b. Two measures in FOUR and one measure in THREE.
    c. Two measures in THREE and two measures in TWO.
    d. Two measures in THREE and one measure in FOUR.
    e. One measure in SIX and two measures in THREE. (Remember, the speed of the takt is the same throughout, as 6/8, 3/8, 3/8.)
    f. Two measures in FOUR and one measure in ONE.
    g. Two measures in THREE, one measure in TWO and one measure in ONE.
    h. One measure in NINE and one measure in DIVIDED-FOUR.
    i. Two measures in TWO and one measure in DIVIDED-FOUR.
    j. One measure of very slow 4/4 and two measures of DIVIDED-FOUR, the speed of the *quarter notes* remaining the same throughout.
    k. Two measures of DIVIDED-THREE and one measure of THREE without the division, *quarter notes remaining the same* throughout (3/4 signature).
    l. Two measures of slow 3/4 and one measure of 9/8, the quarter note of the 3/4 having the same length as the three eighths of the NINE. In other words, each beat of the original THREE is subdivided into three parts in the NINE measure.

m. Three measures in ONE and one measure in THREE, the speed of the quarter notes remaining the same. (See the music.)

n. Two measures in FIVE (3 + 2) and one measure in FOUR, the speed of the beat remaining the same throughout.

o. Two measures in THREE and one measure in FIVE (2 + 3). Pay attention to making the +3 of the FIVE in smaller gestures than the two measures in THREE.

p. One measure in a very slow 4/4 and one measure in TWELVE, each beat of the 4/4 being divided into three parts in executing the TWELVE. Pay attention to the direction of the small beats following One.

q. One measure in NINE and two measures in TWELVE, the takt of the eighth note remaining constant throughout.

r. One measure in TWELVE and one measure in DIVIDED-FOUR, the eighth note remaining constant throughout (12/8, 4/4 Adagio).

4. Make up other studies for yourself similar to those above. Think your coming change and execute it right from the mind itself.

5. Now try the following exercises, the takt (speed of the beats) remaining a constant throughout:

Time-beating in:

(a) 4 2 3 1 4 1 2 4 3 2 1 4 2
(b) 4 1 2 1 3 1 2 1 4 2 1 4 3 1 2
(c) 4 1 3 2 4 1 2 4 3 2 4 1 2 1 3
(d) 3 2 4 1 3 1 2 4 2 1 3 2 3 1 4
(e) 3 4 1 2 4 3 1 2 6 1 2 4 2 6 1 3
(f) 6 2 4 2 6 3 1 4 6 2 1 4 3 6 2
(g) 2 1 3 6 4 3 1 6 2 6 4 1 3 6 1

6. Make up your own series similar to the foregoing. When the more difficult beats have been acquired, practice Exercise 7.

7. Try the divided beats as follows (the takt is the eighth note throughout):

Divided 4/4, 9/8, divided 4/4, 12/8, divided 3/4, 9/8, divided 4/4, 6/8, 12/8, divided 3/4, 9/8. See that the small beats go in the correct direction.

RECOMMENDED REFERENCE READINGS (SEE APPENDIX G)

Earhart, Will, *The Eloquent Baton* , Chapters II-V, pp. 4–38, Time beating patterns; and Chapters IX-X, pp 68–84, "Nine, Twelve, Five, and Seven Beats," and "Divided Beats."

Krueger, Karl, *The Way of the Conductor*, Chapter 11, pp 149–172, "The Conductor's Technique."

4

Time-Beating:
Modern Patterns
and Their Variations
(*The Advanced Instruction*)

The modern conductor is not only a skilled technician and an interpretive conductor: he is also a *creative* conductor in his baton work. He realizes that when he beats a number of measures consecutively alike he is in danger of creating monotony and of losing his audience. Changeless repetition, in musical performance as in other phases of our existence, is the soul of monotony. Therefore, the fine conductor plans as much variation in his time-beating as possible, still remaining consistent with the content of the music. The tip of the stick "designs the music." This means that upon occasion the conductor may completely reshape his beat pattern or even omit it entirely, resorting for a few measures to "phrasal conducting" wherein the hands describe the contour of the music without the presence of the time-beating ictus.

While the suggestions in this chapter may serve to extend the horizon a little into the realm of creative conducting, their immediate purpose is to provide an understandable variation in the fundamental time-beating gestures in order to avoid monotony. No pretense is made here to exhaust all possibilities, but it is hoped that the ideas presented may lay a foundation for future creative work which will be both intelligent and logical.

As the young conductor grows in proficiency, he must learn to yield to the music itself—to become flexible rather than stereotyped. *But in so doing he must not become so original that his gestures are meaningless to the performing musi-*

cians. The fundamentals of guarding the height of his rebounds, of showing clearly where a measure begins, and of delivering his messages to the tip of his stick must not be forgotten or carelessly treated.

The Modernization of the Time-Beating

ONE BEAT TO THE BAR: MODERN

One beat to the bar offers little opportunity to be creative or "modern" in approach. Sometimes, however, this beat makes a definite loop or curve on its reflex instead of the straight-up rebound. This curving reflex contributes to a more legato style. The curve may move outward, inward, to the right or to the left. Certain conductors resort, for a few measures at a time, to making a complete circle of the beat in ONE when the phrasal conducting demands either greater continuity of style or an urging ahead of the emotional drive. When the full circle is used, the lowest point becomes the ictus of the beat. Sometimes the circles are performed first to the right and then to the left, thus showing visually the antiphonal character of the instrumentation of two neighboring measures.

In a passage such as the one shown in Example 12, where a heavier accented measure is followed by one of lighter stress, the ictus point is often varied in space, measure by measure [Figure 26(A), page 40].

The odd-numbered measures might show the ictus as at position (a) in Figure 26B while the lighter, even-numbered bars might move the ictus slightly higher up in space as at position (b).

This method of handling gives variety and "spice" to the time-beating, since the baton itself replaces a monotonous reiteration of a perpendicular ONE with a pattern resembling a two-beat measure and showing the contrasting lilt of heavier (odd-numbered) measures against lighter (even-numbered) bars.

This example, then, opens the door to the great variety which may be obtained by the variation of position-in-space for the ictus-point. Any sudden change in the position of the ictus is instantly noticed by the musicians. Many conductors vary their block dynamics by sudden changes from high to low and from low to high positions in the placing of the ictus.

An interesting variation from time-beating in ONE was recently seen in the handling of the 3/4 section of the Finale of Beethoven's Fifth Symphony. The recipe was as follows: seven measures in ONE, followed by phrasal conducting starting at ♩ ♩ ♩ | ♩ . The three notes were treated as an up-beat to the single note of the next measure and the baton took on a FOUR pattern for the next eight measures, *each beat of the* FOUR *signifying one full measure of*

12. Ludwig van Beethoven, *Symphony No. 6 ("Pastorale") in F major,* Op. 68. Third movement (measures 1–2).

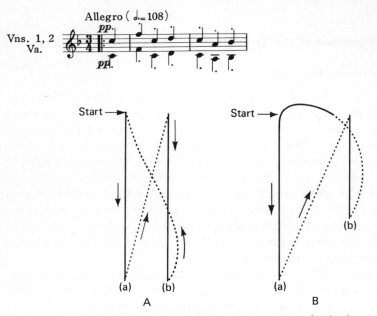

Figure 26. Change in the position of the ictus in time-beating in ONE. *No preparatory beat shown here.*

the written ONE. After the phrasal repetition of these eight measures, the time-beating pattern in ONE was resumed.

TWO BEATS TO THE BAR: MODERN

Far greater variation, in the modern approach, is to be found in the TWO pattern. Figure 27 illustrates what is going on today in this beat. Note that there are four patterns in current use, plus the divided Two. (For the sake of completeness, the traditional pattern is repeated here as (d) of the series.) A four-beat pattern is often substituted for the divided Two. Diagram (e) however shows the usable pattern when it is desirable to preserve the down-on-One up-on-Two appearance. This is helpful when the divided 2/4 is mingled simultaneously with 6/8 in the parts. The musicians with the 6/8 read only the conductor's big down and up beats.

The detailed explanation of the patterns in Figure 27 follows:

(a) *The rigid takt.* One is straight down, Two is straight up. Nothing more is shown. The ictus of One is at the bottom while that of Two is at the top. This type of time-beating is used when there are many rhythms going on

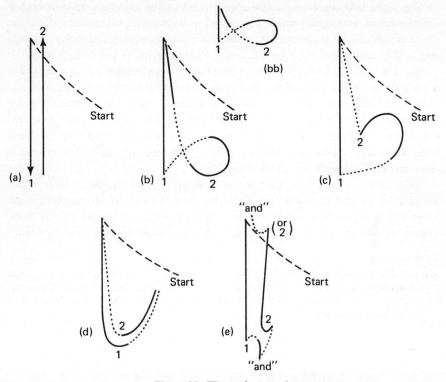

Figure 27. The modern TWO's.

simultaneously in the music, and all that the musicians desire from the conductor is to be shown the most exact definition possible of the takt—and then to be left alone. A passage such as that quoted in Example 13 might very well lend itself to this kind of treatment.

13. Barber, *Medea's Meditation and Dance of Vengeance*. Op. 21 A. Measure 221, rhythm only quoted. © 1956 by G. Schirmer, Inc. Used by permission.

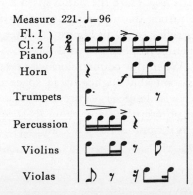

The rigid takt, in TWO, is also much used in the conducting of marches for the band where the musical content is somewhat subordinated to the rhythmic drive. In such cases it assumes a rather staccato character, changing to the traditional TWO for the more melodic trios of the march form.

(b) *The clockwise loop.* The baton rises sharply upward after One and makes a loop outward to the right, coming downward into the ictus of Two. It is as if the rebound after One carried the baton up to the numeral twelve on the face of a clock; the baton traces the clockwise path to the numeral six, where the ictus of Two occurs, and then climbs up ready for the next One. Here again attention must be paid to the rebound after One so that it does not rise too high for good clarity.

This clockwise turn into Two is most valuable when the conductor wishes to carry a phrase into and through the second beat. It is endowed with tremendous sustaining power because of its possible extension of the horizontal line as shown in (bb) of Figure 27. Example 14 is a case in point.

14. Arnold Schoenberg, *Gurrelieder.* Part II (measure 420 of the Alban Berg piano reduction, page 152 of the piano score). © 1912, renewed 1940 by Universal Edition A.G., Vienna. Used by permission of Belmont Music Publishers, Los Angeles, California.

(c) *The counterclockwise loop.* Here the baton spreads its rebound after One outward to the right rather than moving instantly upward. Contrast (c) with the much sharper reflex of (d) in Figure 27. After the outward swing to the right, the baton then moves back toward the down-beat line as it comes into the ictus of Two. When this counterclockwise gesture is used, the ictus for the second beat is somewhat higher up in space than was the ictus of One. This counterclockwise loop serves very well when the phrase ends on Two. To close off the phrase, the hand slows its speed of motion (not the speed of the rhythm) as it approaches Two, and stops still for an instant on Two before continuing.

Example 15 shows an excellent contrast of clockwise and counterclockwise loops. In the third and fourth measures quoted the clockwise loop is practical because the composer so obviously leads the phrase through One into Two. In the last two measures the counterclockwise gesture matches the reverse phrasing, the emphasis on One with the close on Two.

15. Franz Schubert, *Rosamunde*. Overture (measures 340–347).

The counterclockwise loop may also be adapted to the closing of a phrase on the last beat of any measure regardless of the meter. For a complete phrase ending, the beat is brought to a gentle stop on the ictus-point. Great delicacy and charm are possible.

(d) *The traditional* TWO. The traditional TWO depicts well a flowing motion, swinging along with great ease.

Tuxen, before his death the conductor of the Copenhagen (Denmark) State Radio Orchestra, used all four of the TWO patterns very closely juxtaposed in the conducting of a certain Scherzo movement. The music was a 6/8 meter. A staccato section in the rigid takt was followed by the counterclockwise looping for several measures. This gave way to the clockwise gesture which, in turn, was followed by the traditional TWO. Then came a passage similar to that quoted in Example 16, in which the conductor dealt most imaginatively with the rebound after One, changing its height to match the contour of the melody.

16.

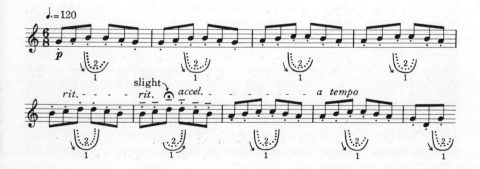

As the melody climbed gradually higher on the second beat the rebound after One likewise gained in height. At the peak of the musical ascent, where a very delicate ritard occurred (measure 6), the reflex in the stick hovered momentarily at a position in space quite startlingly higher than the place where the down-beat began. During the descent of the melody, the rebound of One gradually lost height until the normal relationship of One and Two was re-established. The contour of this time-beating is shown beneath the notes in the musical example.

THREE AND FOUR BEATS TO THE BAR: MODERN

Measures in THREE and FOUR are relatively static so far as modern patterns are concerned. They are standard in shape and direction and relatively unchanged in modern conducting. By this we mean that nothing very universal has emerged in the handling of these beats. The variations which do occur are personal to the individual conductors. However, such time-beating patterns lend themselves easily to the technique of "melding," which may be defined as the combining of two or more time-beating gestures into one longer, sustained gesture of equal duration. The meld will be dealt with in Chapter 18 and need not concern us at this time.

The elongation of the second (or third) beat in FOUR is used. As a *basic* habit, it is not to be condoned. However, as a *modernization* to depict special contours of the melody line, such a variation in size is usable. For example, a measure with a sustained half note, piano, on the first two beats (in FOUR), proceeding to a crescendo on the third and fourth beats, could very well be performed with a small One, Two and a greatly enlarged Three, Four. In this case the out-of-balance contour would be pertinent since it would produce more crescendo from the musicians, with a corresponding heightening of the musical content of the phrase. (Figure 21, page 28.)

An interesting variation in the direction of the second beat in time-beating in THREE was recently used by one of our leading American conductors. He wished to contrast the content of a series of measures where the melodic interest moved, in alternate measures, from the musicians seated at his right to the players on his left. The THREE pattern was beaten in its normal direction (second beat to the right) for the musicians on the right side, but for those on the left the second beat of the THREE was reversed making a down-left-up sequence. This brought with it a fine, flowing interpretation and apparently carried the audience right along with the musicians in following the contour of the music. The pattern might look as shown in Figure 28.

A passage where such treatment would be pertinent is quoted in Example 17. In the first measure the normal shape of the three-beat-pattern would be used, the second beat moving to the right. In the second measure either

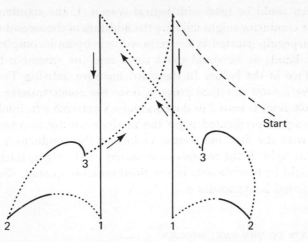

Figure 28. *Reversal of direction in time-beating in* THREE.

17. Johannes Brahms, *Symphony No. 1 in C minor*, Op. 68. Second movement (closing measures).

beat-pattern could be used with logical reason. If the standard beat were chosen, the conductor might indicate the addition of the second violins to the pizzicato arpeggio (started in the cello section) by an inconspicuous motion of the left hand; or he could mold them into the ensemble by using the reversed Two in the baton. In the third measure, moving Two to the left would serve a most practical purpose since the concertmaster (who would play the solo line) is seated to the conductor's extreme left. Such a handling of the passage is predicated upon the modern seating arrangement of the orchestra with the first and second violins on the conductor's left and the cellos on his right. If the seconds were seated on the right, then the reversal of Two would be feasible only in the third measure quoted. (Seating charts are to be found in Appendix A.)

FIVE BEATS TO THE BAR: MODERN

The modern patterns for FIVE are produced in two ways: by deleting one beat from the SIX pattern; and by adding an extra beat to a FOUR pattern. What the choice will be depends upon the composer's phrasal grouping within the measure. Figure 29 deals with the deletion from the SIX pattern.

In (a) the fifth beat of the SIX is missing. In (b), the third beat has been deleted. The former would be used for the 3 + 2 phrasal grouping and the latter for the 2 + 3 arrangement within the measure. *Notice that the long line from left to right, crossing over the down beat shows, by its length, the emphasis of the second phrasal accent within the measure.* It thus replaces the second down-beat of the traditional FIVES. *In all modern 5's and 7's the long lines state the beginning of each accentuation-group within the measure. This is the basic principle.*

Modern FIVES are often accompanied by fast tempo markings which preclude the showing of five pulses by the baton. In such cases the TWO patterns

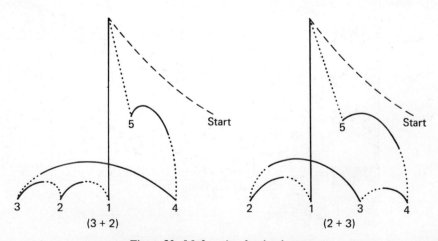

Figure 29. Modern time-beating in FIVE.

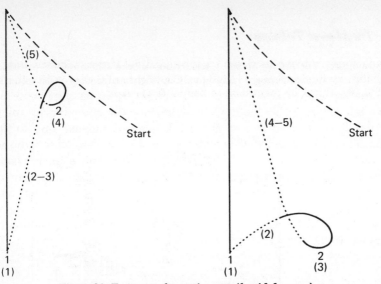

Figure 30. Fast FIVES *beaten in* TWO *(lopsided pattern).*

are adopted and adapted. *While the next several examples are chosen for their clean-cut grouping of various combinations in* FIVE, *the reader will note that some of them will require the 2-beat-per-measure handling.* When this occurs a rhythmically lopsided beat will have to be used, a gesture where one stroke will move slower than the other. In the 3 + 2 grouping, the first stroke will have the longer duration; in 2 + 3, the second stroke. Figure 30 (a) with the high rebound will account for the longer first beat. The longer second beat is shown in (b) since the rebound of One stays low.

Glancing now at Example 18, we see the 2 + 3 grouping.

18. Stravinsky, *The Rite of Spring.* (a) Sacrificial Dance: The Chosen One (measure 155). © 1921 by Edition Russe de Musique. Copyright assigned to Boosey & Hawkes 1947. Reprinted by permission of Boosey & Hawkes.

19. Stravinsky, *The Rite of Spring*. Glorification of the Chosen One (measure 1). © 1921 by Edition Russe de Musique. Copyright assigned to Boosey & Hawkes 1947. Reprinted by permission of Boosey & Hawkes.

Example 19 shows an interesting and controversial excerpt.

Stravinsky's idea here is a 3 + 2 grouping, his double-forte sforzato marking vouching for this phrasing. Figure 30(a) would therefore seem applicable. However, in actual performance, the 2 + 3 grouping in two, Figure 30(b), in which the conductor beats the bass notes of the example, gives a more secure performance by the players. When this solution is used, the second of the two beats is performed as a sudden, forte gesture of syncopation. (See page 68). When beating in two for this example, the ictus of One is followed by a rebound that accounts for One-Two of the five written beats. The second ictus of the measure shows the beginning of Three-Four-Five. The conductor has to think in eighths throughout, keeping them perfectly even, allotting two to the first beat and three to the second.

So much for the combinations of 3's and 2's. The modern composer does not drop the subject here, however. He may write a musical emphasis of 4 + 1, of 1 + 4, or of 1 + 3 + 1. Such phrasal accents were not standard in the traditional fives, but are coming more and more into use in the modern writings. If the composers write them, the conductor has to be able to conduct them.

Let us look at Example 20. Here the interest centers on the important entrances on the second beat of the measure. One could make out a very good case for a change from 3 + 2 time-beating to a 1 + 4 pattern. The latter would come under the heading of an augmented four pattern. These are shown in Figure 31, page 50, and diagram (a) or (aa) would be the form pertinent to our musical example (1 + 4). This would mean a beat-pattern of One followed by a one-two-three-four sequence, the second One being

20. Stravinsky, *The Rite of Spring.* (a) Second part: The Sacrifice (last measure); (b) Games of the Rival Tribes (measure 27). © 1921 by Edition Russe de Musique. Copyright assigned to Boosey & Hawkes 1947. Reprinted by permission of Boosey & Hawkes.

performed in the direction of an "And" of One, and therefore not becoming confusing. Form (aa) shows the dynamic refinement needed in Example 20 (b): a small first beat for the notated rest; a larger second beat for the entrance of the sound.

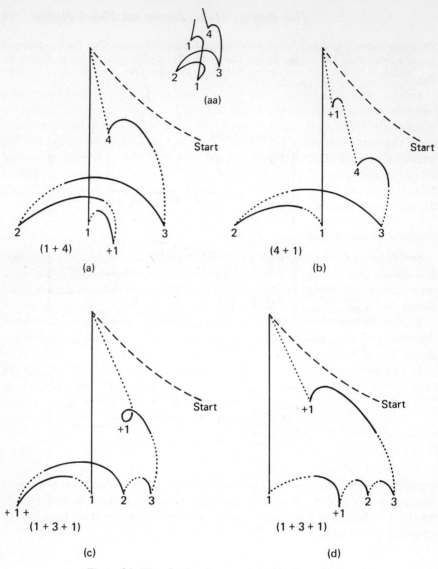

Figure 31. Time-beating in unusual combinations of FIVE.

21. Stravinsky, *The Rite of Spring:* Games of the Rival Tribes (measure 22). © 1921 by Edition Russe de Musique. Copyright assigned to Boosey & Hawkes 1947. Reprinted by permission of Boosey & Hawkes.

If the music read 4 + 1, the normal FOUR would first be performed keeping Four low, followed by an extra added upbeat as shown in Figure 31 (b).

Finally, we come to the 1 + 3 + 1 grouping. (Stravinsky had something like this in mind in Example 21.) In a 1 + 3 + 1 grouping, the conductor is suddenly confronted with the need to *create* a gesture to match the music since there are no *standard* gestures as yet in the instruction books for the handling of such groupings. He would find that his best solution would be either the adaptation of the augmented Four pattern shown in Figure 31 (c), or the creation of a wholly new pattern from a basic THREE. Figure 31 (d) shows the latter solution.

SEVEN BEATS TO THE BAR

Seven beats to the bar may be broken up into the following groupings: 3 + 4, 4 + 3, 2 + 3 + 2, 3 + 2 + 2, 2 + 2 + 3; and certainly someone may write a type of 1 + 4 + 2 in the near future, if it has not already been done.

The SEVENS, in general, spring from the curtailed DIVIDED-FOUR and from the enlarged DIVIDED-THREE. Figure 32 shows the curtailed DIVIDED-FOUR in the 3 + 4 pattern.

In (a) the deletion of the "And" of Two is shown. In (b) the "And" of One is missing. Notice again that the long horizontal gesture from left to

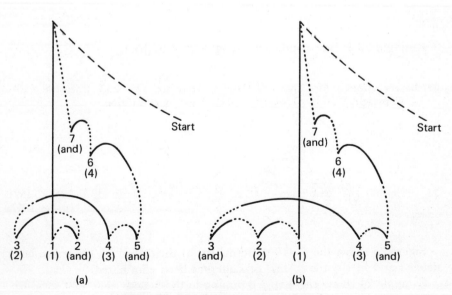

Figure 32. Time-beating in SEVEN: *3 + 4.*

right shows the *beginning of the second rhythmic group*. Notice also that (b) could just as easily be interpreted as a basic DIVIDED-THREE pattern with an extra pulse after the "And" of One.

Examples 22 and 23 show 3 + 4 combinations. The dotted lines are in the scores. In Example 22 the composer says 3 + 2 + 2. Use Figure 32(a).

22. Aaron Copland, *Concerto for Piano and Orchestra*. First movement (measure 4). © 1929 by Boosey & Hawkes, Inc. Renewed 1956. Used by permission.

Example 23 is best conducted using Figure 32(b).

23. Barber, *Medea's Meditation and Dance of Vengeance*, Op. 23A (measure 110). © Copyright 1956 by G. Schirmer, Inc. Used by permission.

Figure 33 shows the 4 + 3 patterns. In (a) the "And" of Three has been deleted and in (b) the "And" of Four has been eliminated.

Example 24 shows the 4 + 3 grouping in the melody line, first measure.

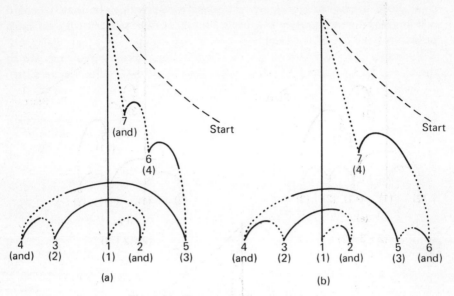

Figure 33. Time-beating in SEVEN: *4 + 3.*

24. Stravinsky, *L'Histoire du soldat.* Music from the second scene (measures 35–37). © 1924 by J. & W. Chester, Ltd. By permission of the copyright owners, J. & W. Chester, Ltd., London.

Remember that whenever the combinations of 3's with 4's occur, the beat is chosen from the deleted DIVIDED-FOUR.

Turning now to the second phase of the time-beating in SEVEN, let us examine the 2 + 3 + 2, the 2 + 2 + 3, and the 3 + 2 + 2. In each of these, one sees *three* groupings instead of two. This suggests the need for *three large basic gestures* which may be divided as necessary for the smaller pulses. Starting with the basic DIVIDED-THREE, an enlargement from six to seven

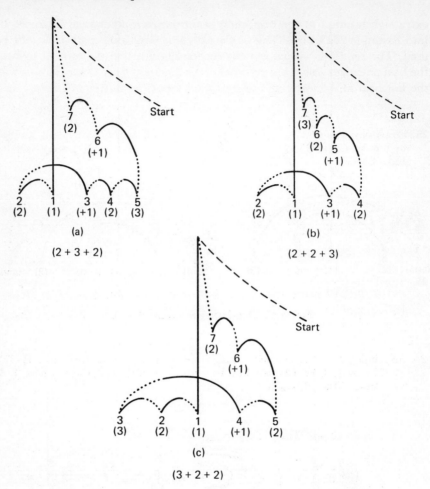

Figure 34. Time-beating in SEVEN *springing from a* THREE *pattern.*

pulses is made by the addition of an extra "And" beat where it is needed. See Figure 34.

In (a) the extra pulse is added after the "And" of the original Two of the pattern. In (b) the extra beat occurs after the "And" of Three, while in (c) the addition is made after the "And" of One. Notice that Figure 34(c) is identical with Figure 32(b).

Example 25 shows an interesting combination of 3 + 2 + 2 (c) followed by 2 + 2 + 3 (b).

SEVENS, like FIVES, can come in fast rhythms, requiring the use of two (3 + 4, etc.) or three (2 + 3 + 2, etc.) lopsided beats. Example 26 is of particular interest when compared with Example 19. In making this comparison the reader will see that Stravinsky has added one extra beat (two extra eighth notes) at the beginning of the measure to change Example 19 into Example 26. In this form of the SEVEN, a fast THREE pattern would be used. The rendition which is most successful with the orchestra is to beat the bass notes showing a big gesture for the Timpani *ff* on Three. In this way the last beat of the measure becomes the longest (by one eighth note).

25. Stravinsky, *Fire-Bird Suite*, Finale (measures 41–42, melody line only). © 1920 by J. & W. Chester, Ltd. By permission of the copyright owners, J. & W. Chester Ltd., London.

*The dotted lines are in the score

26. Stravinsky, *The Rite of Spring*. Glorification of the Chosen One (measure 19) © 1921 by Edition Russe de Musique. Copyright assigned to Boosey & Hawkes 1947. Reprinted by permission of Boosey & Hawkes.

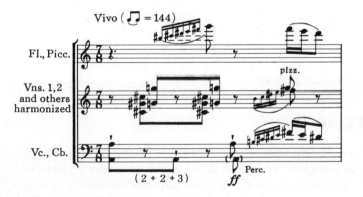

In Example 27, the 2 + 2 + 3 is shown in fast tempo.

27. Stravinsky, *L'Histoire du soldat*. Music from the first scene: Little Tunes beside the Brook (measure 67). © 1924 by J. & W. Chester, Ltd. By permission of the copyright owners, J. & W. Chester, Ltd., London.

ELEVEN BEATS TO THE BAR

In cases where ELEVENS and other odd and rare beats are called for, the basic principle is to use the long gestures where the accents occur, phrasally, and to intersperse these with the short "And" gestures as necessary for the intermediary beats. When the ELEVEN is comprised of eleven equally-accented beats, a simple counting of eleven downbeats is sometimes used. See Example 28.

28. Stravinsky, *The Rite of Spring*. Mysterious Circles of the Adolescents (last measure). © 1921 by Edition Russe de Musique. Copyright assigned to Boosey & Hawkes 1947. Reprinted by permission of Boosey & Hawkes.

Vn. 1 quoted here. Same rhythm in Timp., B. Dr., and all strings

In such a case, the eleventh beat ictus is moved to a place in space different from the ictus points of the other ten beats, thus signifying to the players that the next following beat will be the first beat of the next following measure. The change in placement of the eleventh beat shows the end of the series of eleven downbeats.

The Upward Ictus

Certain conductors use a type of beat in which the playing point, the ictus, comes at the *top* of the reflex. Instead of the feeling in the hand of "bouncing a ball" at the ictus point, the hand acquires the feeling of *tossing* the ball. The instant the ball leaves the hand becomes the instant of the ictus. This phase of the conducting gesture is mentioned here for the sake of completeness, since one does meet it upon occasion and should be able to recognize it when he sees it. It is, however, *not recommended for use as the basic time-beating ictus*. Usually such a beat makes it more difficult for the musicians to acquire a perfect ensemble, and it takes longer to produce the perfection of synchronization. For reference, patterns of the upward ictus are given in Figure 35.

Studies of the conducting gestures of hundreds of directors show that this type of ictus appears more often among conductors of vocal groups than among the leaders of instrumental organizations. Certain vocal conductors feel that such a beat gives "lightness" to the tone and helps to keep the pitch

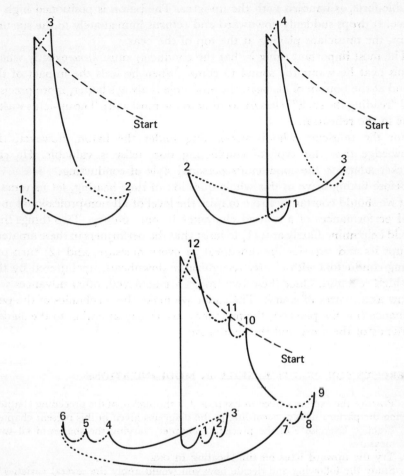

Figure 35. The upward ictus.

from sagging. Let us call attention to the fact that the pronunciation of words helps the synchronization in vocal rhythm. In instrumental music, however, it is difficult to establish easily good rhythmic precision with such a beat. Only much rehearsing makes it a usable device.

While the up-ictus should be avoided as a basic habit, there is one place where it is used to good advantage. This is in the conducting of the One-to-the-bar waltz. It is especially effective in the Strauss waltzes, bringing with it a charming "lilt." In symphonic performances, an occasional beat is performed as an up-ictus, notably in forte brass entrances where the conductor finds that his too-heavy down-ictus forces a bad quality of tone from his musicians. Also, there are instances where the first note of the piece, a double-forte, is handled with the up-ictus. The baton is positioned high in space. It drops suddenly downward and returns immediately to the starting point, the musicians playing at the top of the beat.

The most important thing is that the conductor must *know* exactly where in his beat he wants the sound to come. When he feels the impact of the sound at the bottom of his beat, the ensemble is always better, more precise; and "reading the stick" is less frustrating to the musicians. The up-ictus wastes time in the rehearsal.

For the musician who is performing under the baton, however, the knowledge that this type of conducting does exist is valuable. He can quicker adapt to the conductor's personal style of conducting.

Before taking leave of this whole question of time-beating, let us remark that we should constantly strive to raise the level of all non-professional musical performances of a massed character in our country. Two things that would help immediately are: (1) to insist that the performers in these amateur groups *see* and *recognize* the downbeat in every measure, and (2) turn out young conductors with clearly recognizable downbeats, uncluttered by the too-high rebound. Once these two things are achieved, other advances will follow as a matter of course. The easier we make the mechanics of the performance (for the players), the freer they are to pay attention to the *musical* demands of the score and the conductor.

EXERCISES FOR PRACTICE: SKILL IN MODERNIZATIONS

1. Practice the exercises given in Exercise 3, a through o, of the preceding chapter, varying the pattern designs according to the diagrams given in this present chapter.

2. Practice Exercise 5 of the preceding chapter, varying the shapes of all two-beat measures.

3. Try the upward ictus on time-beating in ONE.

4. Study the following and decide how you would apply the several varieties of TWO to this music:

5. Now try this: use the basic swing to the right throughout the exercise given in No. 4, above, changing to the clockwise loop in measures 2, 5, 6, 10, 12, and 15. Use the counterclockwise loop in measures 13, 14, and 16.

6. Choose the FIVE pattern you believe would be best for each of the following and give your reasons for your choice.

7. What would you do with the following?

8. Choose the correct SEVEN pattern for each of the following:

RECOMMENDED REFERENCE READINGS (SEE APPENDIX G)

Braithwaite, Warwick, *The Conductor's Art*, Chapters II-III, pp 13–21. Excellent exercises for practicing the modern Fives and Sevens are given at the end of each of these chapters.

Grosbayne, Benjamin, *Techniques of Modern Orchestral Conducting*, Chapters V-XI, pp 20–74. These are concerned with time-beating patterns and the reader will find interesting ideas for variety in the gestures.

Malko, Nicolai, *The Conductor and His Baton*, Chapter III, pp 63–108, "Time-beating." The reader will find certain phases of time-beating dealt with which cannot be found in print elsewhere: for example, how to perform the transitions from one type of time-beating to another (pp 95–103).

Scherchen, Hermann, *Handbook of Conducting*. Diagrams showing the up-ictus are scattered throughout pages 151–178.

5

The Expressive Gestures

It has already been stated that every gesture has three parts: the preparation, the ictus, and the rebound or reflex after the ictus. In the following discussion of the expressive gestures, reference will be made to these features.

In general, the expressive gestures may be divided into two categories: the *active* gestures, requiring a response from the players, and the passive gestures, which ask only for silence, no response, from the members of the ensemble. The active gestures are characterized by the presence of much *impulse of will* on the part of the conductor; the passive gestures show a lack of this factor, an expressionless quality that clearly says, "Do not play."

The "impulse of will" is the vital quality in the conductor: upon its strength depend the demanding definition of the rhythmic beat, the decisive leadership of the conductor himself, and the success of the realization of the interpretation, whatever it may be. When the impulse of will is anemic, everything is lost. There is no conducting. When the impulse of will is strong and the technique is weak, the conductor is eternally confronted with feelings of frustration. His muscles tend to tense up and he tries to substitute mental and emotional drive for physical technique. When the impulse of will is strong and the technique is secure, then the ensemble truly has a leader who can unify the musicianship of all into one secure interpretation. Such a conductor has the finely developed technical skill and the confident drive to convey by his gestures exactly what he wants without confusion or misunderstanding on the part of the players, and he appears at ease.

Interpretive technique takes in more than the science of time-beating.

61

By now the student should be handling the standard beats easily and automatically. He is, therefore, ready to add the finesses of the interpretative refinements to his basic time-beating gestures.

Classification of the Expressive Gestures

The following outline will serve to classify and to define the several types of expressive gestures:*

<table>
<tr><td>1. ACTIVE</td><td>2. PASSIVE</td></tr>
<tr><td>Demanding a response from the players:</td><td>Requesting only silence from the players:</td></tr>
<tr><td>Characterized by the presence of "impulse of will"</td><td>Characterized by the lack of "impulse of will"</td></tr>
<tr><td>1. Legato</td><td>1. "Dead" gestures</td></tr>
<tr><td>2. Staccato</td><td>2. Preparatory beats</td></tr>
<tr><td>3. Tenuto</td><td></td></tr>
<tr><td>4. Gesture of Syncopation</td><td></td></tr>
</table>

THE ACTIVE GESTURES

1. *Legato gestures.* The legato gestures are the most common of the expressive gestures. They are those which show the *smooth, flowing connection from ictus to ictus.* They seldom move in straight lines, but instead are curved motions, arc-like in character. The diagrams of the basic time-beating patterns as given in Chapters 3 and 4 show these curves between the beat-points.

The danger in the use of this gesture is that the ictus may become too smooth, lacking sufficient definition of the beat-point. Here the "click" mentioned by Sir Adrian Boult is important. The arm makes much of the motion in the legato gestures but the ictus is defined, in the long motions of the legato, by "give" in the wrist delivering a dip to the tip of the baton.

The legato gesture is, by far, the easiest of the gestures to acquire. It is used wherever the music flows along gracefully without undue stress or effort. This makes it the basic gesture for the time-beating, uncolored by staccato, tenuto, or the gesture of syncopation. The legato gestures lend themselves easily to variation in size. The larger legato gestures are usually associated with the louder passages, although it is possible to perform a large gesture so gently that the texture of the tone may be as fine as a delicate silk veil and correspondingly soft. This is sometimes done.

Gestures for soft passages are, customarily, small. In fact, one can perform a gentle legato in pianissimo with the tip of the stick barely moving, still

---

* This is the *classification* used by Dr. Malko. It appears to be the simplest and most direct route to understanding and proficiency. Malko, Nicolai, *The Conductor and His Baton* (Copenhagen: Wilhelm Hansen, 1950), pp 65, 160–195.

preserving the perfect shape of the time-beating pattern. In this case the arm is static and the motion is centered in the hand through a flexible wrist. Example 29, measure 3.

29. Schubert, *Symphony No. 8* (*"Unfinished"*) *in B minor*, Op. posth. Second movement (measures 92–95).

The "echo" passage, quoted here, is an ideal bit of writing for such a gesture—magnetic in quality, holding the attention of the audience to perfection—but only if the musicians in the ensemble obey the baton in its demand for an exquisitely gentle rendition.

Because of their malleability as to size, the legato gestures are also ideal for describing melodic contour, either of a phrase or of the notes within a single measure. The Haydn Symphony No. 104 in D major ("London") is sometimes conducted with the fourth measure of the introduction as an echo of the third measure.

In the third measure of Example 86, page 144 the third-beat "And" where the first violins enter may be conducted with a larger, but gentle, gesture of the stick. This gives the players the feeling of a longer, but light, bow on this note, thereby producing a delicate emphasis. (Bruno Walter calls such renditions "the accent after the beat.") It is pertinent to the sf in piano passages of a slower nature. Figure 36 on p. 64 shows such a contour in the "And" of the third beat, DIVIDED-FOUR.

The gestures of Figure 36 would all be reduced in size in the performance of the "echo" measure but would retain their *relative variation* in size in the consequent reduction.

The tempo of the music also affects the size of the gestures. In very fast tempos, there is no time for extremely large gestures. Young conductors must be made to realize this, for often in their emotional response to the excitement of the music they "let themselves go" too much, the gestures

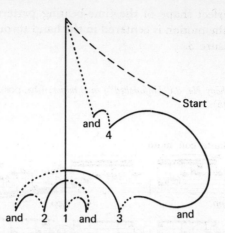

Figure 36. Variation of gesture size in the legato.

become too large and the tempo inevitably slows down. Their first reaction is to blame the musicians for the slowing of the tempo.

When the legato gestures are large, the ictus-point is in danger of losing its definition. However, where the rhythm is safe within itself, this ictus may be purposely smoothed a little, as shown in Figure 37.

Two pages of the *Leonore No. 3 Overture* by Beethoven are given in Example 88 on page 149. In this example, if the conductor is paying attention momentarily to the breadth of the string sound (page 1 of the fragment), the broad legato would be good. If, on the other hand, his attention is directed specifically to the winds, then he must vary his legato so that the second beat of the third and fifth measures will show the requisite staccato.

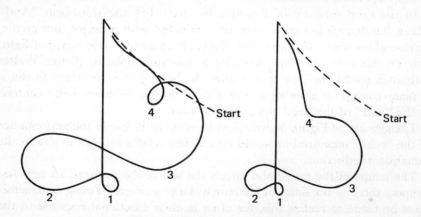

Figure 37. The curved ictus in legato.

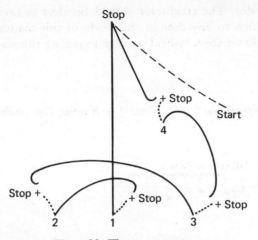

Figure 38. The staccato gesture.

2. *Staccato gestures.* The staccato gestures are characterized by the *momentary stop* of all motion in the stick, hand, arm, *immediately after the reflex*. The student can acquire the feel of this gesture in the wrist if he will practice flicking imaginary drops of water off the end of the baton. The flick is performed by the sudden motion of the hand in the wrist joint, finishing in an abrupt stop, a momentary cessation of all movement. (Look at your hand and arm and see that they do stop.) However, the muscles should not remain rigid during the stop. In slow practice, wait after each flick until you feel the muscles of the arm relax. Figure 38 shows the staccato gesture.

It seems to be much more difficult to hold the baton perfectly still than it is to permit some slight motion to continue somewhere in the arm. Nevertheless, there is no true staccato if motion continues. Correct practice is necessary for good results.

The staccato gestures are used when the composer marks the staccato dot on quarter notes or notes of longer value in tempos other than Adagio, Largo, and Andante. In fast tempos, when the strings have passage work such as continuous sixteenths to be played spiccato, often the conductor will replace staccato gestures with a regular legato, because of the *flow* of the musical figuration. This is most permissible since the spiccato bowing will adequately take care of the staccato dots over the notes without further attention from the conductor. Moreover, the use of the legato gesture in such cases helps the evenness in the iteration of the spiccato sixteenths. (The bowing chart is to be found in Appendix C.)

The staccato gesture should always be used when there is a possibility that the musicians may fail to observe the composer's important staccato dots. It is worthy of special attention that Beethoven was most careful in his use of the staccato dot. The conductor should be alert to notice and to give respectful attention to any dots in the works of this master.

In Example 30 we see a typical passage requiring the staccato gesture in the baton.

30. Schubert, *Symphony No. 8 ("Unfinished") in B minor*, Op. posth. First movement (measure 77).

A type of heavy staccato gesture is sometimes used to indicate accentuation of certain notes in the score. Such a gesture could, if desired, be used on the second page of the *Leonore No. 3 Overture* (page 150) to bring clean articulation and precise ensemble on the first note of each slur throughout the page.

Another excellent place for the heavy staccato is shown in Example 31.

31. Schubert, *Rosamunde*. Overture (Allegro vivace, measure 25).

3. *Tenuto gestures.* These gestures might also be called the *very heavy legato* gestures. They signify great cohesion in the musical line. The hands, in executing these gestures, feel as if they were pulling on tough rubber, trying to stretch it.

The chief characteristic of the tenuto gesture is that the tip of the stick lags behind the wrist and hand. The illusion is built that the tip is very heavy.

This weight in the tip of the stick is the feature which distinguishes the tenuto gesture from the legato. In the tenuto, the tip of the stick is usually *below* the wrist in all vertical gestures moving upward, and lags behind the wrist in the horizontal gestures. In the legato gestures, the tip is, for the most part, *above* the height of the wrist.

The tenuto gesture might further be characterized as the exaggerated "paint brush" stroke, the wrist going first. On the reflex, the wrist appears to be lifting a very heavy hand and stick. As the wrist pulls upward, the tip of the stick falls below the fingers holding it. In appearance, the result is a line of great tenuousness, closely allied to the corresponding musical line.

The motion in tenuto is much more controlled, from one ictus to the next, than it is in the legato gestures. The hand gradually acquires the feeling of covering a shorter distance in a heavier, slower, fashion, taking just as long to do so.

The gesture tenuto is used whenever the composer writes *"ten."* over any note, oftentimes where the wind player would use the "du" tonguing, where the legato-articulated slur occurs in string music (written with a line over each note plus a slur, *louré* bowing), and wherever the sustaining power of the tone is of vital importance. See Example 32, second and fourth measures, second beat.

32. Haydn, *Symphony No. 94* (*"Surprise"*) *in G major.* Second movement (measures 1–4)

In Example 33, the pianissimo might start with legato gestures, move into a soft tenuto in the second and third measures and return to the legato as the third measure goes into the fourth. Such conducting would help the players to feel the legato line and to sustain adequately the last note of the first slur, so that this note would not be clipped in execution. In performing the given gestures, the conductor must guard his tempo.

33. Schubert, *Symphony No. 8* (*"Unfinished"*) *in B minor*, Op. posth. First movement (measures 352–355).

In the continuous tenuto the tip of the stick should consciously "place" each beat-point and then sustain.

There is also a second way of performing the tenuto gesture. The hand bends upward from the wrist and pushes outward with the lower palm stating exactly the length of the note. This is invaluable as a replacement for the cut-off on soft endings. At the end of the gesture the hand retracts instantly. The conductor "stops conducting." The sudden retraction acts as a cut-off. See the last quarter-note, Example 34.

34. Schubert, *Symphony No. 8* (*"Unfinished"*) *in B minor*, Op. posth. First movement (last two measures).

4. *The gesture of syncopation.* The terminology for this gesture is not ideal. In practice, it is the gesture which the conductor uses when he wishes to control an entrance coming *after the beat*. Thus, it should rightly be called the "gesture for entrances after the beat." However, that is a long and unwieldy terminology. So, for brevity, we call it the "gesture of syncopation," G.O.S. for short.

When the musicians have to play after a beat instead of on the beat, the greatest help the conductor can give is to show suddenly and most precisely just where the beat *is*.

This gesture is pertinent to such places as the second beats of measures 1, 2, 3, 5, and 6 of the *Russian Easter Overture* as shown in Example 91 on page 154. The rhythm alone is quoted here in Example 35.

35. Nicolai Rimsky-Korsakoff, *Russian Easter Overture*, Op. 36 (Allegro agitato, measures 58–63).

Allegro agitato

Brasses,
Bns., Timp.,
Va., Vc., Cb.

The use of the gesture of syncopation on the second beat of the measure in Example 35 is a necessity if the winds are to feel comfortable with their afterbeat notes. Their ability to play securely together in such a passage depends greatly upon the conductor's technical accuracy in the execution of the gesture of syncopation. (Note that in the full score, Example 91, measure 4 would be conducted with a simple legato beat, since it presents no rhythmic problems, owing to the rest in the wind parts.) For further emphasis on the importance of giving special attention to such dangerous places as this, let it be stated that the only time this author can remember hearing a professional wind section in one of the world's great orchestras sound insecure in performance was once when their conductor neglected them in a similar passage (Example 39). He simply beat time and left the winds to their own devices. They sounded less than happy in their rendition of the music at that moment.

The gesture of syncopation is one of the more difficult gestures to acquire. Patience will be needed, first for the initial steps in performing the gesture and later on in the development of the precise timing of the gesture for its use in various tempos. But it is worth everything it costs to perfect it. It is the one gesture that will handle hundreds of dangerous places in the music where *no other gesture will be adequate*.

The gesture of syncopation is unique in its performance in that it has *no preparatory motion*. Or, one might say that *its preparation is a dead stop*. See Figure 39, page 70.

To perform it, the hand stops completely on the beat preceding and performs the sudden motion of the gesture of syncopation *exactly on the takt of the beat requiring the after-beat response* from the players.

Applying this to Example 35, the baton would stop dead on the ictus of One and stand perfectly still. It would remain motionless until the exact

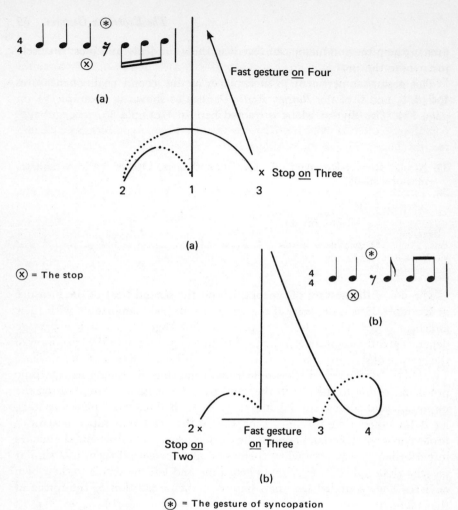

Figure 39. The gesture of syncopation for entrances after the beat.

instant when the ictus (takt) of Two would occur. At the rhythmic pulse of Two, the baton would move *suddenly* upward (direction of the second beat of the measure in cut time) showing precisely where the beat *was*. Psychologically, since the players were not warned by a preparatory gesture that the beat was about to come, they could not possibly play on the beat. It was seen too late. They play, therefore, just after the beat. This sudden and clean-cut definition of the exact beat-point makes playing after it easy for the members of the ensemble. Needless to say, perfect timing and perfect rhythm are the essential ingredients of this beat.

This gesture needs practice and poise. It takes a perfect control of the hand, for the slightest motion *before* the beat-point (ictus) spoils the effectiveness of the gesture. It is one of the most useful of gestures when mastered, since it controls not only entrances after the beat, but also accents after the beat. For producing accents after the beat, use the gesture of syncopation on the beat.

In Example 36, the baton stops on Two and makes the gesture of syncopation on the takt of Three. The stop, here, on Two also produces a cleaner rest on Three. Figure 39(b) shows such a procedure.

36. Tchaikovski, *Romeo and Juliet Overture-Fantasia* (Double bar, Allegro giusto, measure 111).

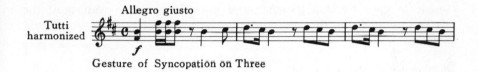

Gesture of Syncopation on Three

In Example 37 the hand stops at the ictus of One and waits until the instant of the takt of Two, then it moves very suddenly upward bringing in its wake the forte syncope after the second beat.

37. Rimsky-Korsakoff, *Russian Easter Overture*, Op. 36. (Allegro agitato, measures 7–10).

The gesture of syncopation can be timed in such a way that the group will respond exactly in the right place within the beat. A very quick, sudden motion of the stick, precisely on the ictus-point will bring an immediate response from the players, especially if it is accompanied by much impulse of will. It is almost as if the conductor's gesture startled them into playing before they could think. A delayed ictus or delayed takt with a sudden motion will place the reaction of the group somewhat later in the beat. (This is of particular value when the conductor wishes to obtain a precise sixteenth note entrance instead of an eighth-note entrance before the next regular beat.)

In slower tempos, a leisurely push forward with the heel of the hand (the lower palm) starting after a stop and exactly on the takt, will produce the desired entrance on the second half of the slow beat.

In Example 38 the use of the slower gesture of syncopation is illustrated. The *Andante non troppo* marking would preclude the use of the faster variety of this gesture. Regardless of whether the motion is to be fast or slow, one must remember that the success of the gesture of syncopation depends upon the complete stopping of motion before the gesture itself is performed and that the motion must not start until the exact moment of the takt. The young conductor must develop patience and poise in order to wait until the precise instant of the rhythmic pulse before moving his hand.

38. Tchaikovski, *Romeo and Juliet Overture-Fantasia* (measure 40).

Tutti, rests.
Vn. 1
Va., octave lower
Vc., 2 octaves lower

Andante non tanto quasi moderato

Let us now analyze a complete passage, as given in Example 39. The quoted rhythm is a series of forte chords performed by tutti winds, timpani and cymbals against a steady flow of unslurred sixteenths in the strings. The bass viols join the winds on the third measure.

39. Tchaikovski, *Romeo and Juliet Overture-Fantasia* (measures 142–146) (rhythm only).

Winds, tutti
Timp.,
Cym.

Allegro giusto

In conducting this passage, the violins are ignored, since there are no rhythmic problems in the string parts. The conductor concentrates his attention on helping the instruments who are playing the dangerous rhythm quoted. When a note comes after a beat, the gesture of syncopation is performed *on that beat.* But when a note comes exactly *on* the beat, then the conductor must make a preparatory gesture before that beat, leading into the beat itself. A complete analysis is as follows: in the first measure, prepare Four; measure 2, use a gesture of syncopation on One and prepare Four;

measure 3, prepare Two and use the gesture of syncopation for Three; measure 4, gesture of syncopation on One followed instantly by Two, then prepare Four; last measure, gesture of syncopation on One and prepare Three. The tutti rests are the smallest of "dead" gestures. (See the discussion of these gestures on pages 73-75 in this chapter.)

This example definitely belongs to the category of advanced conducting. The quoting of such an example at this time is not intended to be a challenge. It is inserted only for the purpose of aiding the understanding. When the skill has arrived to handle it well, the conductor will find that it is possible to produce a perfect rendition of the rhythm of the passage from unskilled players who have no music in front of them. But the conductorial technique must be perfect to do so.

THE PASSIVE GESTURES

1. *"Dead" gestures.* The "dead" gestures are those that are used when the conductor wishes to show the passing of rests (silent beats) or the presence of any single tutti rest. See the tutti rests at the beginning of the second measure of Example 40.

40. Wolfgang Amadeus Mozart, *Così fan tutte.* Overture (measures 11–12).

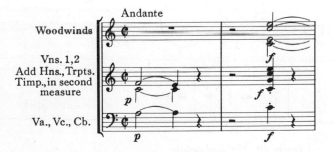

The connotation of this dead gesture is, "Do not play. Be patient and I shall show you when." It must be lacking in impulse of will in order that no one shall respond actively to it.

To perform the dead gesture, the conductor shows *only* the *direction* of the beats by absolutely expressionless straight-line motion in the baton. The gestures are *very small* and no ictus is defined as such in the beat-pattern. On page 74, Figure 40 (a) shows four beats of "dead" gesture; (b) One-Two as playing gestures, Three-Four "dead;" (c) shows One-Two-Three "dead," then a preparatory loop warns that Four will be "active," requiring an entrance into the music.

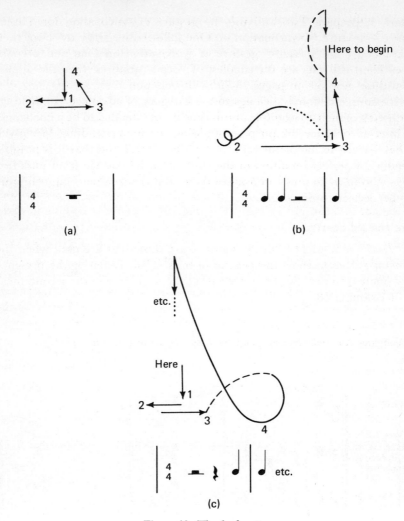

Figure 40. The dead gesture.

Any slight bouncing or curving of the line from ictus to ictus will show impulse of will, or "personality," in the beat and will usually cause some player in the ensemble to respond to it by executing a note. In performing the dead gesture, the conductor's hand should become completely devoid of expression, as if he had disowned it. The straight-line motion shows the passing of the beats in accordance with the takt, but it must show no rhythmic content or feeling in its motions in doing so.

When using this gesture to show the passing of several full measures of tutti rests (such as those which occur when the orchestra is accompanying a soloist) only the first beat of each measure need be indicated. To perform this downbeat as a dead gesture, the wrist permits the hand to drop downward and return with no motion of the arm whatsoever. Such a single, downbeat, dead gesture is also used to show the measure marked Grand Pause (G.P.). In addition to the motion just described, the dead gesture may also be performed by the entire lower arm, moving from the elbow. In this case the wrist should be inflexible.

When tutti rests occur within a measure, they are generally beaten on the takt, but this is not invariably true. In recitatives very often the outline of the several beats of tutti rest is made quickly and not in rhythmic accordance with the takt. The baton stops its motion, thereafter, in a position of readiness for the next playing gesture. As that beat arrives, a preparatory loop is made into the gesture itself. The position of readiness is about in space where the rebound of the last silent beat would normally be if the whole measure were beaten strictly in time. (See Chapter 8, page 107, for the conducting of the recitative.)

In closing chords, forte, interspersed with rests the rests are often not indicated by the baton. Only the chords themselves are conducted. The *timing* of the rests, however, should be exact. A dead gesture One must show the silent measure (**Example 41**).

41. Beethoven, *Symphony No. 5 in C minor*, Op. 67. Finale (last seven measures).

2. *Preparatory beats.* Since the preparatory beat requires no sound from the ensemble it can be classified under the heading of the passive gestures. Therefore, at this time it is good to make a forward step in the refining of the preparatory beat. This beat should attempt to show, in addition to the coming rhythm, also the style and dynamic of what is to follow. The preparatory beat can acquire the several styles listed under the active gestures without losing its passive, "Don't play" character.

The preparatory beat after a fermata, a completely silent measure, or a sustained whole note, is similar in technique to that at the beginning of a piece. It should set the rhythm, dynamic, and style. (The complete discussion of the fermata comes in Chapter 7.)

When the first beat of the measure, at the beginning of a piece, is a rest, the musicians entering on Two, then a very small dead-gesture down-beat is shown, followed by a good preparatory loop into Two. In time-beating in 1-to-the bar this downward preparatory beat (One) shows one full measure of the music. In cases where the score calls for time-beating in One with an entrance after One but before the downbeat of the next measure, then this initial One may be performed as an upward gesture, as stated by Malko.

It has been mentioned that the preparatory beat must be exactly rhythmic when it is to be followed by rhythmic playing. An exception to the rhythmic performance of the preparatory beat may be made when the first measure is comprised of a tutti whole note, or the first sound is a fermata. A sustained tone is rhythmically static. Therefore, the preparatory beat need not necessarily be of a rhythmic character. The gesture following the fermata or the gesture made on the last beat of the sustained tone *must* be rhythmic, however, for it becomes the gesture that sets the pace for what is to follow. See Examples 42 and 43.

42. Beethoven, *Egmont*, Op. 84. Overture (measures 1–2).

43. Beethoven, *Coriolanus Overture*, Op. 62 (measures 1–3).

In the event that the initial sustained tone is a double-forte, a "breathing" gesture may be used to precede the unrhythmic preparatory beat. The purpose of this gesture is to give the players adequate time to set breath and embouchure before the loud attack. The breathing gesture is executed as follows: the conductor raises his hands to call the musicians to attention.

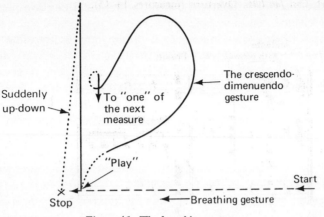

Figure 41. The breathing gesture.

The baton is somewhat to the right side. As the baton makes a definite horizontal motion from right to center front the wind players take the breath. The baton stops still for the barest instant, center front, then rises suddenly and descends immediately and forcefully into One bringing the double-forte attack with it. The conductor will do well to take a breath himself as he executes the breathing gesture. He will quickly acquire the correct timing for this sequence by so doing. Figure 41 depicts these gestures.

Usually a preparatory beat takes the time of one written beat. However, in very slow tempos, the half-beat may be sufficient. This is especially true where the divided beat is used. For an entrance coinciding with a principal beat, the small preceding half-beat could serve as the preparatory beat.

In music where the first played beat is divided into three or more notes, the preparatory beat should be legato, regardless of the ensuing style of the piece. Unless the legato preparatory is used in such cases, the players are not likely to perform with perfect ensemble on those first three or four notes. A *staccato* preparatory beat cannot be efficiently divided into more than two parts, on the first beat, by a large number of players. It is the *line* of the legato motion in the preparatory beat that is unconsciously divided into the requisite number of parts. A baton that is standing still following a staccato gesture of preparation does not show this necessary line.

In Example 44, the baton has to prepare the coming Presto by a legato gesture after the ictus of Four on the last beat of the slow introduction. This legato gesture must set the tempo for the Presto. But if, in so doing, it fails in its legato character, the conductor will get some raggedness in the execution of the first beat of repeated eighths in the first violins. Furthermore, since these players enter after an eighth rest, the conductor will do well to look sharply to the ictus of his first beat for that measure.

44. Mozart, *Così fan tutte*. Overture (measures 14–15).

When the music starts *after* a beat rather than on it, either at the beginning of the piece or after a fermata, there is a little trick which is of excellent worth. Let us examine the two measures shown in Example 45.

45. Carl Maria von Weber, *Oberon*. Overture (measures 22–23).

The musicians have to begin playing in a new tempo on the end of a beat which is preceded only by sustained silence. Showing only the beat on which they enter is highly dangerous. It is impossible to divide anything into equal parts before one knows what the unit is in its totality. To insure excellent rendition of the opening notes of the Allegro, the conductor may resort to the following trick: a small flick of the *left hand* (without any preparatory beat before it) is made in order to show where the third beat of the measure would have occurred *in the allegro tempo*. This is followed, rhythmically, by a gesture of syncopation in the baton on the fourth beat, the entrance beat. The left-hand flick, together with the cleancut gesture of syncopation in the baton, states precisely the duration of the beat in the allegro tempo, which is thus definitely set so that the musicians can proceed securely. Caution: the baton hand has to stand perfectly still during the flick of the left hand. This will need practice and careful attention for a while. If the baton moves during the flick, the entrance will probably be ragged. (Remember the directions for the execution of the gesture of syncopation. It is preceded by a stop in the stick.)

The last aspect of the preparatory beat has to do with entrances where the instruments playing have to execute a very short note (or a grace note) followed immediately by a long note (or fermata). Conducting the very short note as such often causes more difficulty than disregarding it in the conductorial gestures. It is usually safe to arrange beforehand with the players that the extremely short note is to synchronze with the following principal time-beating gesture, rather than to be treated as a special adjunct of the preparatory beat.

ENDING THE PIECE

The orchestral music of Mozart and Beethoven often ends with several loud, tutti chords. These, in general, are played *a tempo,* and only the beats on which the chords occur are conducted. Often such chords are indicated entirely with down-beats. Typical instances are seen in Examples 46 below and 41 on page 75.

46. Mozart, *Le Nozze di Figaro.* Overture (last four measures).

Some pieces end with a rush of time-beating right up to the last note and that note is performed as a cut-off.

A final fermata, or a concluding whole note, can do one of several things. It can sustain full force in forte and cut. It can build to a louder and louder climax. It can diminuendo and rebuild. Or it can diminuendo completely into silence. An upward gesture of support in the left hand is good if the full force is wanted. This will be followed by a cut-off. If the note starts a little softer and builds more and more into the forte, then upward gestures of both hands, palms up, tenuto, will help to increase the power. Sometimes a shaking intensity in the baton is used to add still more vigor to the sound. The forte-diminuendo-crescendo-forte effect may be performed by bringing the hands downward and toward each other for the diminuendo, then turning them palm upward and slowly raising them for the crescendo. Again, a cut-off will follow. For the diminuendo into silence, the hands may approach each other in a downward motion until they are right in front of the conductor, in a low position—just above the music stand. The conductor may then simply stop conducting at the proper moment for the sound to stop, or he may make a gentle gesture of release. When the diminuendo is of the very dramatic kind, ending only when complete silence has occurred, then he brings his hands slowly to center front, moving gradually downward and finally centering the motion in just the fingertips of one hand until the sound is completely gone. When silence reigns, he stands perfectly still for a moment before releasing the audience from the spell of utter quiet.

Another type of ending must be mentioned. It is the hair's-breadth delay of the very last note where no ritard has occurred. It is pertinent to pieces of a light, airy, and often humorous character, that bounce along right up to the end with no ritard. The performance of the last note, just later than the audience expects it, brings with it a bit of a chuckle and a storm of applause. It has a charm that is difficult to match in any other way. Example 47 shows an instance of the delayed last note.

47. Edouard Lalo, *Symphonie espagnole*, Op. 21, for Violin and Orchestra. Second movement (last four measures).

A second example of the delayed last note occurs in the Minuet forms. On occasion the bass instruments have an ending note on the second beat of the measure. This is usually in the form of an octave skip. In cases where there has been no ritard, this last note is generally played a fraction of an instant late. The effect is that of putting a definite period on the end of the sentence.

The necessity often arises, in theatrical performances, to stop the music in the midst of its onrush, as it were. When the "act" finishes, the applause must start, regardless. The old circus bands customarily resorted to their C-major chord, playing it instantly when the act terminated and holding it forte until the applause was well established. In the theater often the tonic chord of the selection being played is used for the ending chord and it is inserted whenever the applause is due. The theater orchestra understands that one of its biggest jobs is to crescendo the endings so that the audience reaction will be enthusiastic, spontaneous and sustained.

Finally, let us mention the old "showmanship" ending. This is used when the theater orchestra is performing on the stage and is itself the main attraction. The conductor wishes to force the applause to start before the orchestra has finished playing its last note. (This presupposes a loud ending.) He can warn the musicians, during the rehearsal, to "keep pouring it on" until the applause starts. He then forces the applause by turning suddenly to the audience while still holding out the last note and, if necessary, jerking the baton upward a little, very quickly. It is almost fool-proof in its results if the conductor has confidence in himself when he does it. The cut-off for the orchestra in performed after the applause has started and while the conductor is still facing the audience. Remember, this is pure showmanship—not formal concert etiquette.

The hand signals customarily used in the Radio and TV stations will be found in Chapter 8, pages 116 and 117.

The gestures used in conducting the four measures of Example 48 are listed below the example on page 82.

48. Christoph Willibald Gluck, *Iphigenia in Aulis*. Overture (measures 17–21).

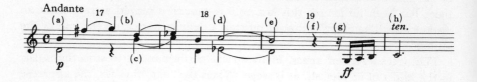

(a) Legato gestures until third beat of measure 19.

(b) Phrasings shown in two-note groups, ending on third and first beats, the ending gesture small, stopping momentarily on the beat.

(c) Entrance indicated (cued) for Oboe II and Violin II.

(d) Tenuto gestures, melded if desired. (Chapter 18 for melded gestures.)

(e) Complete phrase ending. Baton to the right after One, melding Two, cutting on Three.

(f) The cut-off of the preceding half-note *is* Three.

(g) Sudden change of style from legato to brisk double-forte. Gesture of syncopation for loud entrance after the fourth beat. Gesture is made exactly on Four. Customarily the tempo is picked up slightly here.

(h) Tenuto indicated by the composer. Slight melding of gestures is usable here if desired. Two measures later the staccato gesture becomes practical.

EXERCISES FOR PRACTICE: DEVELOPING EXPRESSION IN THE GESTURES

1. Practice applying the gestures legato, staccato, tenuto, dead, and gesture of syncopation to the beat-patterns of Chapters 3 and 4. Watch the tip of the stick in the mirror as you practice, until each beat shows the distinctive style being worked on at the moment.

2. Practice Chapter 3, Exercise 3, applying each style to the examples given. Then change the style in the middle of each exercise, keeping the takt even throughout.

3. Practice the following exercises, repeating each several times without stopping. Be careful not to change the speed of the takt when the style changes to staccato. *Keep the takt steady.*

    a. Six measures in ONE staccato and six measures in ONE legato.

    b. Four measures in ONE staccato, forte, and four measures of dead gesture (silence). Use very small beats for the dead gesture here; center them in the wrist only.

c. Three measures in ONE tenuto and one measure as a gesture of syncopation with the group playing *after* the beat. See below:

d. Two measures in TWO staccato and one measure in TWO tenuto.

e. Two measures in THREE tenuto and one measure in TWO silent (dead gesture).
f. Two measures in THREE with after-beats on the second and third beats (gesture of syncopation on Two and Three) followed by two measures in FOUR legato. Sing the after-beats as you make those gestures.

g. Two measures in FIVE (3 + 2) staccato and two measures in FOUR tenuto.
h. Two measures in TWO with the phrase ending on Two of each measure, followed by one measure in THREE staccato.

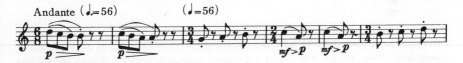

4. In the following exercises, three factors change in the middle of each exercise: the number of measures, the number of beats per measure, and the style. These are a challenge to the mind and they will help to activate the ability to think ahead. Do not be discouraged if they are difficult at first. As you practice, the mental aspect will improve and as it improves you will feel a real technique coming into your hands. Remember to watch your gestures in the mirror as you practice. Repeat each study without stopping, several times or until it becomes easy.

a. Two measures in TWO staccato and one measure in THREE tenuto.

b. Three measures in THREE legato and two measures in TWO staccato.

c. Two measures in FOUR tenuto and one measure in THREE silent.

d. Three measures in TWO tenuto and two measures in ONE staccato. See that your ONE pattern is distinctive from your TWO.

e. Two measures in FOUR legato and one measure in TWO, afterbeats (G.O.S.).

f. Four measures in ONE tenuto and one measure in TWO staccato.

5. Write out musical examples to go with Exercises 3 and 4 above, after the manner of the following:

PROBLEM: Two measures in TWO staccato and one measure in THREE tenuto. (Notice that the "problem" is applicable to each of the following notations, although the music for each is completely different.)

6. Now take a score such as Schubert's Symphony in B minor ("Unfinished"), first movement, and study it through, applying the various types of gestures to the music as written. Where would you use legato, staccato, tenuto? Where should the dead gesture be used? (NOTE: any score may be used here, chorus, band, or orchestra. The Schubert is suggested because it lends itself so well to the first application of the gestures. The orchestral scores will lead the field in variety of gesture within the movement.)

7. Take a score and look for after-beat entrances, or for accents after the beat where the gesture of syncopation would be applicable.

From here on the student should be conscious of both *score* and *interpretive technical means*. This signifies that in studying a score he should carry in his mind the auditory image of the sound he wishes to extract from the musicians at any one place in the music and *how* he is going to conduct that passage to get his results.

As the drill exercises get easy, add to them dynamic variations as the styles change. Use smaller gestures for the *piano* and larger for the *forte*.

Learn the score thoroughly; practice the gestures until they say what they are intended to. Then proceed to *conduct*. Do not spend the time talking. (Further exercises for practice are to be found in Appendix F.)

RECOMMENDED REFERENCE READINGS (SEE APPENDIX G)

EARHART, WILL, *The Eloquent Baton*, Chapters VI, VII, VIII, pp 36–67, "Phrasing" and "Phrasing Beats": "Other Properties of the Beat."

GOLDBECK, FREDERICK, *The Perfect Conductor*, Book III, Chapters I, II, III, pp 146–159.

Kahn, Emil, *Conducting*, Chapter 20, pp 146–154, "Phrasing."

Malko, Nicolai, *The Conductor and His Baton*, Chapter V, pp 123–220, "The Conductor's Gestures." (This is probably the greatest single chapter in print on this subject.)

McElheran, Brock, *Conducting Technique*, Chapter 9, pp 37–46, "Dynamics, Accents, Phrasing, Tempo, Character."

6

The
Development
of the Left Hand

The technically developed left hand plays an important part in the overall musical result. While this hand should be able to beat time efficiently, it should not constantly mimic the rhythmic motions of the right hand. The left hand has its own eloquent language to speak but it must be trained for *independent* action. This takes practice.

First, the left hand should be activated and deactivated without interrupting the rhythm of the right hand. The best drill for this is the giving of isolated cues. Next, the left hand can show a long, smooth crescendo-diminuendo (up-down) sequence while the right hand continues its time-beating. Finally, as true independence is established, the left hand can contour the phrase, indicate a special effect to some group of instruments, aid in the sustaining or cutting off of the sound, show a toning down of dynamic in the accompanying instruments, encourage a solo voice to project, and perform many other necessary tasks. It should be used to heighten the emotional content of the music through gestures that are rhythmically independent of the right hand.

Cues

Cues are given to provide a sense of security for the players, to control the exact moment of the sound, and often to guide the attention of the audience to the instrument or group of instruments they should hear clearly at a given time.

Cues are customarily given under the following circumstances:

1. When an instrument or group of instruments enters the music for the first time after the piece has already begun.
2. When an instrument or group of instruments enters after a long rest.
3. When a single instrument begins an important solo or melodic line.
4. When an entire section takes over the main theme.
5. When melodic interest or rhythmic figures (motifs) are tossed from one instrument to another. (The audience factor is important here, too.)
6. Whenever entrances are tricky and difficult.
7. When the conductor wishes to control exactly the moment of the sound.
8. When instruments enter on *double forte* attacks.
9. When there is a cymbal crash or an entrance of the cymbals for a prolonged passage.
10. When there are isolated pizzicato notes, or chords.

HOW THE CUE IS PERFORMED

The cue is given in the following ways:

1. By the baton, in the manner of a time-beating gesture directed specifically toward a player or group of players customarily seated on the conductor's right or in the center of the orchestra.
2. By the left hand in a special motion (not a time-beating gesture), sometimes with a preparation gesture preceding the cue and sometimes with just an indication on the beat-point. The left-hand cues are used for players sitting left of center.
3. By the eyes, a lift of the eyebrows or a nod of the head. This last is used in very quiet passages where anything other than the most subtle of motions would disrupt the mood. These gestures are also used when both hands are already fully occupied with other necessary conductorial gestures.
4. The two hands should not cross over each other in giving cues.

The Preliminary Drills for Left-Hand Independence

The two hands of the stringed-instrument player perform two entirely different kinds of work at the same time. In like manner the hands of the conductor should be trained to be mutually independent and mutually helpful. The process of building this independence starts with the brain, getting each half of the brain to set up an independent control over the hand that pertains to it. When this is thoroughly accomplished, the two halves of the brain will again coordinate the work of the two independent hands.

The basic drills for this mental-physical functioning are listed below. They must be conscientiously practiced. They are the "etudes," the "scales," that lay the foundation upon which a real manual independence is built.

1. Let the left arm hang loosely downward from the shoulder, fully extended, at the left side. Begin time-beating with the baton hand. Bring the left hand up just in time to indicate a cue on a certain foreordained beat and let it return immediately to its original position of relaxed hanging at the left side. See that the rhythmic precision of the time-beating is not upset by the motion of the left hand. Perform a series of measures, making cues on certain beats. Then perform a series of measures making the cue on a different beat in each measure. Next, plan the cue and execute it almost on the spur of the moment. See that the left hand returns to its position of complete relaxation whenever there is time to do so.

2. Now bend the left elbow and allow the hand to come to a position of rest near the diaphragm. Repeat the preceding exercises but with the left hand returning to this new position each time after the cue is given. In this exercise, the hand should move just in time to perform the cue—with no preparatory gesture.

3. Repeat the same exercises, but bring the left hand into position, ready to perform the cue, a beat or so ahead of the beat on which the cue is to be given. Let the left hand make a rhythmic preparatory gesture as it comes into the cuing gesture. This is more difficult. It involves more control of the left hand and a neatness in the timing factor.

4. The next drill concerns itself with the crescendo-diminuendo motion rather than with the cuing motion. While beating time with the right hand, move the left hand in an upward direction, slowly, from a position slightly in front of the body to a position just a little above the forehead. The palm of the left hand should face upward during this motion. This upward motion should intensify the crescendo in the music. In performing the gesture, feel as if the tone and dynamic were being actually carried up in the palm of the hand. When the peak of the motion is reached, turn the palm toward the players and begin a slow descending motion (decrescendo), gradually returning to the original starting point. During the raising and lowering of the left hand, the time-beating of the right hand must proceed smoothly and without interruption.

The student will find, in performing the motion with the left hand that, at first, it will tend to move in little jerks in accord with the time-beating pulses of the right hand. The goal is to perform the motion with perfect smoothness, separating it entirely from the feeling of pulsation going on in the right hand. Concentrate the eyes and the attention on the left hand itself, keeping the motion smooth and steady. Let the right hand rely on habit as it functions in the time-beating. Later on, two things may be added. The right hand may be required to make very small beats during the softer part of the crescendo line and to enlarge the beats as the dynamic grows in intensity. In the diminuendo, a ritard may be added as the termination of the motion is neared, much as if the softened dynamic were approaching the end of the piece itself.

5. Now comes the last set of drills which is the most difficult of all. This one begins the preparation of the hands for the indicating of two types of articulation simultaneously in the music (as legato and staccato). The need for such a technique comes when, for example, one player or section has a smooth legato melody against a light staccato accompaniment, or against pizzicato articulation in the strings. The conductor wishes to preserve the legato line in the time-beating but finds it necessary to signal a shorter, more staccato style in the accompaniment. Two hands for two things. (The following "etudes" are difficult and belong to the advanced technique.)

We now return to the horizontal and vertical lines mentioned in Chapter 2, page 12. See also Exercises 2 and 4 at the end of that chapter. Using Exercise 4 first, let the left hand move suddenly and instantly from front to the far left side, while the right hand starts at the same instant, moving to the right but moving slowly until it reaches its extreme position. While the right hand is completing its motion, the left hand should stand *perfectly still* at its extreme-left position. (This is difficult, for the left hand will want to continue some slight motion in sympathy with the continuing gesture in the right hand.) When the right hand has finished its outward motion, the fingertips are flipped outward as in the original exercise in Chapter 2, and the left hand now returns instantly to the starting position in front of the diaphragm while the right hand returns slowly. When this has been really conquered—which may take a few days—reverse the motions and let the right hand make the quick trip, while the left hand performs the slow motion. This exercise should be practiced until it is very, very easy. Doing it just a few times and succeeding once or twice is of little or no value. It must be conquered to the point of habit. Concentrate the attention on the hand which is supposed to stand still after the quick motion. See that it does. The fast hand is performing the staccato gesture; the slow hand the tenuto.

6. Adapt the preceding study to the vertical lines of Chapter 2, Exercises 1 and 2.

7. Practice Exercises 5 and 6 above until you can change the quick motion, upon demand, from one hand to the other without stopping, the remaining hand taking over the slow motion at the same time.

8. Finally, perform vertical lines with one hand slowly while making horizontal lines with the other. Then reverse the hands. When the motions are correctly managed in slow practice, add the fast motion in one hand to the

slow motion in the other. It is best to watch yourself in the mirror to make sure that the hands are moving in straight lines rather than in circular paths.

When the hands have accomplished all of the "etudes" given above, the young conductor will find that a real growth in independence of action of the two hands has taken place. He will find that the ability to handle several score problems at once has begun to take shape in his conductorial technique, and also in his mind.

EXERCISES FOR PRACTICE: CUING AND LEFT HAND INDEPENDENCE

Repeat each of the following exercises many times without stopping. Repeat until easy.

1. Beating time in FOUR, cue with the left hand on One of the first measure and on Three of the second measure; on One of the third measure and Three of the fourth measure, and so on.

2. Beating time in THREE, cue on One of the first measure and on Three of the second measure and repeat. Direct the cues toward two different players in an imaginary ensemble.

3. Beating time in ONE, cue on the first beat of the third, fifth and ninth measures.

4. Beating time in FIVE, cue on the fourth beat in the first measure and the second beat in the second measure and continue in the same manner. Use the various types of FIVE patterns, both traditional and modern, and drill each type thoroughly on the given exercise.

5. Beating time in FOUR, cue on the first beat of the first measure, the second beat of the second measure, the third beat of the third measure and the fourth beat of the fourth measure, repeating instantly from the beginning.

NOTE: The student should set himself many problems like those above. Remember, the mind grows as problems are solved. Drill yourself for a few minutes daily. The left hand will gradually come under a control which is quite independent from the right hand. As this happens, add to its problems by having it show style and dynamic in its cuing. It can then, little by little, begin to acquire the feeling for the gesture of syncopation, so that it can control difficult entrances after the beat, independently of the timebeating in the right hand. The well-trained and independent left hand is a wonderful asset.

6. Taking the patterns given in Exercises 3 and 4 of Chapter 3, cue on the last beat of the first measure and the second beat of the third measure throughout.

7. Take also Exercises 5, 6, and 8 of Chapter 3 and cue on predetermined beats as you pass through the measures.

8. Beating time in FOUR, let the left hand show four measures of steady crescendo (upward rise) and four measures of steady diminuendo (downward gesture, palm toward players).

9. Beating time in SIX, let the left hand show a two-measure crescendo, a three-measure diminuendo, a three-measure crescendo and a four-measure diminuendo and repeat.

10. Beating time in FOUR for four measures, the left hand is to show a phrase contour, rising and falling in a curved arc from left to center front, ending the phrase on the second beat of every second measure.

NOTE: The three following exercises are more difficult, but they will come, in time, with conscientious practice. It may take several weeks. Do not expect them to arrive over night.

11. Choose your own pattern of time-beating. Let the left hand make staccato signs on certain beats while the right hand continues with the time-beating. Such gestures are pertinent to indicating isolated pizzicato notes in the strings.

12. Beating time in six, the left hand shows "staccato" to part of the orchestra on every other measure. The right hand continues with the legato time-beating throughout.

13. Let the right hand beat staccato while the left hand shows a cue on a predetermined beat followed by a phrase (legato) of two measures to be played by a solo wind instrument. The time-beating remains staccato throughout.

14. Practice cuing on all of the full-score excerpts in Chapters 10, 11, and 12. Direct the cues to the proper place in the imaginary band, chorus or orchestra. (Seating Charts may be found in Appendix A.)

RECOMMENDED REFERENCE READINGS (SEE APPENDIX G)

Braithwaite, Warwick, *The Conductor's Art*, Chapter VII, pp 46–50, "Use of Left Hand and Arm."

Earhart, Will, *The Eloquent Baton*, Chapter XI, pp 88–93, "The Left Hand and Signaling."

Grosbayne, Benjamin, *Techniques of Modern Orchestral Conducting*, Chapter XII, pp 75–80, "Left Hand."

Malko, Nicolai, *The Conductor and His Baton*, Chapter VI, pp 251–266, "The Left Hand."

7

The Fermata

Every fermata ($\curvearrowright$) is a law unto itself. Only one thing do they all have in common and that is a non-rhythmic execution. *The fermata is held out as a sustained tone with no rhythmic pulsation.*

The fermata is used in two ways:

1. In early church music (chorales), the fermata indicates the ending of the phrase. Sometimes this ending is elongated, but this is not an invariable custom.

2. In other types of vocal composition and in instrumental music, the fermata is written to lengthen a particular note when the drama of the situation demands it or the expressive qualities of the music require such highlighting.

When the young conductor begins working with the fermata, he must clarify his ideas on three points:

1. What the emotional quality of the particular fermata is, and therefore, *how long it should be held;*

2. *Whether it cuts off completely at its termination or leads directly into the next note* with no moment of silence between;

3. In the event the fermata is to cut off completely, *what direction this cut-off should take in order that the baton may be in position to move easily into the next following gesture,* whatever it may be. (Check back on the cut-off diagrams on page 17.) Every fermata should be "solved" in the light of the three points mentioned above before an attempt is made to execute it with the musicians.

Definition of the Fermata

The fermata is a *cessation of rhythm. One does not beat time during a fermata.* The hands simply perform a *sustained tenuto gesture during the length of the sound.*

In general, it is preferred to keep the baton moving slowly during the sounding of the tone, but there are sometimes occasions which warrant the striking of a dramatic pose with the stick and "freezing." When this is done, intensity must show in the baton grip. The tension in the hand keeps the players sounding their tone until a cut-off occurs or the music continues. Upon occasion this intensity is shown by a small but purposeful shaking of the stick. When the baton stands still, there is always the danger that a diminuendo may occur. The sustaining motion may be transferred to the left hand if preferred, the stick remaining static.

Fermatas Classified as to Length

There are two basic types of fermata as to length:

1. The fermata which is determinate in length; the duration is a certain definite span in relation to the speed of the takt, such as twice as long as the composer's written notation of the fermata note. This type of fermata appears in certain places in Haydn and Mozart.

2. The fermata which is indeterminate in length; the duration of such a fermata is left entirely up to the conductor. This is the more common form.

In handling either type of fermata, *no time is beaten.* The takt ceases, but not the sustaining motion in the stick. Be mindful always of the definition of the fermata—a "cessation of rhythm." In the case of the fermata of determinate length, the conductor feels the rhythm within himself, giving the note exactly the length decided upon, but this rhythm does *not* show in the stick. The indeterminate fermata, on the other hand, derives its length from the drama of the music at the moment. If the young conductor will listen to the fermata, it will tell him what it needs for its completion. In the experience of the author, it has been noticeable that novice conductors are afraid of fermatas. They continually cut them off on the exact written length of the note itself, just as if the fermata were not indicated by the composer. One will do well, therefore, to learn to control his own feeling of continuous rhythm so that he can stop it at will. It should not be allowed to control him, nor should it force him to curtail his fermatas as if they did not exist. One is reminded of Wagner's "as if Beethoven cried, 'HOLD my fermata.'"

Except for the early chorales, the fermata must be *longer than the written note.*

The cut-off of the fermata should leave the baton in position to move easily into the next gesture, whatever it may be.

Regardless of whether the fermata cuts off completely or whether the music continues without a full stop, there must be a preparatory gesture following the fermata that will warn the players that the music is about to continue. This preparatory gesture serves the same purpose as does the preparatory beat at the beginning of the composition. It should be only a declaration of intent, not a gesture that commands the sound to start. A more detailed discussion will follow under the excerpts quoted.

The left hand can be very serviceable when it comes to showing the termination of the fermata. It can also help in the sustaining quality of the sound, lending its support by means of the tenuto gesture.

Fermatas Classified with and without Caesura

The word *caesura* means a complete stop, a terminal break. It is indicated in the music by the lines //. (NOTE: caesura lines are not invariably present when the complete cut-off is appropriate. When they do exist, however, they must be observed.)

THE FERMATA WITHOUT A CAESURA

Not all fermatas are followed by a caesura. Sometimes the music continues with the fermata leading directly into the next note, as in Example 49. Here the baton sustains the fermata while moving slightly upward toward the right. When the conductor wishes to continue, the baton then swings suddenly leftward (up to the starting point of One) thus stating Two very definitely and the piece proceeds in rhythm.

49. Beethoven, *Symphony No. 3 ("Eroica") in E♭ major*, Op. 55. Finale (measures 95–96).

Frequently a fermata occurs just before a double bar. This happens often in overtures and medleys. If this fermata is a pause on the dominant seventh chord which resolves on the first note after the double bar, it is best *not* to make the caesura. If the caesura is used, it leaves the resolution chord stranded.

Often, as in Example 50, the fermata just before the double bar precedes a written change of tempo as the bar is crossed. The fermata is then held its due length, after which the baton makes a preparatory loop leading into One of the new measure. This preparatory loop *must be in the new tempo*. In the example, notice that the first beat of the new tempo entails the playing of six notes on the first beat, violins and violas. This should remind the conductor, then, that his preparatory gesture must be legato. (Refer to page 77, paragraph three.)

50. Beethoven, *Nameday Overture*, Op. 115. (Last measure of the slow introduction and first measure of the Allegro).

In the following examples we have several types of fermata without caesura. Example 51 shows a tutti fermata with no caesura. At the termination of the first hold, the baton loops right on into One of the next measure. The cut-off of the second fermata is Two of that measure stated suddenly thus resuming the rhythm. The down-beat of *each* measure must be shown since the fermata occurs on One, not on Two of the preceding measure. Weingartner called this example a "closed harmonic and melodic complex," allowing no break in its sequence.

51. Beethoven, *Symphony No. 1 in C major*, Op. 21. Finale (measures 234–236).

Example 52 also shows a direct continuation of the music, the fermata is held on One, the baton moving slowly toward the right and slightly upward. This motion changes into an outward preparatory loop and Two is stated with good impulse of will, commanding the players to continue the music *on* Two.

52. Beethoven, *Symphony No. 7 in A major*, Op. 92. First movement (measure 88).

In Example 53 the reader will see Beethoven's very careful notation of just exactly what he means. The pizzicato A♭ in the strings is to continue right on the heels of the fermata. Notice Beethoven's notation of the fermata *between the rests* in the string parts. This signifies that the gesture of cutting off the fermata becomes Two of the measure and the strings go right on.

53. Beethoven, *Symphony No. 3 ("Eroica") in E♭ major*, Op. 55. Finale (measures 31–32).

The instruments holding the fermata continue to sound until they see the second beat of the measure. When the cut-off states the third eighth of the measure, the strings continue with no break on the fourth eighth.

Example 54 shows the fermata over the rest which is a tutti silence. Hence, no fermata cut-off is necessary. The conductor lets the silence complete itself, then makes a preparatory gesture into One when he is ready to continue with the music. The left hand can be effective here for the ending of the phrase before the fermata rest.

54. Beethoven, *The Ruins of Athens Overture*, Op. 113 (measures 23–24).

Finally, in Example 55 we find a leading-through on the fermatas with a most interesting articulation in the timpani (stem down in the bass clef line). In the first measure the timpanist is shown his ending note by a gesture of the left hand as the right hand makes its preparatory loop into One of the next measure. In the second measure, the left hand cuts off the timpanist when he has extended his roll as long as he did in the first measure, but now

55. Beethoven, *Consecration of the House Overture*, Op. 124 (measures 200–202).

Beethoven has written a fermata over the rest in the timpani part. This means that the fermata is to be sustained somewhat after the timpanist has completed his task, and he is so warned by the fermata over his eighth rest.

In the first measure, the baton will indicate the beginning of the fermata with a normal gesture to the *left* on Two, but will sustain the fermata by a motion upward to the *right*, thus coming into position for the preparatory loop into One. In the second measure, the baton shows One and moves toward the right thereafter, gradually gaining height for the preparatory loop into the down beat of the next measure.

THE FERMATA WITH A CAESURA

In dealing with fermatas which have the indicated caesura, the first question is, "How long should the caesura last?" Innate musical taste is the deciding factor. But sometimes this taste has to be nurtured. If the fermata is double-forte, the chances are that the caesura will be rather long. If a complete change of mood occurs during the caesura, it will be still longer. If a ritard is shown, leading into the fermata, this, too, will tend to lengthen the caesura silence. If a long diminuendo has led into the fermata, then the period of silence can acquire an intensity that grips all, performers and auditors alike, and one *dares not* break into that overpowering stillness. Let these things complete themselves. Do not shoot them down in mid-flight as you might ducks on the wing.

The reader will find a number of examples of fermatas with caesura in the following pages under specialized handlings. It is not necessary to give further examples here. However, we must mention the notation of caesura lines before a new tempo. In such cases, the composer is telling the conductor, "Finish to here in the former tempo. Set the new tempo *after* the caesura." Example 45 shows such a notation, while Example 65 achieves the same effect by a fermata over the last quarter-rest, to the right of the double bar.

Classification of Fermatas as to Direction of Cut-Off

It has been stated that the cutting off of the fermata must leave the baton in position to move easily into the next gesture. We shall now go more specifically into this phase of the technique.

THE FERMATA ON ONE

See Example 56. Here the cut-off should loop counterclockwise, ending either downward or to the right so that the stick is ready to lead left into the normal Two of the 4/4 measure. If the time-beating were in THREE, the cut-off would go either downward or to the left, since the second beat in THREE moves to the right.

56.

THE FERMATA ON TWO

Example 57 permits the cut-off gesture to move clockwise and downward, counterclockwise and upward, or clockwise and to the left. This is a good place to mention that many vocal conductors prefer the downward cut-off when the caesura exists. The singers take the new breath as the hands rise from the low terminus to conducting position again.

57.

If the time-beating were in THREE, the second beat would be to the conductor's right. The cut-off in that case could move downward, upward, or to the right. If there were a tutti rest on Three, the upward cut-off would be preferred, since it would leave the stick in a high position where the loop into the following One could be made very easily.

THE FERMATA ON THREE

Example 58 shows the fermata on Three. In this case the cut-off may go either downward or to the right. This permits the baton to curve upward and clockwise to prepare Four.

58.

THE FERMATA ON FOUR

Notice that the technique for the handling of the fermata on Four is applicable to the conducting of the fermata on the *last beat of any measure of three or more beats*, since last beats are always upward and first beats downward.

In Example 59 the cut-off would best be made in an upward direction if the caesura is to be of short duration and downward if the caesura is to be long. In either case a preparatory loop into One follows the cut-off.

59.

Thorough practice on the given examples will give adequate technique for the fermatas on beats other than those given, since the gestures are similar. The correct choice of cut-off direction will not leave one stranded.

CAUTION: Remember that the slow-moving horizontal line is the line of sustaining. Vertical lines are dangerous: they tend to move out of sight of the players.

The More Difficult Types of Fermatas

Every fermata requires intelligent study. The composer usually indicates rather exactly what he wants. Of all composers, Beethoven stands out in this regard. This is why his examples have been chosen wholesale for this chapter. His directions are very explicit. They should be followed with complete integrity. If he marks a caesura, observe it. If not, remember that he is showing you that the musical thought is a continuous one, not to be interrupted. A written rest after a fermata with no caesura indication should be given just exactly its own time-value in the tempo indicated. The following special examples will add to the student's understanding.

In Example 60 we have an instance of a gentle *rhythmic interruption* in a *continuous melodic line*. (Compare this with Example 66, page 104.)

60. Beethoven, *Symphony No. 4 in B♭ major*, Op. 60. Finale (nine to six measures from the end).

In this example there is no break: the new instrument starts just as the preceding instrument finishes. In the first two measures, an upward (second beat of the two-beat measure) tenuto gesture is all that is needed, sustained as necessary. This gesture loops, after the sustaining of the fermata, into the next One without interruption. On the last measure, the fermata is started on the downward One and the sustaining motion goes to the right and slightly upward to prepare the stick for looping into the sudden double forte on Two. The gesture Two takes a heavy downward ictus before its rebound, bringing the big tone suddenly with it.

Example 61 shows a triple-rhythm beaten 1-to-the-bar. A caesura is indicated.

61. Beethoven, *Symphony No. 5 in C minor*, Op. 67. Third movement (measures 7–9).

Often the measure preceding the fermata is taken in THREE in order to gain precision in the ensemble for the slight ritard marked by the composer. If the THREE is used, the first two beats of the measure are in tempo, the ritard being reserved for the third beat. The fermata rises upward from the ictus-point of One. The cut-off is made upward and becomes, rhythmically, the first beat of the fermata measure, rebeaten, the musicians playing on the last one-third of the beat.

In Example 62 the caesura lines are missing. The usual solution for handling this famous place is to consider the downbeat One of the third measure as the cut-off of the fermata. However, the author has seen at least one of the great conductors use a very quick cut-off gesture upward with an instantaneous One. In this instance the auditorium was a large one and he may have resorted to this device in order to clarify the written eighth rest for the audience.

62. Beethoven, *Symphony No. 5 in C minor*, Op. 67. First movement (measures 1–6).

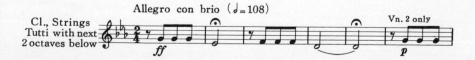

One other comment on Example 62: Your attention is called to the fact that the fermata in the fifth measure comes on the *second* downbeat of that note. Both downbeats must be shown, the second One very small so as not to interrupt the tie.

In Example 63, the cut-off is performed whenever the conductor wishes to end the sound. The following rest is used only for the purpose of making a preparatory gesture into One of the next bar. The rest is a tutti rest.

63. Hector Berlioz, *The Damnation of Faust,* Op. 24 (Last measure of Scene XVI and first measure of Scene XVII, recitative).*

* This type of fermata is very rare. Usually the fermata appears on the rest following the last sounded note, that is, on the *silence*. There are hundreds of examples to be found with notes followed by fermata-rests, but very few with fermatas followed by *rhythmic* rests for the balance of the measure. (See also Example 67.)

Example 64 presents a fermata written against a moving voice. This type of fermata is rather common. Although the fermata appears to begin on the first beat of the measure for those instruments playing the whole note, actually it does not start as a *fermata* until the last beat of the measure. The position of the fermata in the *moving voice* (in this case the first violins and the cellos) states the inset of the hold as such. In conducting this type of fermata, *the time-beating continues until the last beat of the moving voice.* When that beat begins to sustain, the real fermata starts.

The Adagio marking with the cut-time signifies two major accents in the measure, but a time-beating pattern in Four. Beethoven, in writing six notes in this fermata measure, has stretched his phrase with a subtle type of written ritard. Beats One and Three would be emphasized in the preceding measure. They would become rhythmically One-Four of this last Adagio measure, beaten in a SIX pattern.

64. Beethoven, *Fidelio Overture*, Op. 72b (measures 247–248).

In Example 65, the fermata is placed over the rest, indicating two things: (1) the last note before the rest must be given exactly its written value, and not lengthened unless qualified by the word ritard: (2) There is a long moment of silence following the note before the next entrance is made.

65. Gioacchino Rossini, *Italians in Algeria*. Overture (measures 31–32).

In the quoted example, the first beat (One) would be given as a gesture of cutting-off instead of taking the shape of the usual time-beating gesture. This is true in anything but the very slowest of tempos. The cut-off gesture, used in this place, will prevent the lengthening of the last note before the fermata. After the cut-off, the baton stands still as long as the conductor wants the silence to last. Then comes the real problem. Namely, how to get *all* of the players—not just the first stands—to play the next two notes confidently and securely together. One resorts to the "trick" discussed on pages 78 and 79. When the silence is completed, the conductor makes a tiny flick with the fingers of his left hand, which hand is not seen by the audience. This flick tells the players, "Here is Two *in the Allegro tempo*." The baton then beats Three as a sharp gesture of syncopation and everything follows in due course. The flick of the left hand shows the ending of the fermata-rest and simultaneously states Two in the Allegro tempo. When Three follows in the baton in rhythm, the musicians easily pick up the tempo and continue with the music. Careful timing is necessary here to see that Two-Three are exactly in tempo.

When there is no change of tempo after the fermata, and the silence is of rather short duration, the left-hand flick is not needed. The tempo of the piece has already been well established in the minds of the players during the rendition of the measures preceding the fermata. The baton beat alone is sufficient to re-establish the tempo.

Some pieces start with a fermata on the very first note. This is a dramatic call to attention and is usually a double forte. It means *no rhythm* on the first note. Since there is no rhythm to be established, the preparatory beat need not be rhythmic. In the case of the double forte, a "breathing gesture" may be necessary preceding the preparatory beat. See Figure 41 and its accompanying discussion.

Charles Munch, formerly of the Boston Symphony Orchestra, had an interesting formula for this type of entrance. He raised his hands high; they stopped momentarily, then with suddenness descended and rose again, and the big sound came when they once more arrived at the top of the climb.

In Example 66 we have a series of fermatas that playfully interrupt the melody's rhythm but *not its sequence*. Imagine that this same melody has occurred earlier in the piece without the fermatas. In order to perform this music, breaking the rhythm but not the melodic sequence, the conductor has to show *two* second beats in each measure, one to start the hold and another to signify the ending of the fermata and the resumption of the rhythm. The first of the two second beats will show its ictus and move into a slow, tenuto gesture of sustaining. This sustaining gesture will go to the right. This will be followed by a sudden gesture of syncopation also to the right stating "Two" again and proceeding rhythmically into Three.

66.

Allegro moderato giocoso

In Example 67 we have a fermata followed by two beats of tutti rest. When this type of notation is used, it signifies the immediate resumption of the rhythm when the fermata is cut off. The baton shows One and sustains to the right. The gesture of cutting off becomes Three (to the right) while Four (moving upward) prepares for One, the pizzicato chord.

67. Rossini, *Semiramide.* Overture (measures 173–174).

Finally, let us mention a specialized type of fermata. It is that which occurs on a sustained tone or a rest for certain members of the ensemble while one or more instruments perform cadenza-like passages. Here a bi-manual handling is usually best; one hand devotes itself to controlling the non-solo instruments (the fermata) while the other hand beats as necessary, if necessary, to give the needed direction for the cadenza performance. The beat following the cadenza must be made in the correct direction of the time-beating. A good reference score is Rimsky-Korsakoff's *Scheherezade.*

While the foregoing examples provide some methods for studying fermatas, and some solutions for handling them technically, it is important to caution again that every fermata is a law unto itself. Its proper handling is determined by the context in which it occurs. Intelligent thought should be brought to bear upon the problem each presents, and the gestures ought to be practiced in order to insure effective performance of the fermata and efficient resumption of the rhythm thereafter. The fermata is inserted for the chief purpose of making the note *longer* than its written value. HOLD the fermatas!

EXERCISES FOR PRACTICE: HANDLING THE FERMATA

1. Practice diligently on all of the examples given in this chapter.

2. Practice making cut-offs on all beats of the various types of time-beating patterns, picking up the rhythm again on the next following beat. Practice with and without lengthy caesuras. When the caesura is long, use a preparatory gesture before the next time-beating gesture. Make all gestures in the proper direction (preparations and beats.)

3. Make up your mind how you would handle the following problems relative to the fermatas, their cut-offs, and the resumption of the tempo thereafter.

4. See also the fermata exercises in Appendix F, pages 275–276.

RECOMMENDED REFERENCE READINGS (SEE APPENDIX G)

Grosbayne, Benjamin, *The Technique of Modern Orchestral Conducting*, Chapter XIII, pp 81–96, "The Hold."

Malko, Nicolai, *The Conductor and His Baton*, pp 220–239. Excellent examples from the repertoire are given and analyzed in the section dealing with the Fermata.

Rudolf, Max, *The Grammar of Conducting*, Chapters XVIII, XIX, pp 166–201, "Holds."

8

Hints on
Miscellaneous Topics

The discussion of the technical means would not be quite complete without touching upon several things that can present special problems for the student of conducting. These are added in this chapter.

Conducting the Recitative

The recitative has been mentioned in connection with the passive gestures (page 75). However, it warrants a bit of additional discussion here.

The recitative is, fundamentally, an insert, in a vocal composition, which is to be sung as if spoken. It is often relatively unrhythmic in structure, as speech is unrhythmic. Its purpose is to carry forward the story. It serves to brief the audience on what has transpired before the action continues.

Being of a spoken character, the recitative is usually not fully accompanied throughout. Either it is punctuated by single chords which state the harmonic structure or it is supported by sustained tones of a static character which change with the harmony as necessary. The conductor's biggest job in the recitative, therefore, is to see that these chords and changes in harmony occur at exactly the right instant, regardless of the unrhythmic character of the general takt. This requires finesse in the timing plus an understanding of the following points:

1. If a chord is to be articulated *on* a beat, it should be preceded by a secure and well-timed preparatory gesture which says clearly, "Here it comes."

2. If a chord is to be played *after* a beat, the gesture of syncopation will be used, preceded by a warning get-ready motion either in the stick or in the left hand. The latter is usually safer.

The first two chords in Example 68 will be conducted as described in (1) above. The entrance at the end of the second measure will require the treatment given in (2), unless, perchance, the soloist keeps a steady takt throughout this measure, in which case simple time-beating may continue with the gesture of syncopation used on beat Three.

68. George Frederick Handel, *Messiah*. No. 5: Recitative, Thus Saith the Lord (last five measures).

* Customarily, such closing chords are played *after* the singer finishes, starting on the fourth beat and ending on the first beat of an added measure.

3. When the recitative is accompanied by sustained tones, the latter must be played softly and in good balance with each other. They must also be matched against the power of the singer's voice. Since the soloist will take whatever liberties are necessary with the rhythm, the conductor must often resort to a type of irregular time-beating.

Example 69 lends itself to a fairly regular time-beating. The conductor will necessarily remember here, however, that sustained tones have a faculty for sounding a little late with the beat-point. He may have to be doubly alert to anticipate the attacks.

69. Felix Mendelssohn, *Elijah*, Op. 70. No. 12: Recitative and chorus (measures 6–10).

4. The first beat of each measure must be clearly indicated by the baton as the measure passes. This is of utmost importance, since the takt within the measure may vary rhythmically. A simple dead gesture, from the wrist is all that is necessary. In the case of several measures of tutti rest, the conductor may make a series of several quick downbeats, each beat signifying one measure, and then just wait for the singer to finish those measures.

5. After the indication of the first beat of the measure, the baton may do one of several things in handling the rest of the measure. It may show nothing except this first beat, which is often done when the entire measure is a tutti rest for the accompanying instruments. Or it may design the beats within the measure according to a rhythmic takt. This is done when the singer, for the moment, is executing a phrase which lends itself to rhythmic speaking on pitch. Or the baton may design quickly all beats of the tutti rests and stop in a position of readiness for the beat which is to be played by the musicians. The command to play is preceded by a well-timed preparatory beat.

6. The conductor must know thoroughly the singer's part, words and music, if he is to be successful with the timing in the recitative.

Irregular Beats

The discussion of the recitative brings with it the closely related topic of irregular beats, in general. There are countless numbers of places, especially in the modern scores, where the conductor will be obliged to make motions of a time-beating character which will interrupt, so to speak, the *steady* flow of the takt. Let us take as examples the Stravinsky passages quoted in Examples 70 and 71. (It will be noted that the rhythms only are quoted in Example 71. The takt, in each case, is a fast beat, as indicated by the metronome markings which are given in the score.)

70. Stravinsky, *L'Histoire du soldat*. Introduction: Marche du soldat (measures 78–80). © 1924 by J. & W. Chester, Ltd. By permission of the copyright owners, J. & W. Chester, Ltd., London.

71. Stravinsky, *The Rite of Spring*. (a) Sacrificial Dance: The Chosen One (measures 15–19; rhythm only); (b) The Play of Abduction (measures 19–21; rhythm only). © 1921 by Edition Russe de Musique. Copyright assigned to Boosey & Hawkes 1947. Reprinted by permission of Boosey & Hawkes.

In Example 70 the time-beating is in values of the quarter note. In Example 71(a) the takt is the eighth note. In Example (b) the dotted quarter sets the pace, but the continuous eighths should be kept in mind.

The second measure of Example 70 shows the deletion of one eighth note from the second beat. This beat, therefore, will take half as much time as did the first beat in the measure or the measure may be beaten as an extended One. Example 71(a) adds an extra sixteenth note to the first beat of the second measure. This first beat must then be given the value of an extra half-beat. The three sixteenths are *not* triplets. They are entitled to the exact value of an eighth plus a sixteenth. In the third measure, the second beat has an added sixteenth. A THREE pattern with the third beat deleted by one sixteenth is good for this measure. Time-beating in TWO resumes in the fourth measure. Measure 5 uses only one (lengthened) beat. This example is a nice problem in irregular time-beating. The conductor should keep a steady flow of sixteenths running through his mind, assigning the takt of his beat as required.

Example 71(b) is of especial interest in that Stravinsky has written measures which resemble very closely the standard 9/8 bar (3 + 3 + 3) and then has requested a 4 + 5 and a 5 + 4 grouping. This grouping is indicated by his added dotted-line bar-line in the middle of the measure. In practicing this one, the student will do well to count evenly as follows while beating on each spoken One: "One-Two-Three, One-Two-Three, One-Two-Three, One-Two-Three; One-Two-Three-Four, One-Two-Three-Four-Five; One-Two-Three-Four-Five, One-Two-Three-Four; One-Two-Three, One-Two-Three." See that the speaking of each word is done on a steady takt. The 9/8 bars show One and a second beat at the asterisk.

Thorough acquaintance with the music, brilliantly quick thinking, and plenty of secure practice beforehand are the ingredients for success in such places.

Another aspect of the irregular time-beating has to do with the use of the gesture of syncopation. In order that the musicians bring precise responses to this gesture in exactly the right places in the beats, the conductor will find that he has often to make gestures which are not precisely coincident with the takt.

For example, let us suppose the conductor wishes to show an entrance on the second half of the third beat in a four-beat measure. He will make his gesture of syncopation *on* the third beat. This will be precisely on the takt. But suppose he wishes to show an entrance on the *last sixteenth* of the third beat. In this case he may perform his gesture of syncopation just *later* than the takt of Three, thus forcing a later response from the players. Obviously, to do this, the conductor has resorted to unrhythmic timing in his beat in order to insure the exact response he wishes, musically.

The student has already laid the foundation for such accommodations of an irregular nature if he has acquired the ability to handle the fast FIVES and SEVENS of Chapter 4.

Subtle Tempo Variations

If the student will set a metronome going while playing a fine recording of a major work by a major symphony orchestra, he will perhaps be surprised that the two will not continue to coincide in the takt. Music is a living thing and as such it cannot become entirely mechanistic. But, in the hands of a skilled conductor, it can give the illusion of perfectly timed beats without sacrificing the right to breathe freely.

Tempo variations, when they exist and are not indicated by written directives, must be very subtle. It is easier to fool the human ear than it is the metronome. When these variations occur they must be so skillfully performed that they do not call attention to their existence as such. The adding of a bit of tenuto to a certain note in a legato passage may lend color to the whole passage—but, inconspicuously, it has stretched the beat, which stretching is often compensated for by an equally inconspicuous deletion in the next following beat. When the composer himself requests such performance, and wishes it to be of a slightly more obvious nature, he does so through the use of the word *rubato*. It is a delightful word which permits emotion to reign with an authority superior to the inherent majesty of the takt. The French interpretation of the word is one that recognizes irregularities *within* the measure, but keeps the length of the measure itself intact.

When it is necessary for the conductor to hold back the tempo, the addition of more tenuto in the gesture can accomplish it. When he wishes to urge ahead, the use of staccato gestures will help. Also, a factor in urging ahead is the cheating, slightly, of the longer notes.

In very slow movements (especially in Adagio tempos) the entrance of the second theme is usually the signal to relax the intensity and to urge the tempo ahead slightly—enough to negate any monotony that might otherwise prevail.

In Example 72 the tempo is sometimes subtly broadened after the fermata with a *very gradual* accelerando all the way to the end of the piece. This makes for a thrillingly brilliant ending.*

72. Weber, *Der Freischuetz*. Overture (measures 287–292).

Accelerandos and ritardandos marked by the composer are not quite so subtle. The important thing with these devices is that the change of motion in either case be gradual, not sudden, and that both may be brought under control again when the music demands the resumption of its original tempo.

---

* There are two accepted interpretations for the passage given here. The second is as follows: The tempo is slightly slower following the fermata, tutti rest; it then resumes its original brilliance at (a).

The Double Bar with a Change of Tempo

Elsewhere in the book it has been mentioned that the wise conductor marches *across* the double bar in rehearsal before stopping to make comments on the preceding section. Double bars are such natural stopping places that many amateur musical organizations fail to have sufficient practice in crossing them. This can result in unconvincing public performances at such places.

The double bar with a change of tempo is a distinct annoyance to the young conductor (as well as to the players), especially when the change concerns the immediate inset of a new tempo without either accelerando or ritard preceding it. The music to the left of the bar must finish precisely in the old tempo. That to the right must start with secure ensemble in the new tempo. The trick is to show the very last beat to the left of the bar strictly in its tempo and then, following its ictus, to make the preparatory gesture before One exactly in the new tempo. This sometimes entails a momentary pause in the baton after the ictus and before the preparatory gesture—expecially if the new tempo is to be faster than the old. Example 73 is a pertinent instance. The Andante is in FOUR here, the Presto in TWO.

73. Mozart, *Così fan tutte*. Overture (measures 13–15).

Unless the preparatory beat before One is in the new tempo (and is legato), the musicians cannot play these first four notes together. Remember, too, that the conductor has the responsibility to *train these musicians to raise their eyes to the stick* at such places in the music.

The experienced conductor usually has in mind a definite "mathematical" relationship between two tempos, as for example: $\quad \mathord{\half}=\mathord{\quarter}\ ; \quad \mathord{\eighth}=\mathord{\quarter}\ ;$ and so on.

The carrying across the bar of the old tempo for a beat or two before the inset of the new tempo has already been mentioned (page 78 and page 103).

Further discussion is not needed here. Example 74 presents an often-quoted passage.

74. Beethoven, *Symphony No. 1 in C major*, Op. 21. Finale (measures 5–8).

The left-hand, right-hand One-Two is applicable here to set the Allegro tempo, especially since Beethoven marks both an eighth rest and a caesura following the fermata (pages 78 and 103). Another customary method of handling this passage is to make the cut-off of the fermata serve as One of the Allegro tempo, with Two following rhythmically (performed as a gesture of syncopation) and stating sharply the sixteenth rest after which the violins play their run. The dynamic of the fermata and its length are the deciding factors in making the decision as to which method is most feasible. If the fermata is long and the dynamic very soft, the first method is best.

Conducting Accents and Cross Accents

In conducting accents, the conductor's gesture must show that the accent is to occur on the coming beat. The rebound of the preceding beat usually rises somewhat higher and sometimes the baton stops for an instant just before it swings into the accented beat. Stopping the motion momentarily after the ictus of the accent or suddenly retracting the hands helps to prevent a crescendo following the accent.

In non-professional ensembles there is always the tendency to make the accent loud and then to retain that dynamic. Especially is this true in sforzatos. Such a rendition denies the accent completely. An accent is an accent only if the dynamic falls away instantly, following the accented sound. As to the amount of tone on the sforzato itself, the professional rule is "one degree louder than the passage in which it occurs." Lack of understanding of this dictate explains why so many amateur groups "crush" the sforzato in piano passages.

For accents occurring just *after* the beat, use the gesture of syncopation *on* the beat.

Cross accents are regularly recurring accents sounding in one meter but written in another. The most common form is the three-beat measure with the accent coming every other beat: written in Three but accenting in Two. Example 75 is an excellent illustration. The clarinet is accenting in 5/4, the singer in 2/4 and the violas in 3/4, but all parts are notated in the 2/2 measure.

75. Luigi Dallapiccola, *Divertimento* for Soprano voice, Flute (Piccolo), Oboe, Clarinet, Viola, and Cello. III: Bourée (measures 134–136). Reprinted with authorization of Carisch S. p. A. Milan (Italy), owner of the author rights all over the world. © 1956 by Carisch S. p. A.

A good way to practice the cross-accent technique is to make a time-beating pattern in THREE and count One-Two throughout. Each time you say "One" make a large gesture; when you say "Two" make a small gesture, very relaxed; but preserve the three-beat *pattern* throughout in the baton. Beating in THREE, the gestures will then show large on One and Three in the first measure and on Two in the second measure. The dangerous beat is the One in the second measure. It must be controlled so that it is gentle with no great drop.

Accompanying

Almost every instrumental organization will have to do a job of accompanying sometime in its career. It may be that a chorus has been added to the production, or a special soloist is to perform with the group. Or the accompanying activity may be just a simple background for a solo-melody-line within the composition itself. In any case, accompanying is an art in its own right and merits a few words here.

First and foremost: *the soloist must be heard*. This may mean cutting down on the size of the accompanying group, or just an underplaying of the marked dynamics. Second, the conductor, in general, follows the soloist and does his best to give the soloist confidence and a feeling of musical ease in the performance of the number. (After all, the success of his program at the moment depends upon that soloist.) The conductor should know the soloist's part about as well as the soloist himself knows it. He must also know how every note of the accompanying part fits against that solo line. He must be alert to quick adaptation to the soloist, and the musicians must watch with all attention to catch instantly any new subtlety which may be added to their previous rehearsing of the score.

When the accompanying group has an interlude, this interlude should enhance the general character of the drama of the music itself. It should also act as a momentary release—a breath for the audience—from the concentrated intensity of the solo. The interlude should swell out and build up in its own right, furnishing the contrast of the full beauty of the instrumental ensemble to the continuing line of the solo part. In light-opera music, the orchestral interlude should heighten the characterization of the personality being depicted on the stage at the moment. Many times a bit of over-playing in a single measure of interlude can add a humorous touch to the comedy going on across the footlights. In all interludes the accompanying musicians carry the burden of the performance at the moment. They must not let it drop.

Beauty of tone and finesse are the key words in accompanying.

In instrumental works which have lengthy passages for the solo instrument, unaccompanied, the conductor will show the first beat of each measure as it passes, and nothing more. A small, dead gesture is sufficient. When the solo passage happens to be a lengthy cadenza, the conductor tells the musicians that he will begin beating at a certain number of measures before their entrance, and then makes no other motions during the playing of the cadenza by the soloist.

The Radio and TV Hand Signals

The conductor who does radio or TV work, or who takes his school organizations into the studios for special broadcasts, will have occasion to use the standard "hand signals." These have come into being because of the need to maintain complete silence regarding the mechanics of the production during the airing of the show. The broadcast cannot be marred by noises of a technical nature.

The standard signals may vary slightly, but, in general, they are as follows:

1. Raise one finger in the air: Play the first ending and repeat.
2. Raise two fingers: Take the second ending, omit the repeat.
3. Touch the forehead: Go back to the beginning of the piece.

4. Form the letter T with the index fingers of both hands: Play the Theme. (Theme-song.)

5. Cut the throat with the index finger: Cut the music; stop it at once. (The clenched fist also means the same thing.)

6. A circular spinning motion with the first finger, pointing downward: Keep the music going. (It imitates the revolving of the record on the turntable.)

7. A stretching motion, like stretching a rubber band between the hands: Stretch the music out. Fill up a little more time with it.

When the program is about ready to start, the control man will probably say, "Stand by. We're going on the air." The red light in the studio will flash on and also the sign reading "On the Air." It remains on throughout the broadcast. When the one-minute call is given, the conductor *must not* take his eyes from the control operator. The signal for the music to start may come at any moment thereafter. This signal is given by the man at the controls. He raises his hand in a warning, "Get ready" gesture. (The conductor raises his hands in the "ready" gesture too.) At the instant the music is to start, the control man will suddenly point his finger directly at the conductor. (It is one of the greatest "conducting" gestures in the world!) The baton comes down and the show is on its way.

When the program is finished the control man will signal that the studio is off the air by horizontal motions of the two hands in front of his chest; the red light flashes off and it is safe to stop the music.

The school conductor will find that if his musical organization are well versed in the hand signals, recourse to them will be helpful in many unforeseen situations: That forgotten announcement as to whether the first or second ending is to be used; that anxious moment in the processional march when the music runs out and has to be taken "from the top" again.—These can be dealt with smoothly if the hand signals are in working order. There is a great feeling of security between the conductor and his performing group when each knows what to do.

The Metronome

This little beast must not be entirely ignored in a book on conducting. Many are the sins which may be laid at its feet, but nevertheless, it is a good thing for the young conductor to test himself every so often against the metronome. When he does so, he subjects himself to a severe, but conscientious, task-master, and a little disciplining now and then is good for almost anybody.

The metronome came into existence during Beethoven's lifetime. He himself placed metronome markings in his scores, but because of his deafness, conductors do not always accept them as accurate. When the conductor sees metronome markings on scores predating Beethoven, he knows that they are suggestions of the editor of the music, not of the composer himself. When the metronome marking is authentic, it should be observed as closely as possible.

A metronome marking at the beginning of the piece and at double bars with change of tempo signifies that the given note, or its equivalent, occurs the stated number of times per minute, for example, *metronome: quarter note at 126* means that the quarter note value comes 126 times per minute.

At the time the author was studying with Dr. Malko, the following advice was given:

"Sing a common tune—one that is so common it almost ceases to be music. Take the tempo which is your own most natural way of rendering it, and then find this tempo on the metronome. Remember that such-and-such a tune correlates with such-and-such a marking on the metronome. When you have built up a good collection of these tunes together with their metronome markings, you will be able to arrive quite accurately at the marking requested by the composer even when the metronome is not present."

It is, as all of his advice notably was, very good advice.

EXERCISES FOR PRACTICE:
IRREGULAR TIME-BEATING; ACCENTS; METRONOME

1. Practice conducting Examples 68 through 75.

2. Practice the following exercises showing a *change to a faster tempo* when the meter changes. Make the change exactly on One of the new measure, and use a precise preparatory beat *in the new tempo*. Start with several measures in the first tempo.

    a. 4/4 to 3/4
    b. 2/4 to 3/4
    c. 3/4 to 6/8 in SIX
    d. 2/4 to 5/4 in FIVE
    e. 3/4 to 4/4
    f. Divided 3/4 to 4/4
    g. 4/4 to 2/4
    h. 5/4 in a 3 + 2 pattern to 6/8 in TWO
    j. 6/8 in SIX to 4/4
    k. 4/4 to 5/4 in TWO, 3 + 2 division.
    l. 4/8 in TWO to 3/16 in ONE
    m. 6/8 in SIX to 3/4 in THREE

3. Practice time-beating in FOUR, accenting, by large gestures, every third beat in sequence. (In the first measure the accent comes on Three, in the second measure on Two, in the third measure, on One and Four, etc.)

4. Practice time-beating in TWO, accenting every third beat.

5. Practice time-beating in THREE accenting every second beat. (For the exercises above see the suggested routines on page 115.)

6. Familiarize yourself with the radio and TV hand signals until you can execute any of them instantly. Then beat several measures showing first or second endings coming up.

7. Choose five common melodies and gear them to the metronome at your own individual tempo. Check several days in succession on this to see that your own tempo does not fluctuate.

8. Yankee Doodle at a moderate tempo will give 60 (a quarter note each second) beaten in ONE. This can be tested against the speed when one speaks the following: "One thousand one, One thousand two, One thousand three." Do not hurry the speaking. Pronounce clearly. Make a beat on the last word of each group. Check this with 60 on the metronome. It will work with many. When it does not work, try to find your own recipe for 60. It is a very valuable tempo to have at hand.

RECOMMENDED REFERENCE READINGS (SEE APPENDIX G)

Boult, Adrian C., *A Handbook on the Technique of Conducting*, Section 10, p 26, "Accompanying."

Braithwaite, Warwick, *The Conductor's Art*, Chapter IV, pp 22–35, "Sudden Changes of Time"; Chapter VI, pp 40–45, "Indefinite Problems"; Chapter XII, pp 80–82, "On the Conducting of Concertos."

Christiani, Adolf F., *Principles of Expression in Pianoforte Playing*, Part VI, TIME, Chapter XV, pp 259–263, "Tact and Tempo"; Chapter XVI, pp 264–296, "Accelerando and Ritard"; Chapter XVII, pp 296–303, "Sudden Changes of Tempo."

Grosbayne, Benjamin, *The Techniques of Modern Orchestral Conducting*, Chapter XIX, pp 166–179, "Orchestral Cadenzas and Accompaniment"; Chapter XX, pp 180–191, "Recitative."

Matthay, Tobias, *Musical Interpretation*, Section III, pp 60–106, "The Element of Rubato."

SECTION II

Score
Study

9

Clefs and
Transpositions

Before the student begins his perusal of the various types of conductor's scores, his attention should be called to two facts: (1) he will have to deal with the C clefs in addition to the G (treble) and F (bass) clefs, and (2), in the instrumental scores, he will come into vital contact with the problem of the *transposing instruments*. We shall take these up in order.

The C Clefs

The C clefs are not difficult to understand. The small pointer of the printed clef sign points to the line or space of the staff that is to be read as *middle C*, as shown in Example 76.

76.

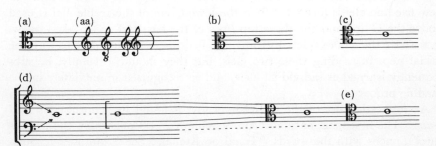

There is a possible C clef for every line and every space of the staff. Those given in Example 76 are the most used in present-day printing, although the reader will come across others as his experience with music scores enlarges.

Example 76(a) is the C clef that is called the *vocal tenor clef*. It designates the third space of the staff as middle C. Since this third space, in treble clef, is also C, the lines and spaces of these two clefs have the same letter names. The use of the C clef sign, however, designates that space as *middle C*, an octave below the corresponding space in the treble clef. When this *C* clef is used for the tenor parts in choral music, it recognizes the fact that the male voice is *an octave below the corresponding female voice*. Nevertheless, it is not used consistently. The other designations for the tenor voice are given in parentheses in Example 76(aa).

Example 76(b) shows the pointer of the clef sign designating the middle line of the staff as middle C. This clef is called the *alto clef*. The viola parts in the orchestra are written in this clef, with occasional lapses into the treble clef to eliminate leger lines for the higher notes. For this reason the clef is sometimes referred to as the "viola" clef. But the violas do not exercise exclusive ownership since the first trombone parts, in the European editions of orchestral works, are often found in this clef. When it is used, the part is often titled "Alto Trombone."

The third C clef, Example 76(c), is the fourth-line C clef called the instrumental tenor clef. This clef is used for the higher notes of the cello and bassoon parts and, in certain European editions, for the second trombone parts which are therefore designated "Tenor Trombone" in such printings. Upon rare occasions the string basses may encounter this clef in their parts. Today the bass clef is customarily used for all trombone parts (especially in American publications), occasionally resorting to the use of the tenor clef for the higher notes of the first and second trombones. The third trombone part is invariably in the bass clef.

The instrumental C clefs are formed as shown in (d) and (e) of Example 76. Starting with the grand staff, we know that between the treble and bass clefs there is one line missing, the middle C line. If this line is extended, it becomes the C line in the C clefs. Thus, for the alto clef, we borrow two lines from the treble clef above it and two from the bass clef below it and our new five-line clef is formed. When the lowest line of the treble clef is used above the C line and the three top lines of the bass clef are marked below it, we have the tenor C clef, instrumental. Bearing this in mind helps with the initial steps in reading these two clefs, but they should, certainly, be subsequently learned as individual clefs, and so recognized immediately in the reading processes.

An interesting use of the C clefs, vocally, is found in Schoenberg's *Drei Satiren*. The first song, entitled "Am Scheideweg" ("Concerning the Departure"), opens with the words, "Tonal or Atonal." See Example 77. Such writing is seldom seen in our day, but, as the example shows, it does exist.

77. Schoenberg, *Drei Satiren für Gemischten Chor*, Op. 28. No. 1: Am Scheideweg (Concerning the Departure) (measure 7). © 1926, renewed 1953 by Universal Edition A.G., Vienna. Used by permission of Belmont Music Publishers, Los Angeles, California 90049.

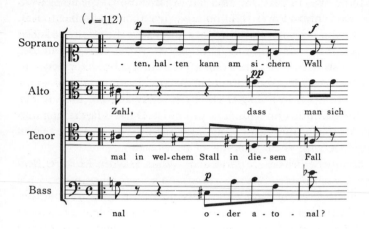

The Transposing Instruments

The transposing instruments may be defined simply as those instruments that *sound pitches different from the notes actually written in the score.* Obviously, the first question is, "Why?"

With the exception of the string bass which sounds an octave lower than notated, the transposing instruments are all wind or percussion instruments. The resonance of a wind instrument depends upon the length of its air-column. What this length is must be determined, for the particular type of instrument, by three things: (1) the range of the notes it is to play, (2) the resulting efficiency and tone quality produced by the chosen length, and (3) its adaptability to the size of the human hand. The shape of the instrument, the manner in which the air is set into vibration and, according to some authorities, the material of which it is made, all add their bit to the resulting tone.

Through years of experimentation and improvement, certain standard instruments (as to length of air column) have emerged as functioning most efficiently for the player. This means that such instruments cover their entire usable range with good quality and fairly easy execution.

Certain of these resulting instruments are known as C instruments. These sound pitches identical with the piano when playing their written notes. Such instruments are the flute, oboe and bassoon, plus the professionally used trumpet in C favored by many symphony players today. Parts that are *written* to be played on C instruments are notated exactly as if they were to be played on the piano, pitch for pitch. The piccolo in C sounds an octave higher than written. The bass clef notation for the trombones, euphoniums (baritones), and tubas sounds as written. However, when treble clef is used (and it is found sometimes in parts for amateur organizations) the notes written will sound a major ninth lower than notated (trombones and baritones).

The instruments which are not built in C are named for the pitch produced by the basic (open tone) air column. Thus we have the clarinets in B♭, A and E♭, the English horn in F, the French horns in F, the saxophones in B♭ and E♭, and the trumpets and cornets in B♭ (most commonly encountered) A, and C.* Trumpets in F and D also exist today and are used in the performances of the baroque oratorios. The piccolo in D flat is fast falling into disuse. A complete table of the transposing instruments is given at the end of this chapter, together with their intervals of transposition.

Now a word about the brasses in particular. When Haydn, Mozart, Beethoven, and their contemporaries were writing, the horns and trumpets were not provided with valves as they are today. (By use of the valve mechanism, our present-day instruments have control over the complete chromatic range.) Instead "crooks" were used. These were of varying lengths, and each crook placed the instrument in a certain key. The crooks were removable and when the music modulated, the player had to have time to make the exchange. The use of the crook permitted the following notes to be played in the given key: root (not playable on some instruments), octave (not used on the trumpets and cornets), fifth above, double octave, third, fifth, out-of-tune seventh above the double octave, plus scale-wise progression thereafter, including the raised fourth; in other words, the succession of notes playable on the trumpet as open tones today. If the D crook was in the horn, the D major series would sound, and so on.

On the French horn, the player could also make other pitches by inserting his hand into the bell of the horn, but the tone quality changed on these notes and composers did not often write them in their scores.

Since these early horns and trumpets would necessarily play in the key of the crook, it is easy to see that accidentals had little or no place in the writing of such parts in those days. The composer stated the crook to be used and that took care of the situation. The accidentals of that key functioned automatically.

With our modern valve horns, any and all accidentals are playable. The contemporary notation of the horn parts is generally without signature and with all accidentals marked in as they occur. In classifying a score as to the period in which it was composed, much can be inferred from the presence or absence of accidentals in the horn and trumpet parts.

* The trumpet in C (the instrument) is being used widely by professional players today who transpose at sight music written for the other trumpets.

The conductor will feel insecure with the early horn parts unless he is acquainted with the transpositions of various crooks in use during the eighteenth century. These will be explained in the next section under Rules for Transposition.

The Two Basic Rules for Transposition

There are two basic rules for transposition which can be mastered quickly by the young conductor. The first rule tells the conductor exactly what pitch should *sound* for each note written in the score. The sounding pitch is called *concert pitch*. The second rule tells the player what to do about it when the composer calls for an instrument other than the one the player has in his hands. The future school-music conductor must be well versed in both of these basic rules, especially if he is to handle an orchestra where music of the classical period may be encountered.

THE FIRST RULE FOR TRANSPOSITION

Most prevalent are the transpositions that *sound* a pitch somewhat *lower* than the written note. The difference between the written note and the sounded pitch is called the *interval of transposition*.

To determine the interval of transposition, proceed as follows:

Write on the staff the note C. (In treble clef the third space is best; in bass clef use middle C.) *Next to this note write the pitch of the instrument designated by the composer* (clarinet in B♭, trumpet in A, French horn in F or D or whatever is called for). The *drop* in pitch from the C to the name of the instrument will tell you the interval of transposition. The C represents any note written by the composer. The name of the instrument represents the sound that will occur when the written note is played. Each written note will sound as much lower as the interval of transposition states.

For safety's sake, let us take an example: the score calls for clarinet in B♭. The note C is written on the staff. Next to it a B♭ is placed, showing that each note the composer has written will actually *sound one whole tone lower*. (CAUTION: this also signifies that the composer has had to write each note one whole tone *higher* than he wanted it to sound.) Refer now to Example 78. This will state the most common of the transposition intervals.

A very few instruments transpose upward. These are: piccolo in D♭ (a minor ninth higher); soprano clarinet and trumpet in E♭ (a minor third higher); trumpet in D (a major second higher), in E natural (a major third higher) and in F (a perfect fourth higher). The student will have to memorize this short list of upward transpositions. Applying the first rule of transposition to these cases, the C will be written on the staff and the key-notes of these instruments will be written on the staff *above* the C. Each written note in the part will then sound at the resultant interval above. (The composer will have had to write it that much under pitch.)

With the exception of the four trumpets mentioned immediately above, the early instruments with crooks all transposed downward. These were: trumpets in B (natural), B♭ and A; French horns in B♭ alto (one whole tone lower), A, A♭, G, F, E, E♭, D, C basso (an octave lower) and B♭ basso (a major ninth lower). The designation "Horn in C" generally refers to the "C basso." For further specific information, see the Table of Transposition Intervals at the end of the chapter, page 131.

78. Common transposition intervals.

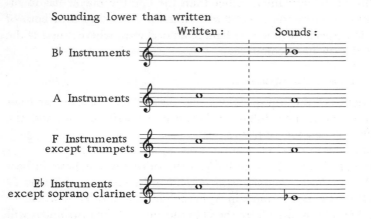

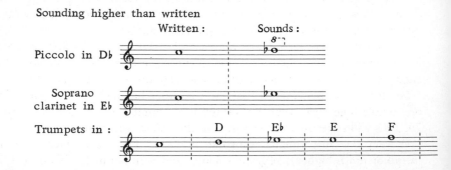

When horn parts are notated in the bass clef, the transposition interval is the inversion of the interval in the treble clef. This is due to the fact that the direction of the notation is reversed in bass clef writing for the horns, each written note rising to the concert pitch *above* instead of dropping to the concert pitch below. This is a traditional form of writing for these instruments and is not strictly adhered to in modern works. When the composer chooses to lay aside this custom he will call attention to the fact by a brief sentence in the score and parts.

NOTE: It is suggested that the student spend much time with this first rule before going on to the second rule. It is imperative that he know first how his score should *sound*. The ability to transpose must become automatic.

THE SECOND RULE FOR TRANSPOSITION

This rule tells the player what to do when his instrument is not built in the key specified by the composer. Here again the rule is simple: the player writes on the staff *the key of the instrument he has in his hands* (as "horn in F") *and next to this the key of the instrument called for* ("horn in D," for example). The relationship between the instrument he has in his hands and the instrument called for will state his interval of transposition. He will have to read each note of the written part, transposed by that interval. In the case of the example given above (horn in F to horn in D), each written note will be read downward a minor third. If horn in A were called for, the A would be written *above* the F since in the table of horn transpositions that is the A designated by "horn in A." Example 79 will help to clarify this point.

79.

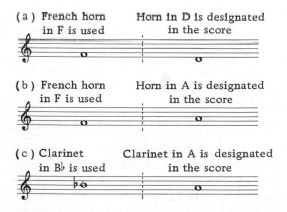

(a) French horn in F is used — Horn in D is designated in the score

(b) French horn in F is used — Horn in A is designated in the score

(c) Clarinet in B♭ is used — Clarinet in A is designated in the score

It is difficult to think quickly "a minor third lower." A note on a space will drop to the next space below, a note on a line to the next lower line. When this is done the new part will have to be played with the correct number of accidentals (in the correct new key). To find out what the new key is, we may apply the rule just given: take the key-note of the *written part* (in this case the Horn in D part), and send it through the interval of transposition.

The resulting note will be the tonic of the key for the horn in hand. Be sure to notice whether the original key is major or minor and keep the same mode in the new key. Apply the signature of the new key to the transposed notes (the new notes). For example let us say that the Horn in D shows a one-sharp signature (or that the F is sharped throughout the part) thus stating the Horn in D is to play in its G-major key. Dropping G a minor third (the interval of transposition) we have E. Using an F horn, the player must play in four sharps (the signature for E-major). Two of the sharps take care of the D major of the D horn, one more sharp accounts for the F-sharp appearing in the D part, and the fourth sharp cancels out the one-flat inherent in the F horn itself.

While the subject of transposition is complicated at first, the reader will find that after solving a few problems according to the rules given, he will feel much more comfortable with the processes involved. Such problems are to be found at the end of this chapter in the Exercises for Practice.

Certain C instruments sound at the interval of the octave as follows: piccolo in C, xylophone, chimes, and celesta all sound an octave higher than written; the glockenspiel, two octaves higher; string bass and contrabassoon, one octave lower than notated.

When the bass clef is used for the bass clarinet, the written notes sound only one whole tone lower, whereas, when treble clef is used, the written pitch drops a major ninth.

Contrabassoon parts are occasionally written at concert pitch (*Iberia* by Debussy, *Parsifal* by Wagner) and Wagner also notates the glockenspiel in its sounding range.

In examining the following Table of Transposition Intervals, it is interesting to note that, except for the bass clef notation (when used) for the bass clarinet, the bass saxophone, and the French horns, the transposing instruments are written in the *treble clef notation*.

IMPORTANT: When the conductor wishes to name a pitch for a wind player whose instrument is a transposing instrument, he specifies "concert" G, "concert" F, and so on. When he says "concert" he tells the player, "This is the *sounded* pitch, *not the written note*." If the conductor wishes to name the written note, then he should specify "written G," etc.

The foregoing hints will provide a fairly adequate working knowledge for the young conductor. However, he is urged to contact one of the fine books on *Instrumentation* (see list below) and to study this subject more comprehensively. For the terminology, style and manner of execution of the many types of bowing for the stringed instruments, the reader is referred to the chart in Appendix C, page 260, herein.

Table of Transposition Intervals

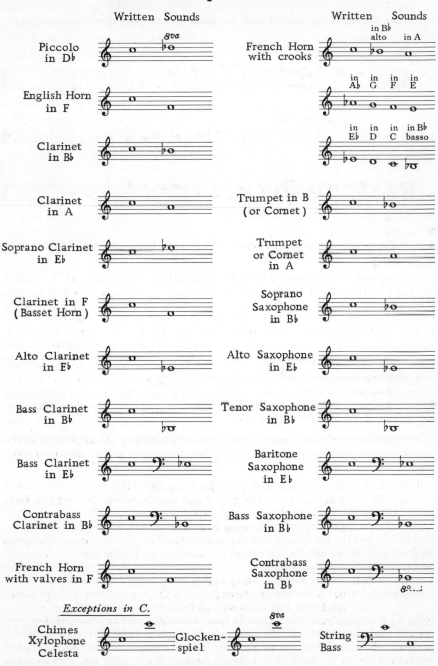

Timpani sounds as written in all modern notations.

EXERCISES FOR PRACTICE: SKILL IN CLEFS AND TRANSPOSITIONS

1. Play the following examples on the piano, or on your major instrument.

2. Refer to the orchestra scores given in Chapter 11 and play through all of the C clef parts.

3. Refer now to the scores for both orchestra and band (the latter are in Chapter 12) and play through on the piano the correct *sounds* for clarinets, trumpets, cornets, French horns, and saxophones. (The piano is a "C" instrument.) Apply the first rule for transpositions. Write the C, then the key of the instrument itself, and proceed to play each note of the written part, sending it through the correct interval of transposition . Be alert in the reading of the trumpet parts. You may find one or two which will transpose upward.

4. Reading from the bottom upwards, play each *sound* called for on the first beat of each measure. Make the correct transposition for each instrument as you come to its part. Remember, the string basses sound an octave lower than the cellos when they are playing the identical written notes.

5. Sing Exercise 4 above, without help from the piano. Sing the *sound* for the transposing instruments, not the written note. Place the pitches within your own voice range.

6. Work the following problems: (See also pages 282–284.)

a. The composer writes for Horn in C and the instrument in hand is a horn in F. What is the interval of transposition for the player?

b. The composer specifies Trumpet in D with no Signature (the key of C for that horn), and the instrument used is a trumpet in B♭. (The D trumpet transposes up from B♭.) What will the interval of transposition be for the player? What will be the key of the transposed part?

c. Horn in E♭ is called for. Horn in F is being used. What is the interval of transposition? What is the key for the new part if the original had a C signature?

d. A band conductor has no bassoon in his organization. He hands the part to his E♭ alto saxophone player and tells him to play the part as if the clef sign were printed treble instead of bass, the notes remaining just as printed. He also tells him to play in the key of three sharps, the original part being in the key of C. Marked accidentals are to be handled as follows: marked sharp, raise the corresponding note a half tone (written A sharp in bass clef, bottom space, would read F𝄪 in treble clef notation, the F being already sharped by the three-sharp signature): flatted notes lower the corresponding treble clef note by half a tone (E♭ in bass clef would read C natural in treble clef, the C being sharped by the three-sharp signature and then lowered the half tone, since the E is flatted). Will the notes sounded on the saxophone be identical with those sounded in the original part, or will they be off by an octave?

7. Write out the first four bars of *America* in unison (or sounding in octaves) for the following instruments: violin, clarinet in B♭, French horn in F, trumpet in A, trombone in bass clef, viola in alto clef (C clef), bassoon in tenor C clef (instrumental), and alto saxophone in E♭. Remember that the written note must be *higher* than the sounding note for the transposing instruments. The tone drops as it goes through the instrument. Use the concert key of G-major.

RECOMMENDED REFERENCE READINGS (SEE APPENDIX G)

Goldman, Richard Franko, *The Concert Band*, Chapters II-V, pp. 18–146. Very complete information on band instrumentation and the functions of the instruments.

Kennan, Kent, *The Technique of Orchestration*. Complete information on the instruments of the symphony orchestra.

Lang, Philip, *Scoring for the Band.*

Pietzsche, Hermann, *Die Trompete* (The Trumpet). The new American edition is filled with excellent information of a detailed nature on this instrument, its history, transpositions, uses in the literature.

Piston, Walter, *Orchestration*. This is another fine, and recent, book in this field.

Rimsky-Korsakoff, Nicolai, *Principles of Orchestration*, Vol. I. Chapter I, pp. 6–35. The manner of presenting the instruments in this book is unique. It is highly recommended since certain information is available here which is not obtainable in other places. The resonance and power of the various instruments is compared on pages 33–35.

Schwartz, Harry W., *Bands of America*. An extensive history of the band movement in America (exclusive of the public schools) beginning with 1853 through 1956.

Wagner, Joseph, *Orchestration, A Practical Handbook.*

———, *Band Scoring.*

10

Mechanics
of the
Choral Score

The first experiences with reading score present many new problems. These may be enumerated as follows: (1) the problem of the position of the several parts on the page; (2) the problem of spanning with the eyes a wide range of page *vertically;* (3) closely related to number two, the problem of reading the notation of the rhythm in a vertical direction so that cues may be properly made; (4) the problem of the instant recognition of the proper octave of the particular voice or instrument in the score; (5) the problem of the frequent encountering of the C clefs; (6) in vocal music, the parallel reading of words and music; and (7), in instrumental music, the problems presented by the transposing instruments and the shifting of the melodic line.

The present-day four-voice choral score, written on four staves, furnishes an excellent introduction to the problems of score reading. In the first place, all parts are singable. In the second place, the line-space letter names are those of the treble and bass clefs, even when the vocal-tenor C clef is used. (The C clefs are explained in Chapter 9 on page 124.)

It is suggested that the college student begin conducting with a choral score wherein the tenor part is written with the C clef sign. This will give him some experience in seeing the clef in its easiest form and in becoming cognizant of the octave in which this clef sounds.

Construction of the Choral Score

Choral scores range from two to a dozen or more parts for the singers. Example 80 presents a two-part work.

80. Johann Sebastian Bach, *Cantata No. 212* ("*Peasant*"), for soprano and bass voices. First duet (measures 1–5).

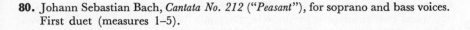

In some scores, the piano merely doubles the voice parts, lending support thereby, but not adding to the musical thought. Example 81 shows such a use of the piano.

In other scores, the piano plays an entirely independent part and in many cases must be conducted as such. Example 82 presents an excerpt from a recent score where the accompaniment is given to two pianos requiring some definite attention from the conductor.

In still other scores the piano part is entirely lacking and these are called scores for *A Cappella* performance, that is, for unaccompanied voices. Example 83 shows an *A Cappella* work with a piano part marked "for rehearsal only."

The study of three-part scores (as for three women's voices) makes an excellent background for the later study of the orchestral scores of Haydn, Mozart, and even Beethoven where three-part writing is often employed. The young conductor can gain valuable experience in working with the three-part voicing. The auditory recognition of such a structure, harmonically, will come in aptly in many places in scores of larger form. See Example 84.

It is interesting to compare this writing with the three-part structure shown in Example 88, pages 149–150.

Scores for large choral ensembles may divide one or another part, as first and second soprano, first and second tenor, and so on. Or a work may be written for a double choir comprised of two choral groups which are relatively independent of each other. Such writing is often encountered in opera scores, and a case in point is shown in Example 85, page 140.

In examining this excerpt the student will see that it is comprised of two solo voices; a five-part choir which, in the staging, is a group of townspeople standing outside of the church; and a second choir which depicts the singing of the people inside the church. Attention should be paid to the brackets in the form of heavy vertical lines outlining these two choirs on the score. These heavy lines are placed at the beginning of the staff, before the clef signs. They will later on become a helpful part of the orchestral score-study.

Now let us look at the music itself. Notice that in the second measure, only five tones are actually being sung. The solo voices double the notes written on the two top lines of the "External Chorus" parts. (Santuzza is the soprano and Lucia the contralto.) When the second choir enters in the second mea-

81. Antonin Dvorak, *Stabat Mater*. Blessed Jesu, Fount of Mercy: anthem for mixed voices (words adapted by the Rev. Benjamin Webb) (measures 1–12). Taken from MASTER CHORUSES. © 1933 by G. Schirmer, Inc. Reprinted by permission of G. Schirmer, Inc.

82. Copland, *The Tender Land*. Choral Square Dance: Stomp your Foot, for male voices with piano duet accompaniment (words by Horace Everett) (measures 1–20). © 1954 in U.S.A. by Boosey & Hawkes, Inc. Reprinted by permission.

83. Orlando Di Lasso, *Good-Day Sweetheart*. Chanson for mixed voices, a cappella, from the A Cappella Chorus Book, edited by Christiansen-Cain (words by Pierre Ronsard, trans. A. C. Curtis) (measures 1–11). © 1933 by the Oliver Ditson Co. Reprinted by permission of Theodore Presser Company, Bryn Mawr, Pennsylvania.

84. Giovanni da Palestrina, *Tell Me, What Master Hand.* Canzonet for female voices (edited and trans. Henry Coates) (measures 1–7). By permission of Novello and Co., Ltd.

85. Pietro Mascagni, *Cavalleria Rusticana*. Scene and Prayer (Schirmer's Standard Secular Choruses, No. 2415, page 30). Reprinted by permission of G. Schirmer, Inc.

sure it, too, is singing the same pitches as the first choir. The independence of parts is established by the rhythm and the words. In the third measure, the four tones are expanded into seven tones through the splitting up of the soprano and bass parts in both choruses. The piano part as given here is a reduced orchestral part and shows a typical independence from the voices.

The study of these many types of choral scores carries over into instrumental score-study by laying the foundation for the quick recognition, in the instrumental score, of the number of parts actually occurring at any given moment. (A distinction should be made here in the reader's mind between the number of instruments playing and the number of rhythmically independent parts appearing on the page.)

Many times an instrumental score of from ten to twelve lines, fully orchestrated, will, upon analysis, boil down to a simple three-part structure such as a melody, a counter-melody and a chordal accompaniment. The detailed discussion of Example 88 (pages 149 to 151) in the next chapter will bring further light to bear upon this point.

In approaching score reading of any type, it is a good idea to learn to scan the page, beat by beat, from the bottom upward. It is also a good idea to form the habit, right from the beginning, of grouping notes by their relationship to the quarter note. By far the largest part of our music is written in meters where the quarter note is the unit of the beat. It helps, therefore, to be able to recognize instantly "what makes one beat" throughout the score, and this in turn facilitates the reading of a number of parts simultaneously. The whole rhythmic system of the parts on the page seems to mesh, like a good clutch and the gears on the car, when this habit is established. The vertical reading will gradually become an habitual part of the horizontal reading.

"But why read from the bottom upward?" you ask. The answer is, "Because the *foundation* of the harmony is its bass note whether reading vocal or instrumental works. Furthermore, the string parts in the orchestral scores give the clue most of the time to the whole score, and they are printed at the bottom of the page." In the band score, the bass instruments in each family also occupy the lowest lines for that group of instruments.

The foregoing discussions have served to introduce the reader to the mechanics of the score itself. The next two chapters will build upon the foundation laid here. For the handling of the chorus as such, we refer you to Chapter 13, *Interpreting the Choral Score*.

EXERCISES FOR PRACTICE: BEGINNING THE SCORE READING

1. Take any easy four-part choral composition, preferably with the C clef tenor printing, and play the voice parts on the piano, reading from the bass note upward on each beat. As soon as one beat is played, sustain it with the pedal and immediately begin to prepare the hands on the notes of the next beat, again *starting with the bass*

and proceeding upward. It will be slow work for those who are not expert pianists. If you yourself are one who belongs in this category, do not worry about the rhythm at first. Just get the mechanic established of the upward reading and the recognition of the notes in the various clefs. Place the fingers silently, one at a time, on the proper note as you look at each part and when all notes are correctly under the fingers, play the chord. Sustain it with the pedal while you place, silently, the next chord.

2. Sing each part throughout (same composition as in Exercise 1). Jump an octave in the part as necessary to make it fit your voice. Pay attention to the half-step and whole-step intervals as they occur. Concentrate on the pitches this time through, and let the words go. In singing long skips, the unskilled singer will do well to imagine mentally the sound of the missing scale-tones between the terminal notes of the skip. In this exercise, start with the soprano line.

3. Sing the notes on each beat vertically upward from the bass note. Place the pitches in your own voice range. Such an exercise is also fine if played on your major instrument, whatever it may be.

4. Conduct the number throughout, handling an imaginary chorus.

5. Now give the words a run-through, beating their articulations instead of the time, just as a practice routine. Sustain with the hand the syllables falling on the long notes of the music.

6. Practice conducting all of the longer examples given in this chapter. Imagine the sound of the voices and piano as you do so. Pay attention to the mood as set by the accompanying words of the poem. Try to depict it with your gestures.

RECOMMENDED REFERENCE READINGS (SEE APPENDIX G)

Crist, Bainbridge, *The Art of Setting Words to Music.* This book contains analyses of the works of many composers. Many things of interest and help to the young conductor in the vocal field may be gleaned therefrom.

Crocker, Richard L., *A History of Musical Style.* This book is filled with vocal examples. Traces the development of vocal music in all of its aspects.

Davison, Archibald T., *The Technique of Choral Composition.* The ranges of the various voices may be found on page 17.

11

Mechanics
of the
Orchestral Score

The orchestral score is introduced immediately upon the heels of the vocal score for two reasons: first, because the orchestral score, during the two hundred years of its existence and development, has become quite standard as to form, and second, because it may be presented *in toto* in a somewhat simpler form than the score for full symphonic band.

In the following discussion, the subject matter will be interspersed with many references to the several illustrations of full-score pages. By studying these the reader will be able to achieve a modest understanding of the gradual development which has led up to our modern school of orchestral composition. In the process of doing so, he will also expand his ability to encompass more parts on the page and he will encounter the more difficult rhythmic problems in the conducting. This, in turn, lays a foundation for the study of the expanded score form necessary to the fully instrumented symphonic band, together with its problems of twentieth century repertoire.

First Acquaintance with the Instrumental Score

Let us now examine the first page of Symphony No. 104 in D major ("London") by Haydn, often called the Second Symphony. (Example 86, next page).

The following items should be noticed:

1. The woodwind family occupies the top lines of the score, the brass family comes next, then the percussion, and last, the strings.

2. At the beginning of the staves, to the left of the clef signs, appears a heavy black line which groups the instruments of each family by bracketing them together. The reader will recall the similar bracket-lines for the choruses in Example 85.

86. Haydn, *Symphony No. 104 ("London") in D major*. First movement (measures 1–5).

3. Within each family, the instruments are placed on the page from highest to lowest, the highest occupying the top line for that family. The one exception to this is the position of the French horn parts. The horns occupy the top line of the brass family because they so often correlate with the woodwinds when the rest of the brasses are not playing. They are therefore placed in the most favorable position for the conductor to see them easily in this relationship.

4. The bar-lines between measures break at the end of each family of instruments in a great many editions, thus giving the conductor further help in seeing the instruments in their proper relationship.

5. There is also a curved bracket in the left margin joining the first and second violins. This curved bracket is used in the majority of editions whenever *identical* instruments occupy more than one line of the staff. For example, if there were four French horns instead of two, they would, of necessity, be written on two staves and those two staves would be bracketed. (On occasion the conductor will find straight lines for the bracket rather than the curved printing.)

6. The student will notice next that in orchestral scores the names of the instruments are often printed in foreign languages: Italian, German, French. Italy was the cradle of the stringed instruments, and the symphony orchestra as such began its development with the compositions of Haydn who was Austrian. The English-speaking countries did not produce their greatest orchestral writers until long after the "professional" vocabulary had been established. The few terms the musician has to learn should not bother him greatly; and being annoyed by them is rather childish when one compares our musical vocabulary with that needed by the medical student for his work.

Most troublesome will be the following terms:

		Singular	*Plural*
French horn:	(Italian)	corno	corni
Trumpet:	″	tromba	trombe
Bassoon:	″	fagotto	fagotti
Cymbals:	″	–	piatti
Trombone:	(German)	Posaune	Posaunen
Viola:	″	Bratsche	Bratschen

With this introduction to the obvious difficulties, the reader is referred, for further information, to Appendix B, pages 258-259.

7. Next we see that certain instruments are marked "in A" or "in D," and so on. These are the transposing instruments, discussed in Chapter 9. The young conductor must continue to advance himself in the handling of the transpositions.

8. If there is a solo instrument (as in a concerto for solo violin and orchestra) the solo line usually appears in the score just above the string parts. Chorus parts, when they exist, are given a similar place on the page.

9. When the harp is used, it, too, may be placed after the percussion and before the strings.

10. In music written for younger orchestras, a condensation of the score often appears as a piano part, printed on the two lowest lines of the page.

87. Rossini, *The Barber of Seville*. Overture (measures 1–9).

11. The very first page of the score lists all of the instruments needed for the performance of the work, together with their transposition. In symphonies of several movements, the instrumentation for the single movement only is listed on the first page. Therefore, to know what instruments are needed for the performance of the entire work, the conductor must look at the first page of each movement.

12. After the first page, many scores list only the instruments playing during the measures occurring on each particular page. If, at a certain place in the music, only cellos and two woodwinds are playing, the score will be narrowed down to just three lines, omitting the staves on which the other instruments would be written. With a three-stave score, there is room on the page for several lines of the music instead of just the one line possible when the scoring for full orchestra is needed. The printer calls attention to this fact by placing a pair of heavy lines in the margin, signifying the break in the score and telling the conductor that the page has not been completed when one line of music has been played. These heavy lines are similar to the caesura lines appearing after a fermata (page 94). See the left margin of Example 90.

13. If the reader will now look at Example 87, he will see that the instrumentation calls for "Timpani in H—E." In German language printings the

H is used to designate B natural, as distinct from B♭ which is normally printed as B. The composer here is calling for the timpani to be tuned to B natural and E.

14. Occasionally, in early scores, the notes for the tuning of the timpani were stated by letters and then only C and G were written in the score. The drum which was tuned to the tonic of the key would play all notes written as C, and the other drum, tuned to the dominant of the key, would play the notated G's.

15. By observing carefully the variety in clefs and key-signatures at the beginning of each page of score, the student can soon learn to recognize the part written for each instrument. (Not all scores designate the instrumentation after the first page of the score.)

16. In general, the transpositions are given only on the first page. If the transpositions change within the movement, the composer writes the words, "Muta in—." This means "Change to —" (whatever the new transposition is). Such marking occurs most often in the French horn, trumpet, and timpani parts. Occasionally one sees it in the clarinet score.

In actual rehearsal, remember to specify "written" or "concert" pitch when discussing notes with a player of a transposing instrument. (See page 130.)

The Score in "C"

Some scores are written entirely in C scoring, that is, as if none of the instruments were transposing instruments. The exact pitches are notated throughout, just as they will sound. This makes it somewhat easier for the conductor. Prokofieff is the great modern exponent of this form of writing. The story goes that Prokofieff, in his student days, asked his teacher, Glazounow, "Why not write the score always in C and transpose only the parts for the players?" Glazounow is said to have looked the young man up and down rather coldly and then to have replied, "Young man, if it was good enough for Beethoven, it is good enough for you."

Nevertheless, today we find a fair number of Prokofieff's scores in C with the transposed parts for the players only. Recommended for perusal might be the *Lieutenant Kije* Suite and the Fifth Symphony by this composer.

When the C scoring is used, the composer either specifies French horn in C, trumpet in C, and so on; or he writes, "Score in C, parts transposed." When the players read from C parts today, they must transpose to fit the instrument played upon. Either the player writes out his part in full in the transposition, or, if he is professionally efficient, he will read it correctly at sight.

A score in C is to be found in Example 88.

Beethoven used the C scoring here for a reason different from Prokofieff's. In this case, the piece was in the key of C. Beethoven therefore specified that

88. Beethoven, *Leonore Overture No. 3*, Op. 72a. (measures 378–389) Score in C.

(*Continued*)

88. Cont'd.

all instruments be in C and expected that C instruments would be used in the performance of the number. If the modern clarinetist is reading from the original C part, he will have to play each note *one whole tone higher* than written in order for it to sound correctly on his B♭ clarinet. (In studying this excerpt, remember that the French horns in C sound an octave lower than notated and that the trumpets sound as written.)

While we have this example in front of us, let us look at another phase of score-reading from the conducting standpoint. The page appears to be heavily scored. But look more carefully. Notice that in the first six measures there are actually only three rhythms going on: (1) the quarter-half-quarter-note rhythm of the first measure, prevalent at the top of the page, (2) the reiterated notes in the strings which correlate in pitch with the woodwinds, and (3) the rhythm of the trombones and timpani. Or, reducing still further the scoring, one might say that it is even simpler: only two parts, the melody in the woodwinds and strings doubling each other, and the distribution of the harmonizing notes among the brasses and second violins. Many of the greatest pages of orchestral music (and the *Leonore No. 3* belongs in this category) are as simple in construction as this when analyzed, so do not be afraid of many notes on a page. Take courage from this example and stop and see just what is going on.

The Score Not in "C"

The more-often-encountered score is that in which all notes are written as fingered on the various transposing instruments. In such scores, the interpretation of just how these notes will sound is left to the conductor and his knowledge of the transpositions. The reader will quickly see that most of the scores quoted herein belong to this category. We are speaking at this time of the orchestra, but this manner of score-notation is well-nigh invariable in the full scores for band. Since these facts obtain, the future conductor will do well to acquire fluency in reading transpositions.

The Orchestral Score, Historically

The very early scores for orchestra are confined to the strings with or without the addition of a wind instrument or two. Among these early scores we find the *Brandenburg Concertos* by Bach. See Example 89.

89. Bach, *Brandenburg Concerto No. 2 in F*. First movement (measures 1–2).

* Cembalo and Violoncello are on a separate line from the Violone di ripieno in the original score. *Ripieno* is the tutti instruments as distinguished from the solo instruments (*concertino*), which appear on the four staves at the top of the score.

The full wind-string orchestra as we know it today began to develop with the work of Franz Joseph Haydn. Quite common in his day were the scores for oboes, bassoons, French horns, trumpets, timpani and strings, with sometimes the addition of the flute. (See Example 90.)

90. Mozart, *Symphony in D major ("Prague")*. First movement, beginning.

The clarinet entered the orchestra symphonically about the middle of the eighteenth century. Examples of its use may be found in the works of some of the Mannheim composers and in Mozart's Opera, *Idomeneo* (1780), and his symphonies K. 297 in D major (Paris, 1778) and K. 543 in E flat major (Vienna, 1788,). The composer himself added clarinets to his symphonies K. 385 ("Haffner") and K. 551 ("Jupiter"). His last concerto was written for clarinet and orchestra in 1791. The trombone was introduced for the first time symphonically by Beethoven in the Finale of his Fifth Symphony, but the instrument had already established its place in church music performances and as a functional part of the opera orchestra. Under Berlioz, Wagner, and Tchaikovski, the orchestra was still further enlarged in instrumentation, and in our day such novel effects as the recorded song of the nightingale,* the use of cow bells, and even the typewriter are accepted to add a bit of color to the performance.** Other "sound effects" have also been tried, but one hesitates to accept them as "music."

Some of today's rhythms are very complicated, and our harmonic structure encompasses the free use of all twelve tones of the chromatic scale, uninhibited by tonality. Instrumentation is whatever is needed to make the sound-effect desired.

The next excerpt, Example 91, is interesting from the standpoint of the syncopated accents and the articulation of the chords at odd moments. (Page 154.)

As the instrumentation has expanded and the rhythms and harmonies have become more intricate, so has the job of the conductor grown in size. See Example 92.

(In the original of Example 92, cello II and bass each occupy a single line of the staff.)

Finally, let us quote a page from Stravinsky's *Rite of Spring*. "The Sacrificial Dance: The Chosen One." Here we see the very essence of modern orchestral problems. (Example 93.)

---

* *The Pines of Rome* by Respighi.
** *The Typewriter* by Leroy Anderson.

91. Rimsky-Korsakoff, *Russian Easter Overture*, Op. 36. (Allegro agitato, measures 58–65).

92. Darius Milhaud, *Concertino d'été* for Viola and nine instruments. (measures 111–112.) © 1952 by Heugel & Cie. Editeurs, Paris. Reprinted by permission.

93. Stravinsky, *The Rite of Spring.* Sacrificial Dance: The Chosen One (measures 1–10). © 1921 by Edition Russe de Musique. Copyright assigned to Boosey & Hawkes 1947. Reprinted by permission of Boosey & Hawkes.

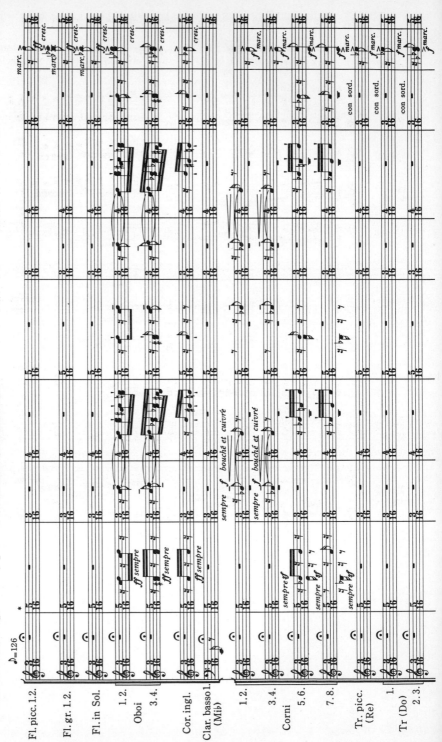

156

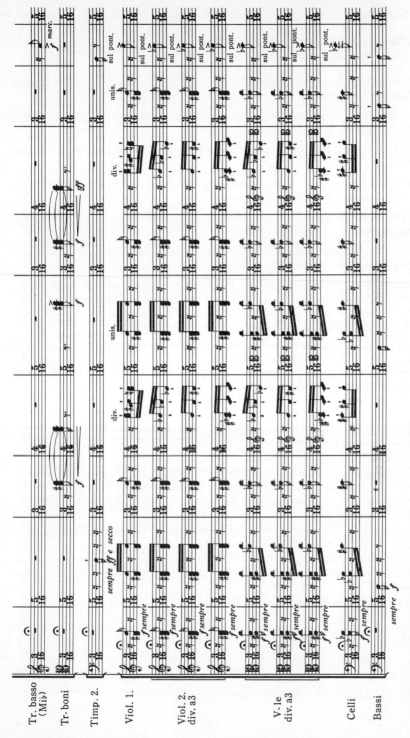

* The student will find editions in which the second and fifth measures of the passage quoted read 2/16, 3/16 instead of 5/16 shown here. NOTE: *Bouché et cuivré* in the French horn parts mean "muffled (stopped horn) and brassy."

157

**EXERCISES FOR PRACTICE: ACQUAINTANCE
WITH THE ORCHESTRAL SCORE**

1. Memorize the order of instruments in a standard score such as the *Leonore
No. 3 Overture*, Example 88.

2. Familiarize yourself with the order of instruments in the larger form of the
score. See Appendix B, Part 1.

3. Study all of the full-page excerpts in this chapter, comparing format, transpositions, and so on.

4. Analyze each excerpt for the number of parts actually sounding. Notice where
the scoring condenses to three or four parts.

5. Go through the score sheets and name each instrument when it enters after a
few beats of rest.

6. Take the viola part (middle line is middle C) and play it through on the piano
or on your own major instrument.

7. Practice the time-beating gestures for all of the excerpts given while either
singing or thinking-in-pitches the melody line. Pay attention to the switching of the
melodic outline from one instrument to another. If necessary, mark these changes
lightly in colored pencil.

8. Refer to Appendix A. Study the seating charts for the standard grouping of
instruments in the several types of orchestras given. Then practice the excerpts in
this chapter, directing your attention to the place where this or that instrument
is situated in the orchestral setup.

RECOMMENDED REFERENCE READINGS (SEE APPENDIX G)

Gal, Hands, *Directions for Score Reading.*

Jacob, Gordon, *How to Read a Score*, Chapter VI, pp. 39–46, "Aural Imagination."
    Very fine examples stressing solo passages for the various instruments of the
    orchestra are to be found herein, as an aid to recognizing these instruments by
    ear.

Krueger, Karl, *The Way of the Conductor*, Chapter VII, VIII, pp. 83–104, "History
    of the Modern Orchestra."

Read, Gardener, *Thesaurus of Orchestral Devices.* A large book containing hundreds
    of musical examples showing the various uses of the instruments in their many
    aspects.

Rood, Louise, *How to Read a Score.*

12

Mechanics
of the
Band Score

The band score is largely a product of the twentieth century. During its emergence as such it has gone through many growing pains. An examination of the scores of the twenties and thirties will show great variation in the order of the instruments on the page. The size of the full score for band is necessarily larger than that for orchestra since the modern American symphonic band includes in its regular instrumentation many instruments which are used only upon occasion in the orchestra or are not used at all. These include the small E♭ clarinet, the English horn, the saxophones, cornets, baritone horn (almost exclusively a band instrument), and the alto and bass clarinets, which are orchestral instruments in the best sense of the word, but which are not an invariable adjunct of the fine orchestral score. In the band the sousaphones largely replace the orchestral tubas and the snare drum is almost everpresent.

At the time of the writing of this text we can safely say that the score for full symphonic band has established itself with dignity; that it is settling down into a standard form and that, as such, it is here to stay.

Not only is the full score a reality, but there are also the many types of abbreviated scores ("condensed scores") which are also accepted as standard now. In general, these scores in the smaller forms are entirely in C. They might be compared to the orchestral theater-scores called the piano-conductor.

The Piano-Conductor Score

The piano-conductor score (which originally was printed for orchestral use, the piano making up for the lack of complete instrumentation) is a C score of three lines. The top line carries the important melodies, annotated as to what instruments are playing the parts. Beneath appears a piano part that fills in the harmonies and strengthens the melody line wherever it may be thin. The two staves for the piano are bracketed as such. Many band scores of the present day use a comparable form.

The advantage that the piano-conductor score has is that it can be quickly and easily played on the piano, without transposition, and the conductor can thereby familiarize himself immediately with the sound of the music. Its great disadvantage is its lack of precise information as to which instrument is playing which note of the harmony. The conductor has only a general idea of what is transpiring when he uses this score.

The Modern Three-Line Band Score

The modern three-line band score is a derivation from this piano-conductor score-form. It may be played rather adequately on the piano since all parts are in C, but it is not written in a piano medium. The lowest line is devoted to the bass clef instruments and the upper lines are used as seems best for the other instruments of the ensemble.

Let us now examine the first page of a fine three-line condensed score for band. The Williams *Symphony in C minor* is a true band classic of the twentieth century. The full score is available, but for the purpose of presenting the various types of scoring, we have chosen this page in condensed form. (Example 94.)

We see here an excellent exemplification of what the condensed score deals with. Notice that when two lines will do instead of three (as shown on the bottom staves of the page) the composer has reduced the score accordingly and has clearly annotated the instrumentation.

The reader will further notice that at the beginning the *two* lowest lines of the three are used for the bass instruments, since the symphony opens with

94. Ernest S. Williams, *Symphony in C minor* for band. First movement (measures 1–32). © 1938 by Ernest S. Williams. Copyright assigned by Edwin H. Morris Music Company to Charles Colin 1958. Reprinted by permission of Charles Colin, 1225 Sixth Ave., New York 19, N. Y.

a heavier scoring in the low instruments. On the second set of staves this bass clef sign changes to treble clef for the horn entrance two measures before rehearsal number One. Such changes are very typical of the three-line scoring. Each line is used *as needed* with clef and instrumentation changing in the most functional way. The three-line score is greatly used in editions for school bands where much doubling of parts exists among the instruments of the several classifications.

In the fifth measure of the Williams work, notice the extra line for the percussion (Tam-tam). This writing of the percussion parts on a single added line is also typical of the condensed score. When the timpani part becomes prominent, it will usually be found on the bass clef scoreline with the other bass clef instruments. Observe its entrance on the third measure after the rehearsal letter 1. The "plus" sign here means "add" the timpani to the instrumentation at this point.

Let us now refer to several measures of another work. Example 95 is taken from the *Bolero* of Moszkowski, arranged by Philip Lang.

95. Moritz Moszkowski, *Bolero*, Op. 12, No. 5. Arranged for band by Philip J. Lang. (a) measure 1; (b) measure 5; (c) measure 37. © 1948 by Mills Music, Inc. Used by permission.

Here the score shows the two top lines devoted to the treble clef instruments and the lowest line reserved for the *lower notes* of the score, not necessarily the bass clef instruments (measure 1). At letter A the high clarinets enter and later on the flutes and oboe are scored on the top line. At measure 37 notice that the middle line makes a quick switch to carrying the brilliant cornet entrance. (Remember that *cor.* in band music means *cornet*, whereas in orchestral scores it signifies horns. The instrumentation in band scores is customarily given in English.)

The Modern Four-Line Band Score

The four-line score is used when the disposition of the instrumentation and harmonic structure will not condense clearly into the three-line pattern. The four-line score can be a little more specific in the information it gives to the conductor. Example 96 is taken from the transcription for band of the Coronation Scene from *Boris Godounov* by Moussorgsky, made by Erik Leidzén.*

Notice that Mr. Leidzén has devoted the second line of his score to the French horns, even though they are doubling the muted cornets in the first measure and the second and third clarinets and saxophones in the second

96. Modeste Moussorgsky, *Boris Godounow*. Coronation Scene. Transcribed for the Goldman Band by Erik Leidzén (measures 3–4). Copyright 1936 by Carl Fischer, Inc., New York. Used by permission.

* (Respectful tribute should be paid to two great arrangers for band, Mr. Leidzén and Lucien Cailliet. Their contribution to the recognition of the musical worth of the fine symphonic band has been of untold value, not only to the bandsmen themselves but also to the music profession as a whole.)

measure of the example. Notice, too, the change in clef sign for the purpose of keeping the notes on the staff rather than on leger lines. This fine notation makes for a clean-cut appearance on the page and an easy handling of the musical problems by the conductor.

The Solo Instrument in the Score

For the stand-up solo, many scores for band resort to the typical piano-conductor setup on the page. The solo instrument (or solo ensemble such as trumpet trio) is placed on the top line of the three-line score. The band accompaniment is written on the two lower lines, bracketed so that they look exactly like the former piano part, but marked "band" instead of "piano." Example 97 shows the first two measures of such an arrangement of scoring.

97. Clifton Williams, *Dramatic Essay* for solo trumpet and band (measures 1–2). Copyright 1958, Summy-Birchard Company, Evanston, Illinois. Used by permission. All rights reserved.

The Full Score for Band

So now we turn to the full score for band, similar to the scores for orchestra with which the student has already familiarized himself (Chapter 11). Our first extract is a score involving modern rhythmic problems. Example 98.

This type of scoring is presented here first, because it will not overwhelm the reader with a great multitude of parts such as are found in some of the other scores quoted in full-page examples in this chapter. This smaller score makes an excellent steppingstone from the fewer lines of the orchestral score to the many lines of the full score for symphonic band.

In conducting example 98, the student is cautioned to make the eighth notes of even length throughout and not to permit them to become triplets-on-one-beat in the 3/8 measures.

Check up on the doubling of voices during study of the later-quoted scores. Notice what type of dynamic marking occurs. Are the dynamics balanced by the composer, or do they follow the early orchestral tradition of marking the same dynamic for all parts and leaving the subsequent balancing to the players and the conductor? Is the melody line scored so that it will project easily, or will the accompanying parts have to be softened? These questions are very important in dealing with scores for school use, since school organizations vary greatly in instrumentation and individual efficiency.

Our next Examples, Nos. 99 and 100, give excerpts from the Fauchet *Symphony for Band*. It pre-dates, by a dozen years, the Williams Symphony, and score-wise is an interesting example of the musical form of several movements adapted to the band medium.

Here the reader begins to see the dimension which a score for large band can assume. The conductor will notice the close resemblance in setup to the orchestra score. The bar-lines break at the end of the small groups of instruments, just as they do for *families* of instruments in the orchestral score. Here Mr. Fauchet has grouped the clarinets together as a family. The bassoon appears as a maverick, at first glance, being placed with the flute and oboe. But this is not illogical, since oboe and bassoon together form the double-reed section of the band and the flute is often in octaves with the oboe. The upper middle section of the score is given over entirely to the single reeds, clarinets and saxophones.

At the bottom of the score come the brasses. Notice the extra bracket grouping the staves occupied by instruments of identical name. The percussion is placed on the very lowest lines just as in many other types of scores for band.

We now come to the largest of large scores for the band in Example 101. We find that the number of lines in the score has jumped from the twenty-five of the Fauchet Symphony to a total of thirty-one in the Wagner-Cailliet score.*

In this score, the double reeds are grouped together after the flutes, followed in turn by the single reeds. The brasses occupy the lower section of the score. Note that the position of the trombones and baritones will be found to be reversed in certain other scores for full band.

One further point should be noticed here and that is the enharmonic writing of the signatures, sharps in the flutes, double reeds and low brasses, and flats in the rest of the instruments. An alto saxophone in E♭ playing in a five-flat signature comes out in the key of F♭ major, concert, which is, enharmonically, E major for the C instruments. (Circle 4 on the excerpt.)

For interpretation of the band score see Chapter 14.

---

* Blank staves for the drums and the timpani, which appear below the harp on the original score, are omitted in Example 101.

98. Frederick M. Breydert, *Suite in F* for band. Finale (measures 1–11). © 1954 by Mills Music, Inc. Used by permission.

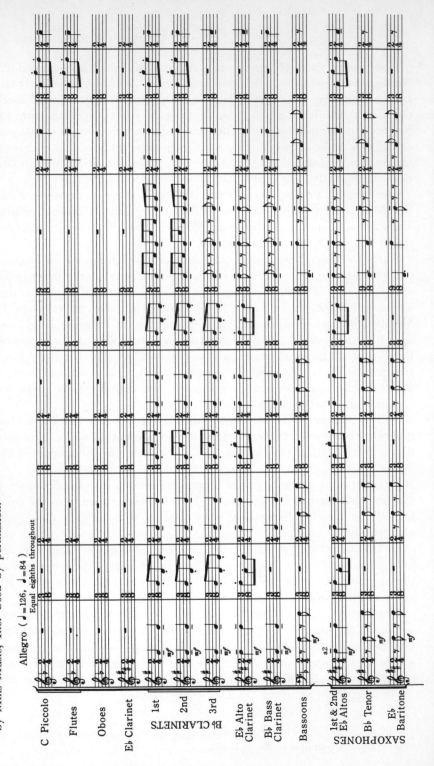

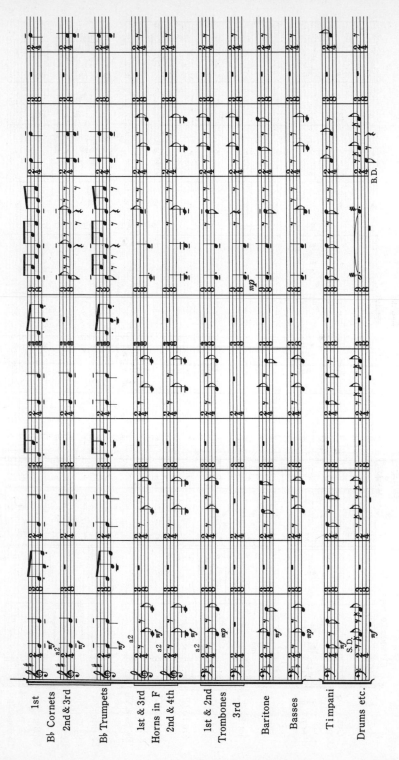

167

99. Paul Fauchet, *Symphony in B♭* for Band. (Arranged by Gillette) First movement. (a) (page 17). Copyright 1926 by Evette & Schaeffer. Copyright 1934 by M. Witmark & Sons. Copyrights renewed. All rights for the United States and Canada controlled by Warner Bros–Seven Arts, Inc. Used by permission.

169

100. Fauchet, *Symphony in B♭* for Band. (Arranged by Gillette) First movement. (b) (page 29). Copyright 1926 by Evette & Schaeffer. Copyright 1934 by M. Witmark & Sons. Coryrights renewed. All right for the United States and Canada controlled by Warner Bros.-Seven Arts, Inc. Used by permission.

101. Richard Wagner, *Lohengrin*. Elsa's Procession to the Cathedral. Arranged for band by Lucien Cailliet (page 5 of the full score). Copyright 1938 by Remick Music Corporation. Used by permission of Warner Bros.-Seven Arts, Inc.

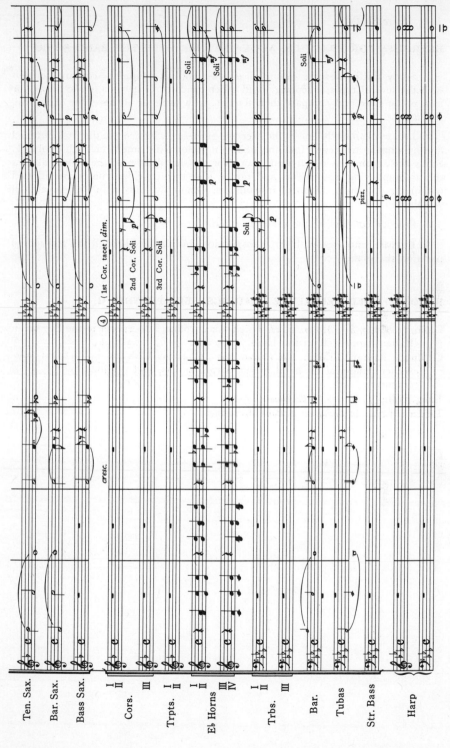

173

EXERCISES FOR PRACTICE: ACQUAINTANCE WITH THE BAND SCORE

1. Study the band-score examples as given in this chapter. Acquaint yourself with the several types of scoring. Find other band scores in your music library or at a music store and compare their formats with those given here. See Appendix B, Part 1.

2. Locate the melody line in the excerpts given here. Notice whether it is doubled and by what instruments. Imagine what tone color will come from such doubling. Study the accompanying rhythms. Look for the distribution of the chords among the accompanying instruments and notice how the individual notes are allotted within the particular group of instruments. Obviously, only a full score can tell you this.

3. Practice conducting the excerpts given.

4. Increase your ease with the transpositions by playing through the transposed parts on the piano.

RECOMMENDED REFERENCE READINGS (SEE APPENDIX G)

Gallo, Stanislao, *The Modern Band*. This book introduces the reader to the European (Italian) approach to the band.

Goldman, Richard Franko, *The Concert Band*, Chapters VI-VIII, pp 147–211, give excellent material on band music, arrangements, and originals by the great composers.

Lang, Philip J., *Scoring for the Band*.

Leidzén, Erik, *An Invitation to Band Arranging*.

13

Interpreting
the Choral Score

Choral music has come through several periods in its development historically. The very early music, largely church oriented, was sung *a cappella* (unaccompanied). There was no recurrent accentuation. The words themselves were the important thing. Stress was laid on a level, continuous dynamic for all long tones.

Choral Style

This style gradually succumbed to the idea that long notes should be made to "come alive." The *bel canto* school of singing took over. This was a style of great lyricism, stressing beauty of tone and the legato line. The sustained vowel sound, when interrupted by the articulation of a consonant, would be interrupted as little as possible. One should feel the legato line as continuous throughout, in spite of the consonant interruption. Instrumental accompaniment by stringed instruments became popular. Gradually the musical sound emerged from its background position to become an active entity in the song itself.

Schubert is recognized as having had an extraordinary talent for catching the spirit of the poem and transferring that same spirit to the music. He started the process of giving the accompaniment something important to say in its own right, thus adding to the content of the words. Schumann, in his turn, carried through on this idea so that the *Lied* became a duet of sorts between the voice and the piano.

Choral music relies heavily on the words to set the style for the rendition. Here there is a divergence from instrumental music in that the latter, having no words to articulate, depends for its stylistic changes largely upon the musical customs of the historical period in which it was written and upon the personal attributes of the composer himself.

Let us examine for a moment the language aspect of style. A language such as Italian, which has many words ending in vowels, lends itself naturally to *bel canto*. In contrast, a language that bristles with consonants (as does German or Russian) will acquire a somewhat harsher type of articulation and therefore a different stylistic sound in making its musical contribution.

Dynamics in choral composition have an emotional basis. The emotion states the dynamic. (One does not sing a lullaby with either the same dynamic or the same emotional content one would use for an operatic cry of anguish.) In instrumental music the process is often reversed. The dynamic sounded induces the emotion in the listener. Emotions become tangible in choral music because the words demand it. They exist equally in instrumental music, but they are intangible.

With this in mind, certain things of a practical nature may now be dealt with.

1. *Horizontal motion.* The horizontal or forward motion in each voice in a choral composition should have a certain inevitableness about it. Wide skips between notes in the horizontal line are always difficult and especially so in the inner voices. Notice these as they occur in the score and solve their problems before the rehearsal begins. Much valuable knowledge is gained through attention to the horizontal line of the choral score.

2. *Vertical relationship.* The vertical relationship of the parts is their harmonic relationship. Good ensemble is dependent upon the vertical synchronization of the parts. The best way to study this facet of the score is to sing each beat from the bottom upward, bass to soprano. This clarifies the harmonic outline in the conductor's mind.

3. *Difficult entrances.* There are times when the singers have difficulty in accurately locating their entry note following several beats of rest. Often the conductor can clarify such places by calling attention to the sounding of the same pitch a beat or two before by another voice. Example 102 is an excellent illustration of this.

In the given example the entrance of the new part is made each time on the identical pitch as the *last sung note* in the preceding voice before the new voice enters. In the first measure of the example, the alto sings B on the eighth note just before the soprano enters on that same pitch. Each entrance is similar.

It is the conductor's job to clarify such difficulties for the singers. He will do well to search diligently during his score study for ways in which he can better these entrances after rests, should such help be needed in the rehearsal. Assurance on the part of the singers means confidence for the conductor. It works both ways!

102. J. Lamont Galbraith, *Out of the Silence* (measures 12–15). © 1919 by The Oliver Ditson Co. Reprinted by permission of Theodore Presser Company, Bryn Mawr, Pennsylvania.

4. *Breathing in long phrases.* When long phrases must be sustained, the conductor may suggest "staggered" breathing in which the singers do not breathe simultaneously, but each catches a quick breath and re-enters the music as individually necessary thus preserving the sustained tone-quality. A breath taken just after a strong beat is less noticeable than one taken before the strong beat. This is true also in slurred passages. If the breath is insufficient to carry through the slur, take the new breath after a note that falls *on* a beat and preferably a strong beat of the measure.

5. *Tone quality.* The conductor of the vocal group is working with what might be termed the most *personal* type of music, namely, the instrument within man himself. In everyday life, subjective attitudes are usually apparent in the speaking voice. The choral conductor should face this fact and train his singers to set the mood of the song itself, regardless of their individual and personal feelings at the time.

To get the message of the song across to the audience, one emphasizes the important words and pays good attention to the phrasing.

Any spoken vowel, when sustained, will take on the pitch of a musical tone. The skillful choral conductor is always conscious of the beauty of tone produced by his singers on their sustained vowel sounds. In score study, notice where the long vowels occur. Good vowel sound is accompanied by the proper opening of the mouth as the tone comes forth, without tension in the throat.

Many beautiful effects may be accomplished by giving the third of the chord special attention whenever the tone quality is weak or thin. Strengthening this note will add luster to the sound. The third of the chord is also one of the links in fine intonation. When a chorus begins to flat, it is frequently because the voices singing the third of the chord have been careless in perfecting the intonation. The seventh of the scale is also dangerous in this respect. Perfect intonation enhances tone quality.

6. Since the choral profession is apparently divided on the next point, we shall briefly state the two views without urging the acceptance of either. The problem concerns the vowel that is slurred over several notes. Example 103 is pertinent.

103. Palestrina, *Tell Me, What Master Hand* (quoted in full in Example 84). By permission of Novello and Co., Ltd.

won - drous

One hears, at times, the articulation of a soft "h" attack in the slurred vowel as the pitch changes. Certain very fine teachers argue against the use of this device for two reasons: (1) It tends to interrupt the legato line which is the main reason for the writing of the slur; and (2) it tends to build breathiness into the tone. Other very fine teachers sanction its use to prevent the glissando which often mars slurred runs in vocal execution. Some opera singers use it, some do not. The young conductor of vocal groups is advised to talk with the finest vocal teachers he can contact on this point. Perhaps the use of this device may depend upon the size of the auditorium and the heft of the accompaniment.

7. *Final consonants.* The ending of most tones is given more special attention in choral music than in instrumental performance because of the fact that many English words end in a final consonant that must be articulated cleanly and together by the singers. This is especially true of *sustained* tones ending in a consonant. The cut-off should be shown in such cases.

Final S sounds cause much trouble. They should be spoken softly and placed late in the beat. Final D's and G's, when given clean-cut pronunciation, add immensely to the clarity of the words. There is a tendency for choruses to sustain final M's, N's and R's, instead of the vowel preceding them. These letters, too, should be delayed until the last possible moment.

The clean articulation of the consonant makes the speech understandable.* Since the words carry the story of the music, if they cannot be understood,

---

* There is the story of Chaliapin, the great Russian basso of the recent past, standing backstage in the opera house during rehearsal and singing over and over the Russian word for God (*Bog*), fighting out an articulation of both consonants that would freeze the blood of the audience when the dramatic moment should arrive.

there is no point to singing them. Their ultimate sense depends upon the distinctness of the consonant and the correctness of the vowels.*

The choral conductor should listen constantly and consciously to the words as his chorus sings them. Too often his own familiarity with the song gives him the illusion of good pronunciation on the part of his singers. Listen to *hear* what your chorus is saying.

A fine exercise for diction is that of having the whole chorus sing together one of the Gilbert-Sullivan "patter songs." It is great fun and an excellent exercise for the tongue.

The Operetta

If the show has music, the music must be good. If it is an operetta, everyone should have fun performing it.

Here are some useful hints: (1) Drill the chorus, the soloists, and the orchestra each separately first; the chorus for words and action; the soloists, to know their parts thoroughly—the whole show depends on them when they are soloing; the orchestra to mark cuts, to check the parts for wrong notes, to indicate the number of verses, and sometimes "cue lines." Stage-exit repeats will have to wait for a stage rehearsal. Anything that can waste time in the full rehearsal should be taken care of beforehand. (2) Have the chorus and soloists on stage first without the orchestra. Get all stage-business taken care of before bringing in the orchestra. (3) At the first stage rehearsal (without orchestra) make sure that everyone on stage can see the conductor in the pit. Also assign certain leaders who must watch the conductor more intently (preferably strong singers). (4) After the speaking parts, it is better to "crash the last line" with the orchestra introduction than to have a wait. The wait kills the show. A good stage show must not be allowed to sag. Call the orchestra to attention before the last speech starts. Also, train it to *get the music ready for the next number as soon as the end of the previous number is played.* This saves fumbling when it is time to play. (5) Bring the orchestra "into the act." Their introductions and interludes (even one-measure interludes while the singers take a breath) "set the mood" and must be so played. Orchestra dynamics should *project on the interludes;* build them up for those single measures that are important. (6) One fine opera conductor told the author, "Always *one really slow number* somewhere in the performance. The change of pace sparks the rest of the performance." (7) One solo violin is more apparent dynamically than are two violins playing in unison. (8) Tell the soloists, "In general we shall follow you, so feel free to lead. How-

* The young choral conductor is urged to study diligently the Marshall book on English Diction. (See the Reference Readings at the end of this chapter.)

ever, there are certain places where you will have to follow the conductor or the orchestra will not be with you. These places concern entrances on a fraction of an up-beat (usually occurring after fermatas), when the orchestra must play either *with* the singer or on the first beat of the following measure. In such cases the singer must take the cue for continuing from the conductor." (9) In school performances where the solo voices are weak (especially in the Junior High School) have the orchestra use the real "musical comedy style," very short notes articulating the beat but with little or no sustaining power. Strings: off-the-string bowings (spiccato), using a position near the frog of the bow and lifting after all short (quarters or less) notes. If the music calls for sustained tones, drop them back to double-piano immediately after the attack, to let the voices through. (10) Do *not* use the piano with the orchestra in performance if it is possible to avoid it. It usually leads out too loudly and the orchestra is blamed for the excessive dynamic. Warn the soloists on stage (and the chorus) that there will not be quite as emphatic an articulation from the orchestra as from the piano. Get them to listen intently to the orchestral sound during the rehearsals.

Finally a word about who is to conduct the performance. In the professional theater it is always the orchestra conductor. In school performances sometimes the choral teacher conducts the performance. Warning: If the school orchestra conductor is the man for the job, he will have to train himself to remember to give the chorus a good cut-off sign on their last sung note in each selection. If the chorus teacher conducts, it will be necessary to remember to *conduct* all orchestra afterludes (the orchestral measures that continue after the chorus or soloist has finished singing). Too often the school orchestra is left stranded at such places and the piece ends badly.

In choosing the operetta the choral conductor should consider carefully the abilities of the voices at his disposal. He should also set up committees among the chorus members to take care of much of the nonmusical business (ticket sales, publicity, costumes, and so on). The dramatics coach and the customary stage crews should be enlisted to help as well as the orchestra conductor.

Working in the pit, the performance conductor will have the problem of being remote from the singers on the stage. He will find that at times he will have to raise his hands higher than usual in order that his cues may be seen by the stage performers. Also, the sound of the orchestra may reach the audience before the sound from the stage. This should be checked out during rehearsals by going back into the auditorium to listen.

Very important is the consciousness of what is called "dramatic timing." This includes many things, not the least of which is the tempo at which the show must move. Whatever happens, it must not be allowed to sag for a moment. Care should be taken not to fall into the habit of using your own pulse-rate as the tempo-beat in piece after piece. It creates an amateurish monotony in the overall performance. On stage, the performers should be taught not to "crash a laugh." They should learn to wait until the audience "simmers down." The next line should be heard. Finally, the timing of the dramatic pause emerges: the length of the fermata and the silence after it, the "moment of suspense," the drama of surprise, the timing of a bass drum beat or a cymbal crash—all have to be intelligently dealt with. If a stage performance has music with it, the music must be good.

The legato line: In choral conducting the legato line of the beat tends to become more important than the ictus. Phrasal conducting and word artic-ulation will, at times, replace the steady reiteration of the beat as such. The speaking of the words is relied upon to hold the singers together to some extent. In instrumental music the beat alone does this. Therefore, if the choral conductor becomes the pit conductor, working with the orchestra as an accompanying medium, he must see that his *beat-pattern* is readable at all times. The down-beat (first beat) of every measure must be clearly recognizable. Contrariwise, if the instrumental conductor does the perfor-mance, he will do well to pay a little more attention to his horizontal lines and not over-emphasize the perpendicular gesture in his time-beating. Each conductor has something to learn from the other.

The fine choral performance carries the audience with it by presenting clearly the literary content of the words and the beauty of the music. The excellent rendition of either factor should never be made the excuse for a poor rendition of the other. The words tell the story. The music heightens the emotional color. Each must justify the existence of the other.

EXERCISES FOR PRACTICE: CHORAL INTERPRETATION

1. Take the assigned score for class performance and study it following the seven headings given in this chapter. Thereafter try to synthesize these various aspects into a single, total interpretation of the piece. Set the mood and see the composi-tion in its entirety. The audience is not interested in details. It is interested in the *song.* Failure to synthesize brings with it the same result one gets in plucking the feathers from a bird one by one. In the end, most of the beauty is gone.

2. Prepare to conduct the song without looking at the score. Leave the speaking of the words to the singers who are reading the music and turn your attention to the mood and the sound of the final result.

RECOMMENDED REFERENCE READINGS (SEE APPENDIX G)

Braithwaite, Warwick, *The Conductor's Art* Chapter XIII, pp 83–98, "The Conduct-ing of Choral Works." Part III, pp 101–176, is entirely devoted to the problems of the conducting of Opera.

Coward, Henry, *Choral Technique and Interpretation*, pp 69–87, "Words, Articulation, Diction;" pp 88–111, "Musical Expression;" pp 203–248, "Analysis of the *Messiah.*"

Crist, Bainbridge, *The Art of Setting Words to Music.* This book is excellent from the standpoint of analysis of the music. Scattered throughout are analytical discussions of specific works. These are valuable in their relationship to interpretation.

Davison, Archibald T., *Choral Conducting*, Chapter V, "Choral Technique," pp 44–73. The instrumentalist, particularly, is urged to read this chapter.

Finn, William J., *The Conductor Raises His Baton*, Chapters IV-VI, pp 95–223, "Dynamics."

Howerton, George, *Technique and Style in Choral Singing*. Part II, pp 79–187, deals with styles of the several historical periods of musical composition and of the various countries and geographical influences as applied to choral singing.

Jones, Archie M., *Techniques of Choral Conducting*, Chapter III, pp 37–45, "Diction;" (Tables on the specific pronunciation of words, vowels and consonants in Chapter III); Chapter IV, pp 46–56, "Choral Interpretation;" Appendix E, pp 108–134, Interpretative Analyses.

Marshall, Madeleine, *The Singer's Manual of English Dction*. A comprehensive and very complete manual of this important aspect of singing.

14

Interpreting
the Band Score

Only in the twentieth century has the band come into its own. Certain of the leading present-day composers have recognized it as a serious musical medium and some excellent compositions have been forthcoming. Its repertoire needs many more of these and the ranking composers are being urged to write for the wind organization as such.

Since this is true, the repertoire is obviously, to a large extent, a twentieth-century product. It is shunted into three channels: (1) the fine original works for the symphonic band mentioned in the first paragraph; (2) the twentieth-century arrangements of great orchestral works which were written originally by the masters of the past for whom the band was, in their day, a closed door; and (3) music created specifically for instructional purposes, training materials for bands of all ages and all levels of advancement.

Comparing the writing for the band and the orchestra, we find certain differentiations pertinent to each of them. For example, in the band, the chordal tones of a harmony might be distributed among the clarinets (two B♭, an alto and a bass), or among the saxophones, or the four French horns, so that the chord would be complete within the individual section. In the orchestra, such a harmony would, of necessity, have to be distributed among the instruments of the woodwind *family* as such, or the brasses or the strings, the harmony being completed within the family but not necessarily on like instruments.

One of the greatest points of dissimilarity in the writing for the two organizations stems from the ability of the orchestra to capitalize on the individual tone color of the solo wind instrument. The string-tone background in the orchestra serves to highlight the solo quality of the winds, their individual and unique colors, in a way which is very limited in the band. Thus the orchestral palette is more colorful, the band more opaque in color texture, weightier in quality against the soloist.

The orchestral wind player will find himself often using his finest solo tone in order to *project* his playing, whereas, the same player sitting in the band will be more conscious of *blending* with his section so that he alone does not protrude unduly. In this phase of interpretation the band is closely linked to the customary choral practices. In band and chorus, the blend of tone is of paramount importance. In the orchestra, the solo character of the wind tone is of first concern much of the time.

With these ideas in mind, we can see the basic difference in the writing for the two organizations, band and orchestra.

The band composition, especially on the school level, keeps most of the instruments playing most of the time. This is fine from the standpoint of interest and technical development, for it is much more gratifying to play than to count rests. Wind *technique* is developed through band participation, but *solo tone* is developed through orchestral playing. (The top players in most school bands need the enriched curriculum that orchestral playing will give them. Also, they should be introduced, as early as possible, to the "professional repertoire" for their instruments—a repertoire which is, regardless of one's personal prejudices, an *orchestral* repertoire. It is the repertoire they will *hear* for years to come.)

The Basic Problems

These remarks spotlight the need, now, for focusing attention on the basic problems of a good *sectional* sound.

INTONATION

The first of these is intonation. When many instruments are playing in unison, it is difficult to get purity of tone unless the intonation is impeccable. The rougher the band sounds, the more likely it is that the intonation is bad. Sound waves which are sent out into the air, each fighting for its individuality of intonation, create a huge turmoil that sounds anything but pleasant. Tones which are projected with consonant intonation and, therefore, a consonant purpose, result in a tone quality much more in keeping with the chief purpose of Music as such.

Good intonation results (1) when the players are taught to hear what is actually going on, and (2) when they are taught to adjust pitch instantly on their instruments. Every wind instrument has a certain amount of leeway in intonation which can be utilized by the player. The careful adjustment of pitch is a part of the technique of skilled performance. Band members should be instructed on how to make these adjustments on their individual instruments, and they should be expected to make them as necessary for the over-all good intonation.

The ability to make fine auditory distinctions and correspondingly quick adjustments is also the foundation upon which success with the second basic problem of the sectional sound depends. This second problem is *balance*.

BALANCE

Since the band color is the sectional color it is, comparatively, a rare thing when the melody line in a band arrangement is played by one solo wind. The conductor should, therefore, study his scores to determine what the sections are doing as individual units and how each fits into the blend of the entire score. For example, which section has the melody line? Is it doubled by another section in unison or octaves? If so, what is the resulting dynamic power of this melody when played with the composer's markings and *by the particular musical organization being conducted*? If the melody does not project as it should, how can you, as conductor, change the balance in order to give the composer his desired sounds? In your organization, is it best to strengthen the melody, or can you best make some deletions in the accompanying voices, still preserving the original harmony?

The melody line should be clearly heard and understood by the audience. This often means great *tempering of the accompanying instruments*, a thing which the conductor has every right to insist upon. When the score is written by a fine band composer, he will have taken care of much of the balancing— provided his music is played by an adequate musical organization. The rest is left to the conductor of the particular band in question. Chordal accom-paniment of a sustained character is especially dangerous dynamically. It is so natural for over-enthusiastic playing of the "easy" spots to cover the melody line completely. *The conductor's ear must be the judge, not the written page*.

Not only should the melody-accompaniment balance be perfected, but the equalizing of dynamics within each section must be given attention. A triad, distributed among three clarinets, will sound bad if two of the players per-form at one dynamic and the third player produces a distinctly different degree of loudness. The chord notes should be balanced by the players within the section and then, retaining that inner balance, be fitted into the whole score at the properly synchronized dynamic level. This is a basic part of the conductor's job in the interpreting of the ensemble type of writing found in the band score. It must be given conscientious attention by the conductor. When perfect balance is accompanied by good intonation, then the organiza-tion begins to produce a really fine tone quality.

One further word about balance. It is greatly influenced by the response of the players, individually, to the baton. It is easier to produce a given amount of tone on some instruments than on others. This is probably the greatest factor in unbalanced sounds. Each musician should be trained to know what it takes to produce the several degrees of dynamic *on his own instrument* (and in his several registers), and should try faithfully to deliver each at the right time so that he will blend with his fellow bandsmen in achieving the finest ensemble effect possible.

Another factor that has a vital impact on tonal beauty is the conductor's general style of conducting. The director who replaces technique with cheerleading in his gestures can expect a rougher quality, less accuracy in attacks and releases, and poorer intonation from his band than the conductor who has taken the time and trouble to acquire a good, controlled conductorial technique. The very best of the band directors are not wild men with their arms. Their baton work is neat, precise and not overly accented on the ictuspoints. In this connection, special care should be taken where loud brass entrances are indicated. Over-enthusiasm in the stick often produces the burble in the player's horn as he responds too anxiously. A definite and not-too-heavy ictus, followed immediately by a tenuto gesture is a fairly safe recipe for the loud brass entrances. Such a handling helps to produce the richness desired from the full-throated brasses without forcing an initial cracking of the tone. Naturally, there must be good impulse of will on the conductor's part in the showing of the attack, but it should be controlled *technically* in the stick so that it does not run away with his gesture.

ATTACK AND RELEASE

As for clarity of attack, this depends greatly on a preset embouchure and a ready breath. The players who have been trained to take their breath as the conductor makes the preparatory part of the beat will be more likely to produce a good simultaneous attack than are those who have not consciously acquired this habit. Student entrances are often muffed and often late because the players have waited too long in preparing the breath.

Closely connected with the conducting of attacks is the handling of releases. The band conductor should pay very special attention to the manner in which he indicates the release of the tone. The too-sudden, too-sharp cut-off in the baton can produce from the players an explosive release of the breath creating an unpleasant accent instead of a precise ending of the tone. When this happens, the cut-off should be tempered down, retaining its accuracy, but deleting a little of its enthusiasm.

Transcriptions and Arrangements

In the performance of the modern original compositions for the band, the conductor has recourse to the customs of our times. "Traditions" are twentieth-century in almost every respect. Therefore, these works are not so dangerous. However, in the interpreting of the great orchestral works arranged for band, the conductor must be careful. Ignorance shows up quickly in this aspect of band conducting. The conscientious musician will listen to a number of recordings of such works. He will talk with the finest orchestral conductors with whom he can make contact. He will improve his knowledge of the orchestral repertoire at every opportunity, for then only will his readings of the great classics of all time have the true flavor of authenticity.

A word is pertinent here about transferring the early classical orchestral style of execution to the wind instrument medium. All tones rendered in this style should sound as if they were cut from the same piece of material. Shorter notes (such as sixteenths) will be executed with as much breadth as possible. They will not be softened or lightened as much as in the modern compositions. Even when each note is tongued, a staccato style should not result. In *allegro* movements longer notes, such as eighths among sixteenths or quarters among eighths, should be spaced. Wind players will learn much about this style of playing by listening to a fine classical rendition on either cello or violin. It is, typically, a "string" style.

Nearly all of the material as to style, classifying the score, use of staccato and legato, dynamic variation and tempo, given in the next chapter on *Interpretation of the Orchestral Score*, can be applied to the conducting of the *arrangements* for band. Study it carefully, whether or not you ever expect to conduct an orchestra. Poor musicianship is not forgivable in front of the band any more than it is in front of the orchestra or chorus.

One last observation concerning arrangements: in making the transfer from orchestra to band, the violin parts are frequently divided between clarinets, flutes and oboes. This often presents problems for the woodwinds. A fast spiccato passage in the strings may be much more difficult when transcribed for the woodwinds, due to the rapid tonguing involved. Therefore, the original tempo for orchestra may have to be slightly modified in band. This is usually no detriment if a composition is originally of perfect construction. The great masterworks are. Consequently, they will sound very convincing and enjoyable when played slightly slower. Only poorly constructed works need fear the light of slow performance where the bad writing can be clearly distinguished as such. The perfection of the original construction is the cue. Once the transfer has been made, the result must needs be a fine *band* performance. Whatever slight adjustments may have to be made, they should be accompanied by confidence. After all, the *sound* is the thing!

EXERCISES FOR PRACTICE: BAND INTERPRETATION

1. Study the excerpts given in Chapter 12. Apply the factors of balance to them. Think what the resulting dynamic would be when melodies and accompanying figures are played by professional as opposed to amateur organizations. Imagine what the

problems might be in an amateur organization and figure out what you might try in your effort to solve these problems for good musical results.

2. Listen to a recording of a fine symphony orchestra work (such as the "Jupiter" Symphony of Mozart, K 551, in C major) and imagine how it might be transcribed for band. Try to compare and contrast tone qualities of the two mediums. Do this without recourse to a score.

3. Practice conducting a recording or two and decide wherein your own personal interpretation might differ from that of the recording. Use a score for this and refer to the composer's markings.

4. If live groups are available in the classroom, find something which will be fairly complete with the available instrumentation (this may be anything from a small ensemble to something of band-size proportions) and rehearse the number. Listen carefully for clarity of balance, projection of the melody line, good intonation.

RECOMMENDED REFERENCE READINGS (SEE APPENDIX G)

While there are many books devoted to the organization and management of the band, there is practically nothing in print on band interpretation. The reader may be referred to the articles by William D. Revelli which ran for many years in the *Etude Magazine*, starting about 1935. However, this magazine is no longer in print.

Goldman, Edwin Franko, *Band Betterment*.

Prescott, Gerald R. and Lawrence W. Chidester, *Getting Results with School Bands*.
    An excellent and comprehensive handbook filled with practical suggestions for the administration of the school band.

Worrell, J.W., "Music by the Masters," *The Instrumentalist*, XIV, No. 3 (1959), pp 46–47, 92. A list of masterworks that have been arranged for the school band.

15

Interpreting the Orchestral Score

The orchestral conductor is working in a field of endeavor that has many great traditions. A lack of knowledge of these traditions marks him as less than efficient in his handling of the repertoire. There is not room to go into specific instances in specific compositions here. But certain general aspects of the subject can be dealt with modestly in the following discussion.

The composer for orchestra recognizes the solo character of each wind instrument in the ensemble. He paints with their colors against the string background just as an artist chooses his reds, yellows and greens. This factor permits a wonderful clarity to develop in the scoring for orchestra. The orchestral wind tone is also used sectionally and may combine with the strings to produce double-forte passages of great breadth and power. These two approaches to the winds of the orchestra should be borne in mind as the young conductor listens mentally to his score during score-study.

The percussion section in the orchestra is used somewhat more sparingly than it is in the band, with the exception of the timpani. In the orchestra the percussion is a means of highlighting the musical thought. This may span the entire range of brightness from the merest outlining of a delicate pianissimo rhythm to a burst of magnificence that will rival the sun itself in brilliance. The percussion is used only where it is needed, only when there is a real reason for its entrance into the musical thought. Each utterance from this section of the orchestra, be it a murmur, a simple statement, an unrelenting intensification of the emotional content, or a thunderous climax, must be made with the utmost sensitivity to the dramatic content of the music at that instant. The young conductor will do well to study his percussion parts with all of this in mind. He should challenge his imagination when he deals with these instruments. He must know their *raison d'être* whenever they enter the score.

And now comes the string section, that magnificent foundation of the whole orchestral structure. *The strings are the resonance of the orchestra.* The acoustical principles on which the stringed instruments are constructed are such that these instruments pick up added resonance from the other instruments of the orchestra through the action of the physical law of sympathetic vibration. This resonance can function only when the intonation is excellent. And intonation is excellent only when the conductor's ear (and the ear of each of his musicians) is trained to recognize perfect accord and to cure the faults when they exist. The intonation of any group starts with the demands of the conductor.

The ability of the strings to vibrate in sympathy with the sound waves sent out by the other instruments is the thing that gives to the orchestral tone that added glow, that spark of extra life, which nothing else in the musical sphere can equal. It is a law of nature and cannot be repealed.

Mutual respect must exist between the conductor and his string players. The conductor who knows only enough to whine and snarl at his strings will get nowhere. He must have arrived at that state of knowledge where he understands the problems of these instruments and how to make suggestions which will be truly constructive for them in their handling of the music. He himself should not be frustrated in his relations with the stringed instruments. He should realize that his string section has the largest mass of technique possible to any section of his ensemble, (the longest range per instrument, specialized types of bowings, harmonics, double stops, and so on). He should realize that they are constantly using, in their seven positions, what would amount to seven transpositions for the wind instruments (seven sets of fingerings). He should understand that a fine violin section, playing music of the Tchaikovski-Wagner-Brahms period, will wind in and out of these seven positions as casually as a professional clarinetist may read music for an A clarinet on his B♭ instrument. He should understand that there are as many as twenty-two usable fingerings for the production of the sound of the E on the third leger line above the staff in the treble clef when it is played on the violin. The fingering system of the stringed instruments is so extensive and so flexible that almost anything can be accomplished, *given a little time to figure it out.* But, this being true, the player cannot always guarantee to choose immediately, in sight-reading, the finest solution for the problems presented.

The conductor should also understand that while his winds perform the staccato in *one* way, varying its length as needed, the strings have actually six distinctly different styles of bowing for staccato notes: martelé, slurred staccato, spiccato, sautillé, ricochet, and staccato volante. (The reader will find a table with detailed explanations in Appendix C.) Each is a complete and separate style of bowing. Each is a specialized technique and must be mastered as such through many hours of concentrated study. The young conductor should know these things, and respect his string section. It conquers problems unknown to his winds.

The many bowing styles are not interchangeable. There is a proper place for everything, and each should be used in its place. The speed of the passage determines the type of staccato bowing which the strings will adopt to play it facilely and musically.

Let us now turn our attention to the orchestral traditions.

The Orchestral Traditions

The period in music history during which an orchestral work was written influences its interpretation, tempowise, dynamically, stylistically, in tone color and types of technique used on the instruments. A thorough knowledge of music history helps to give an *authentic* interpretation. A knowledge of the composer's life and personal philosophy helps to produce an *understanding* interpretation. Musical genius and sincerity on the part of the conductor, added to the other factors, can result in a *great* performance.

A conductor should be able, when necessary, to place a score in its correct historical setting, just by studying the clues on its pages. To illustrate, let us look at Example 104(a).

104.

This single line of music shows a driving continuity of sound, suggesting breadth in the tone and a relatively stable dynamic. One "feels" the contrapuntal style in the straightforward line of the music. No peculiar rhythmic abstractions are shown. If accents and dynamic variations between notes are inserted, they make no musical sense and actually sound ludicrous. Solid tone and continuous breadth are best. We conclude that the music is "late Baroque" or "early Classic," dated somewhere near 1650 to 1750, the time of Bach and Handel. (Both were born in 1685.) If this example were a score of four lines, each part would show the same characteristics as this single line.

Example 104(b). Here several things strike us simultaneously: The openness and clarity of the writing, the chord-tone structure, and the block-dynamic markings. This one has to be "late Classic," the Haydn-Mozart period. If this one were a full score, we might find the second violins, violas, cellos-basses, reiterating eighths throughout, forming a chordal harmony among themselves. The vertical harmonic style has superseded the polyphonic horizontal style.

Example 104(c). Now suddenly the first two styles seem to have merged into a still more advanced form. We are startled by the *notated* sudden and extreme dynamic markings, *ff* to *pp*, and also the *pp–cresc–ff* that repeats itself. Emotionalism is obvious on the page and strength is replacing lightness. We enter the "post Classic" or "early Romantic" period.

What do we see in Example 104(d)? Bristling accidentals, strange accents, odd rhythms battling at cross purposes, a discordant harmony: obviously Twentieth-century music.

These four great periods of musical composition are the milestones. The transition periods between them have been peopled by musical geniuses who have taken music where they found it and, by their combined efforts, carried it forward to the next milestone. Retracing this path we find some interesting *sequences:*

In tonal sound. Modes, major and minor scales (horizontal), chords (vertical), chromaticism, the whole-tone scale, twelve individual tones with no family ties, discord, sound-effects with infinite pitch (electronic music), and finally sound-effects with no pitch (tin cans dropped on the stage as part of the performance).

In Rhythmic Notation. Music without bar-lines (indeterminate note values), music with bar-lines (determinate note values), whole-beat notes (♩, ♩, 𝅝), fractional-beat rhythms (⁴₄ ♩. ♪ , ♩. ♩ , ⸰ ♫ ♪ ⸰), unbalanced rhythms extended or deleted by *half a beat*, staggering and unrelated rhythms in simultaneous performance, and finally notes and silences whose duration is controlled by a stop-watch—completely non-rhythmic. (The several language dictionaries define rhythm as a stress plus a relaxation, *repeated*.)

In Interpretation. First, we find that the conductor was free to show both the duration and the probable pitch of the note by his hand gestures—no written score being read by the singers; second, a period of free creativity in relation to what actually was notated (embellishments and solo cadenzas at the pleasure of the soloist); next, the composer begins to notate the embellishments and what he wants as a cadenza exactly as he wants it. Then comes the period of the worship of the *printed* note: artists write cadenzas that have become "standard," to make up for the oversight of the original composers. Finally, the performer is denied any creativity whatsoever. Every dynamic, every slightest nuance is stated; rhythms become mechanistic (if they exist at all) to the extent that the performer has to be a computing machine controlled by an electric current, and the conductor (poor man) stands on the podium, stop-watch in hand, to give the composer exactly what he has requested in his own handwriting. We said, "Finally . . ." but not quite; history is beginning to repeat itself. The "composer," in some instances now says "Well, *you* make it up as you go along . . . .!"*

The Instruments in the Score

Traditionally, the stringed instruments have formed the core of the massed instrumental performance. Prior to the seventeenth century, ensembles were formed by the "consort of viols." Gradually the string family developed into the string orchestra, adding now and then a trumpet or flute (the Bach Brandenburg Concertos and the Telemann Suites), and then the early orchestra of Haydn and Mozart materialized: Strings, plus two oboes, two bassoons, and two French Horns, with Timpani. The timpani entered the orchestral picture between 1670 and 1700, in the works of Locke, Lully, and Purcell. It was not long before the flute and trumpet became permanent members of the ensemble, with the clarinet being used in the Mannheim orchestra during Mozart's lifetime. (For full information on the brasses, see pages 126–130.) Today the brasses progress chromatically and diatonically instead of being limited to the chord of nature series.

Until the time of Mozart, the violins were limited in range from the G below middle C to the E on the third line above the staff. The instruments before his time had a short neck. With the advent of the longer neck the range

---

* In the last movement of the G-major Violin Concerto, at the end of the hustle and bustle of the little Allegretto, Mozart writes two of the funniest notes in all composition:

They clearly say: "So what?" (Finale: Rondeau, Allegretto, last measures.)

could be expanded. Mozart took the first violin part up to the very end of the E string—so high that the last reiterated half-step could be played only by rocking the finger back and forth.

Achieving Authentic Orchestral Interpretations

The Pre-Bach and Bach-Handel Periods. The period of the early string orchestra was the period of the chamber sonatas and concerti grossi of Corelli and Vivaldi. It is the period of the on-the-string bowings, the broad *détaché* strokes. (Détaché does not mean detached in the sense of staccato. It simply means "unslurred." Each note has a bow to itself.) In polyphonic music, the forward motion of the line should be interrupted as little as possible by the change of direction in the bow-stroke. One can see a close relationship between this and the *bel canto* principle that the legato line of the sung vowels should be interrupted as little as possible by the consonant articulation. It is the characteristic of the period. (See Chapter 13, pp 175, 176.)

It is interesting to note that Bach did not use any staccato dots in the autograph copy of his famous Six Sonatas for Solo Violin.

In spite of the customary lack of staccato markings in music of that period, the currently accepted style of execution requires that certain notes be spaced. For example, an allegro notated in sixteenths and eighths (semi-quavers and quavers) will retain the smooth détaché for the sixteenths, but will slightly space the eighths. Just how "authentic" this is we cannot prove, but it is today the generally accepted style for music of the polyphonic period. See Example 89, page 151.

In Bach's day, the bows used on the stringed instruments were still the old-style "viol" bows. These had an upward curving stick that negated many of the bowing techniques in use in our time. During the latter half of the eighteenth century the modern bow was designed by Tourte in Paris. Almost immediately bowing technique expanded. Mozart had access to the spiccato bowing (the bow bounces off the string after every note) that was denied to Bach. "Authentic" interpretations take cognizance of this fact.

Traditionally trills started on the upper note, the trilling note, rather than the written note. Where the trill is indicated on a dotted note, it is usually terminated on the dot in order to permit the written note to re-establish its place in the melody line.

The Haydn-Mozart (Classic) Period. As we have seen, big changes have taken place. Polyphony has given way to harmonic writing, the violin range has been expanded, new bowings have come into use. A transparency and clarity of string sound emerges, and attacks are better controlled. In Paris, Lully is insisting on uniform bowing in the orchestra. Composers are notating more dynamics in the scores, but they are of the "block" type. A forte is a forte all the way until a piano marking makes its appearance and then everything is piano. The dynamic markings in the score are identical for all instruments at all times. By tradition, therefore, it is customary for the performer to play *one degree louder than marked if he has the melody and one degree softer than marked if playing an accompanying part.* This gives two degrees of dynamic difference between the melody and its accompaniment, resulting in clarity and projection of the most important part.

Although the block dynamic now appears in the score, Stamitz in Mannheim is training his orchestra to perform the most exciting of crescendos and diminuendos, and thereby influencing vitally the composers of the day.

When two consecutive measures are identical, often the second measure is played softer as an echo of the first, even though no such dynamic is stated in the score. It is again a "tradition." Conductors today use the effect with good conscience when they feel that it is appropriate. (For example, the fourth measure of Haydn's D-major "London" Symphony, Example 86).

Regarding embellishments, we shall mention only those that are still vitally important in the orchestral repertoire today.

During Mozart's lifetime the appoggiatura and the acciaccatura ("grace notes") were undergoing a change. The appoggiatura, written as a small note but showing exactly half the rhythmic value of the following larger note (Example 105(a)) is played *on* the beat and becomes the first (and accented) note of a group of notes of equal value Example 105(b). Notice that the slur is retained.

105.

Modern editions are often printed like (b) in the example even though the score still retains the original notation (a) in tact. The use of the appoggiatura notation signified that the small note was not part of the vertical chordal harmony on that beat but that the following large note was.

The mordant (∿) is the single trill and can be treated as such.

The Turn follows the contour shown by the shape of the sign. Usually it proceeds upward first (Example 106(a)), but the upside-down form is used in performances of Wagner's *Rienzi* (b). When the Turn is written in conjunction with a dotted note, it is performed so that it terminates on the dot (c). The main melody line is thereby re-established before the music proceeds.

106.

These are the chief relics today of the very fancy embellishment customs prevalent in pre-Mozart times. Readers interested in pursuing this subject further are referred to the Recommended Reference Readings at the end of this chapter. One's musical taste can help greatly in making the embellishment sound logical and musical, but the conductor must be definite in telling the orchestra exactly what he wants whenever one of these markings appears in the score.

The Beethoven-Schubert Period. Here we come to the late Classic or early Romantic period—actually a transition period. Clarity now becomes strength; simple joyousness seems to acquire a certain passion; charm changes to nobility, and elegance is the order of the day. This period synthesizes what has gone before and lets it "grow up." Brilliant, full-powered climaxes pour forth from the orchestra. In Beethoven's hands the piano-subito of the block dynamic develops into wave after wave of crescendo from piano to forte. The climax is delayed until the tension of suspense has been created.

Beethoven writes sustained chords alternating between strings and winds and requests that they be connected from section to section (Example 107).

107. Beethoven, *Symphony No. 1 in C Major.* First movement (measures 8–10).

The science of notation is perfected in Beethoven's careful work. No composer ever notated so precisely what he wished to convey as did Beethoven. Scholarly musicians pay attention to every dot on the page. His notation of the fermata is a masterpiece of clarity, and the fermata itself is used in greater variety than by any other composer. While Beethoven capitalizes on the repetitious motif, it never becomes boring.

The solo wind sound begins to emerge more fully in this period, with von Weber, Beethoven, and Schubert, but it is not as thoroughly exploited *color-wise* as in the next following period.

Musical form becomes very important. Beethoven, the perfectionist, adds the extra blank measure at the end of the first and last movements of his First Symphony in order to complete the form. In handling this, the conductor customarily uses a high rebound after the last chord in each movement, then holds his hand still at the top of the rebound for the requisite amount of time to account for the extra measure, after which he "releases" the audience.

We mentioned that Lully had demanded uniform bowing from the Paris musicians. The basic "rules" for when to use down-bow and when to use up-bow were emerging as an adjunct of the orchestra.* They are most perfectly exemplified in Beethoven's writings and when they are applied to his scores, everything works out perfectly. He must have been bowing-conscious as he wrote.

Schubert added a personal type of lyricism to the orchestral sound; Mendelssohn, a personal quality of brilliance. Schumann's orchestrations are inclined to be "thick," and sometimes have to be very slightly altered for clarity. In his works, dynamic balance demands an exacting control to "sort out" the score.

Late Romanticism and the Nationalistic Schools. Berlioz' name is synonymous with huge orchestras and great outbursts of brilliant color, a display of splendor. He brought "program music" to the fore. Liszt contributed the Symphonic Poem as a casual "form" in its own right and made the world conscious of the contribution Hungarian music could make to the symphony orchestra. Wagner came on the scene, changing opera into music drama and apparently ending thereby an era. Brahms, who needed no "program" for his writing returned to the "pure" form of music, adding his great symphonies to the orchestral repertoire. Brahms disliked the bar-line. One pays special attention to the "long line" in conducting Brahms.

The second half of the nineteenth century sees the "nationalistic" schools coming to the fore and stepping across into the twentieth century—Sibelius in Finland, Debussy to Ravel in France, Strauss and Mahler to Hindemith

---

* In orchestral bowing the basic principle from which the rules and the exceptions spring is: *Measures start down-bow. The down-bow matches the conductor's down-beat.* There are many exceptions, however. Refer to the Recommended Reference Readings at the end of this chapter.

in Germany (not to forget Bruckner), Tchaikovski to Stravinsky in Russia, Bartók in Hungary.

New interpretative elements bring their influence to bear. First, the "impressionistic" music of the French School. Here the orchestral sound takes on an unrealistic quality. Color is pre-eminent. The bow once again moves farther from the bridge, taking some of the high *component harmonics* out of the sound. But *audible harmonics* as such come into their own in the orchestra as color factors. The splendor of Berlioz' color changes to muted shades in Debussy's writing. The French period is above all else a period of experimentation in orchestra coloring. All possible facets of the orchestral palette are explored. These are further enhanced by the momentary projection of an inner voice, a new color, emerging and then subsiding (Debussy's *en dehors*). The conductor uses a lighter hand on the baton and explores in depth the inner voices. Dynamics arrive at a most refined state. Finesse is imperative. Discords creep in but are not projected; they are, rather, used as a color factor.

Bartók brings the peasant songs, the close harmony, and the odd-beat rhythms for the conductor to deal with: another style with its own peculiar sound.

In Germany with Bruckner and Mahler the symphony takes on extraordinary length. Strauss does the same with the symphonic poem, and Hindemith sets up the "mental" approach to music-writing. Richard Strauss presents the conductor with still more problems in balance, and his works contain many subtle beauties that should be given prominence in the rendition.

In Russia Tchaikovski is adding a Russian flavor to the Schubertian lyricism and to Beethoven's emotionalism. And Tchaikovski is doing something else: He is exploring chromaticism fully and subtly upsetting the bowing customs that Haydn, Mozart, Lully and Beethoven initiated. The down-bow up-bow sequences are often reversed in order to account for the short swells and diminuendos that now come to the fore. (The peak of the phrase is best if it arrives on the down-bow, with the little swell preceding it being taken on the up-bow.)

Finally comes Stravinsky, and the twentieth-century sound blazes forth.

Contemporary music. The problems now become more mechanical for the conductor. How does he beat beats that are shortened or lengthened by a half-beat? The "lop-sided" rhythms come to the fore, and discords cease to be a color factor but become brutally apparent in their own right.

Music is now comprised of twelve individual sounds that have no family connections. The scale is done away with. Rhythm staggers instead of walks. New devices are tried *ad infinitum*. Even the definition of music has become confused. All "sound effects" are being classified as music. Sound effects are interesting, true (but this author refuses to dignify them with the title of music). Disjointed and dismembered "melodies" are scattered among the silent beats. Orchestral bowings have only one rule: Grab the accent—wherever it falls or is marked—on the down-bow. Dynamics are to be played "exactly as marked" regardless of the outcome. The duration of notes and silences is being geared to the stopwatch . . . and with this approach the shackles are clamped firmly into place.

(All of this, seemingly, because a music critic in Beethoven's time objected to a famous discord!)

Progress? or the final stages of dissolution?

Music is for the ears—its only excuse for being.

Some Professional "Tricks of the Trade"

In music of all periods, when a note is tied over to a sixteenth in fast tempo and this sixteenth is the first of a group of four sixteenths, for the sake of good ensemble the tied sixteenth is replaced by a sixteenth rest—a complete stop in the bow (Examples 108 and 109).

108. Beethoven, *Symphony No. 3* ("*Eroica*") *in E♭ Major*, Op. 55. Finale (measure 1).

109. Mozart, *Don Giovanni*. Overture (measure 56).

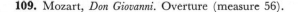

Sustained tones against figuration usually sound late with the beat when they change pitch. This must be especially guarded against in the brasses. To cure it, the player of the sustained sounds keeps the rhythm of the sixteenths (the figuration) running constantly through his mind.

The staccato dot does not always mean staccato in string music. In passage work where slurred notes are interspersed with unslurred notes the dot on the latter simply calls attention to the fact that the composer did not want them slurred. If the tempo is fast and forte, such notes will be played with a broad détaché bowing, *not* staccato (Example 110(a)). If the tempo is presto, and the unslurred notes come in pairs, they will probably both be taken on up-bows, the bow coming off the string *after* each unslurred note (Example 110(b)).

110.

One often sees this figure printed thus: ♪ ♫ and marked *forte*. Unless the tempo is fast enough for both sixteenths to be taken up-bow, staccato volante (the bow coming off the strings after each sixteenth), they will be played broadly, on the string, one note per bow-stroke, and not staccato. The eighth, however, *will* be staccato. It is the eighth that is spaced, not the sixteenths. As a very skilled section leader in one of the major symphony orchestras once remarked, "They're always writing it that way but none of us ever play it that way." In fast tempo obviously there is no time to stop after each sixteenth.

The slide from one position to another on a stringed instrument can be accomplished in two ways: either silently so that the slide does not sound or audibly connecting the first tone to the second. The latter is called the *portamento* shift. Such a shift is an adjunct of the Romantic Period. It is sentimental in sound and should not be used in Mozart's music or music written before his time. It is considered bad taste to use it in the early writings. But in Tchaikovski one finds it upon occasion acceptable and colorful. Certain contemporary writings have carried this effect to such an extreme that it has become nothing more than glorified caterwauling.

The "Orchestral" Dynamic

The meaning of dynamic markings in the orchestral score is something quite different from their signification in solo music. In the latter, one can accept the dynamic at face value. But in the orchestra the indication is only a general thing open to all kinds of variation and hundreds of interpretations. The underlying reason for this statement is the fact that no composer can predict beforehand the musical prowess of every orchestra that may play his music. Therefore, the orchestral dynamic becomes a law unto itself and the conductor is its guardian.

Let us take two examples: The composer has written a melody line in the lower flute register to be played by the second flute alone. It is accompanied by sustained tones in the string sections (first and second violins, violas and cellos without basses). The strings are marked piano, the flute mf, and the tessitura of the string chord is from the treble staff downward, the first violin being on the third-line B. With the full string section playing only *piano*, in that range the flute will not be heard. The strings will have to get down to a triple-piano, or they will have to attack their note *piano* and instantly drop "out-of-sight." Obviously it was the composer's intention that the flute be heard or he would not have written the melody in the first place. Therefore, the conductor must continue to re-write the dynamics until that melody does project.

The second example concerns the drop to one section of instruments immediately after the double forte tutti orchestra. Refer to Example 44. The composer has marked a *piano* on the music for that sole surviving section. If that section actually plays piano, the audience will hear nothing for a beat or two. *The called-for piano already exists when the majority of the players stop-playing.* The remaining section must support the burden of that orchestral *double-forte* by continuing its own *double-forte* for at least one more beat and then making a gradual diminuendo to the required piano. The skilled professional knows this. The unskilled conductor does not and often demands the *immediate* piano thus ruining the overall effect. The musicians are helpless in such cases, because the first rule of orchestral playing is "Give the conductor what he asks for." The professional is heard to remark with a shrug, "If the conductor says black is brown, it's brown."

Where a certain note is repeated several times, then a new note enters, returning immediately to the given repeated note, the note that changes the pitch should be projected slightly louder. Leading into the changing note by a small crescendo makes a fine effect. Also repeated notes or sustained tones (winds or strings) leading into a melody line should crescendo just before taking over the melody. The first note of the melody is the most important one, because it establishes the beginning of a theme and must take the audience with it.

Balance

As has been stated previously, balance concerns itself, first and foremost, with the projection of the melody line, the thematic material.

The melodic line is clearest heard when it occupies a place in the orchestral range not touched by other instruments in the scoring. The closer the other instruments are to the pitches sounded by the melodic line, the harder it is to project this line. The more the accompanying voices are moved away from the range of the melodic line, the easier it is for the line to stand out. Bearing this point in mind will help to foresee the problems which may be encountered when the rehearsal starts.

In tracing the melody line in the score, attention should also be paid to its "solo" character. Is it played on only one instrument or by one of the string sections, or is it doubled by other instruments? The written strength of the melody line states within itself what leeway the secondary accompanying instruments may have, dynamically. Also, the range used on the particular instrument that is playing the melody affects its ability to cut through. A flute melody written *on* the staff will not project as well as if it were written an octave higher. The accompaniment in such a case will have to have great delicacy. If flute and oboe double the melody in octaves, the tessitura will tend to lie in the oboe octave. The flute tone blends with the first harmonic of the oboe and is, thereby, absorbed by the oboe tone.

Sustained tones in accompanying harmonies are especially dangerous to the melody line in that they penetrate the consciousness of the listener more potently than do the moving voices. Thus, they become one of the greatest problems of balance and of melody-line projection. The more "amateur" the ensemble is, the more aggravated the problem becomes. It is so easy to play with great authority on a sustained tone.

The fine professional players know how to execute a sustained tone so exquisitely that it can blend itself into the quiet texture of the whole chord and lose its individual identity for the time being. It is a wonderful art.

Monotony

The synonym for monotony is unvaried repetition. It has no place in music. Music is fluid. It is constant motion. It is not a static art. The conductor's gestures, too, should be endowed with that ever-changing variety that is music. Continuous and unchanging repetition of any gesture can kill a performance for the audience.

The story goes that Glazounow learned one English sentence for his guest conducting appearances in England: "Gentlemen, please play what I shall design with the tip of my stick."

While clarity is basic in good conducting, monotony can be avoided by changes in size of gesture, changes in position in space, changes in style—a thousand styles to fit a thousand composers—changes in intensity, changes in speed of motion, and changes in emotional textures. By combining and re-combining these factors, the baton and left hand can live music. There is nothing more deadly than the rut of constant, unvarying time-beating in both hands.

EXERCISES FOR PRACTICE: INTERPRETING THE ORCHESTRAL SCORE

1. Take any five pieces (or symphonic movements) written by the great masters of orchestral composition. Look them through and decide what you think the tempo should be for each. To do this, sing the melody line throughout the work. Check the accompanying parts for convincing rhythmic performance against the tempo chosen for the melody, Check the fastest notes in the various parts to see whether they can be played effectively by the individual instruments at your tempo. Come to a definite conclusion as to what your tempo should be. (See Exercise 2 below.)

2. Now take the metronome and find out what the tempos are which you have chosen. Annotate these in the parts and use the results for class discussions.

3. Choose from among these five works the one which interests you most. Jot down how you would *classify* this piece. What style would *you* use in conducting it? What type of tone would you desire from your ensemble? How would the dynamics be handled? What would you do to balance the score if your string section numbered 10, 10, 8, 6, 4? (The first number designates the first violins, the second number, seconds, and so on down the score.) The brass and woodwind sections would be standard as shown in the symphony orchestra seating charts in Appendix A.

4. Sing each part through, just as if you were playing it on your own instrument. Be exact and strict with yourself in this exercise. Check your pitches after you sing each note. Use the piano. Stay with each part until you are really acquainted with it and can sing it *correctly* (or hear it as it really is in your mind's ear) without using the piano. Change octaves for your vocal range as necessary.

5. If you cannot sing it yourself, you do not know it well enough to conduct it. You will be bluffing!

6. Practice conducting the piece before you get in front of the class, the orchestra, the recording or whatever you use in the classroom.

RECOMMENDED REFERENCE READINGS (SEE APPENDIX G)

Bakaleinikoff, Vladimir, *Elementary Rules of Conducting*, p 23, "Style."

Blaukopf, Kurt, *Great Conductors*. This book is devoted to character sketches of a number of the great conductors and gives many hints on their interpretative means.

Braithwaite, Warwick, *The Conductor's Art*, Chapter VIII, pp 53–66, "On Style in Conducting;" Chapter IX, pp 67–71, "Choice of Beats;" Chapter X, pp 72–76, "Ensemble in Unusual Passages."

Christiani, Adolf F., *Principles of Expression in Pianoforte Playing*. This book is probably the greatest treatise available to the English-speaking student on expression in music. Starting with the section on "Melodic Accents" (p 138) and reading to the end of the book, one can pick up information not obtainable from other sources. In reading the book for uses other than pianoforte playing, the word "accent" may be interpreted simply as "stress" or "swell" in the tone.

Crocker, Richard L., *A History of Musical Style*. A very complete history of music approached through the music itself. Pp 355–526, the development of the orchestra via composition.

Goldbeck, Frederick, *The Perfect Conductor*, Book I, Chapter VII, pp 35–49, "On Melody, Dynamics, Phrasing;" Book III, Chapter I, pp 104–106 particularly, concerning the conductor's influence on the musicians, and his readiness for rehearsal.

Green, Elizabeth A. H., *Orchestral Bowings and Routines*. The whole book is applicable to this subject. It goes into the generally accepted professional customs underlying good orchestral bowing (when to use the down-bow and up-bow), and gives teaching information on the routines of orchestral playing for the string sections.

Krueger, Karl, *The Way of the Conductor*, Chapter X, pp 127–148, "Some 19th Century Conductors." Ideas on various styles may be obtained from this chapter.

Malko, Nicolai, *The Conductor and His Baton*, pp 205–209, "Dynamics," (gives some technical tricks with the baton to make the conducting of dynamics more effective); pp 210–219, "Kynetics," "Agogics." These two sections refer to speed, tempo and leading.

Mozart, Leopold, *A Fundamental Treatise on the Principles of Violin Playing*. Section on Embellishments, Chapters 9–10–11, pp 166–214. An authoritative discussion by a great teacher of that time.

Thomas, Theodore and Frederick Stock, *Talks About Beethoven's Symphonies*. Two great conductors give much information to the young interpreter.

Weingartner, Felix, *On Conducting the Beethoven Symphonies*. Here a great Beethoven interpreter tells his ideas. Very valuable to the young conductor.

16

Preparing
the Performance

The nature of the conductor's sounding instrument precludes his practicing thereon six to eight hours a day. The act of rehearsing the musical organization is a *performance for the conductor*, but a rehearsal for the musicians. The conductor's "practice" is his mental preparation of the music and his drilling of his hands to interpret to his "instrument," by sign language, the results of his mental deliberations. A good conductor knows that he cannot afford to waste even one precious minute in the "live" rehearsal. Therefore, it behooves him to be superbly prepared before he makes the music sound on the instrument itself, be that instrument the chorus, the band or the orchestra.

If a problem confronts him during rehearsal which he is not prepared to solve, he should check it with a pencil and continue the rehearsal. The solution should then be worked out in detail before the next rehearsal. Valuable rehearsal time should not be used to mull over the conductor's problems.

The conductor and the musicians each have a responsibility to the other. The conductor owes the musicians *efficiency*. In addition to his knowledge of the music, the conductor should recognize his responsibility for (1) clarity of time-beating gestures; (2) confidence and definiteness in leadership, based on thorough knowledge; (3) honesty in error; (4) the giving of cues for certain difficult and dangerous entrances; (5) the recognition of technical difficulties in the parts for the various instruments and a readiness to help in any way he can; and (6) an understanding of what is *possible* on the several instruments at diverse tempos and dynamic degrees.

The musicians owe the conductor accurate, efficient and pleasing-to-the-ear renditions of the notes and rhythms. They owe him *attentive participation* in the rehearsals and performances and instant response to any requests he may make, whether these are by word of mouth or by his conductorial gestures. They owe him their ears and their eyes as well. Furthermore, the members of the ensemble should give the conductor a certain perfection of intonation in performance. This is *not* an absolute standard. It is a flexible standard. Intonation varies as the chord varies. Good intonation means the adaptation of the individual note to the chord as a whole. The members owe the conductor dynamic sensitivity of an *ensemble* character—a knowledge of when to play louder, when to play softer, than the composer has so marked.

Musical history is full of anecdotes of musical organizations and conductors who have not been overly fond of each other, but, for the sake of *music*, they have had to work *together*.

Preparing the Music Itself

Without excellent preparation of the score, there is no conducting. In the strongest of words, THE CONDUCTOR MUST *KNOW* THE SCORE.

THE STEPWISE APPROACH TO THE SCORE

The following steps are approximately in the order of usage, but they should not be interpreted as being invariable rules which must be adhered to. In any case, step 1 makes a very safe beginning.

1. Look at the list of instruments required for the rendition of the score as set forth on the *first page of each movement*. Memorize this list, together with the transpositions called for. Notice whether one or more than one of each instrument is designated. (Refer to the language chart in Appendix B.)

2. Glance through the entire score noting form, style, climaxes. Place the score in its true setting historically and decide on the style of interpretation best fitted to it. Count the measures in short phrases throughout and mark the start of each phrase below the score.

3. Trace the melodic line throughout. Know what you will want to project. Play the melody line on the piano or your major instrument.

4. Pay attention to contrapuntal structures (imitations). Play them on the piano. Follow them from instrument to instrument in the score. Check on the bridge passages between melodies. See how the score hangs together *in toto*. Find where themes are doubled and note the instrumentation for such doublings throughout the score. Outline this on paper if necessary. Then go through a second time and compare the instrumentation of the thematic material with that of the accompanying passages, checking probable balance. Remember that if the audience cannot hear the themes, the melodies, your performance is only a glorified percussion ensemble.

5. By this time, undoubtedly some idea of your tempo has taken form. Study this through next. (Page 18.)

6. Notice whether the score is balanced by the composer as to dynamic

markings, or whether all instruments are marked the same throughout, regardless of their momentary importance. Try yourself to hear the melody through the accompaniment. Start to *use your own auditory imagination*.

7. About this time the real *raison d'être* of the work should make itself apparent. Consider again what it is trying to say, what the style, mood, and emotional content are.

8. Sing through the part for each instrument now or hear it clearly in your mind's ear to acquaint yourself with what each instrument is going to do. Check your cymbal crashes!

9. Pay attention, next, to the countermelodies and the important driving rhythms which should be felt in the total musical effect. Decide on their dynamic relationship to the whole. Notice where accompanying rhythms are derived from the thematic material.

10. Give the work a run-through, analyzing harmonic content. Relate this to the form of the composition.

11. Go through the score synthesizing all you have studied so far, and trying to hear the various tone colors in your mind. Feel the dramatic climaxes and the periods of genuine calm. Try to see the work as a whole. Total it up. Hear it in its entirety as if you were listening to a finished performance on a hi-fi set.

12. Now return to the parts for each instrument and really learn them this time. Sing and play each until it becomes as familiar to you as the melody line itself.

13. If the music is for amateur performance, go through next paying attention to what may cause trouble in each part for the players in your organization. Think out a means of clarifying each problem for the player who may have difficulty. (This phase of the score study will be presently enlarged upon.)

14. Practice *conducting* the score, applying the expressive gestures and paying particular attention to the places where the players may have trouble. Decide how you may help if it becomes necessary.

RECOGNIZING THE DANGER SIGNALS

As the conductor gains in experience he will gradually come to recognize certain things (in studying a new score) which will tell him, before he ever stands in front of his group, that trouble lies ahead. Let us glance at these under three headings: (1) Rhythmic Difficulties, (2) Problems in Intonation, and (3) Ensemble Factors.

1. *Rhythmic Difficulties.* If the conductor is working with school groups, he will experience difficulties now and then with three basic notations: the half note (not being held out through the second beat), the dotted quarter and eighth (the eighth coming too soon—often before the *second* beat of the dotted quarter takes place), and, in measures starting with an initial quarter note

followed by faster notes, the fast notes starting almost invariably before the second beat has fallen. Learn early in your school career to recognize these specific notations as trouble-makers. Cure these difficulties by the following clear-cut explanations to your players:

The note (or rest) following a half note *starts on Three.*

The note following a dotted quarter (in quarter time) must wait until after the second beat has fallen. It is played *after the second beat.*

The note (or rest) following the first quarter note in the measure comes *on Two.*

When your students can think clearly on these three points, they will be better sight-readers.

The conductor can help with the dotted-quarter-plus-eighth figure by using a gesture of syncopation (pp. 68–73) on the dot.

The dotted eighth with sixteenth will also cause inaccurate playing. However, this is not so much a matter of sight-reading as it is a matter of technical precision on the player's part. The younger musicians tend to perform the sixteenth too soon. (This results in a 6/8 rhythm, a quarter and eighth in fast 6/8 time.) The cure is to stress the long sound on the dotted eighth. When this note is long enough, the sixteenth will come late enough. Thinking a steady background of sixteenths can help to perfect the accuracy.

Rhythms in cross accents, such as two-beat rhythms notated in three-beat measures, will cause trouble. As the conductor beats his steady THREE, the youngster should count steadily, "One-Two. One-Two." He will find by so doing, that he can play the passage rather convincingly almost at once.

In measures where some players have a half note and triplet quarters (in 4/4) against a steady reiteration of quarter notes by the rest of the ensemble, the conductor will do well to help the triplet rendition with his baton. He may do this in two ways: either by changing to 2/2 time-beating in the measure in which the triplets occur, or by actually beating the triplet in the baton after warning the players of the steady quarters to keep them steady and disregard the baton for the moment.

Quick entrances on short motifs, in allegro especially, either on the beat or after the beat, will need help from the conductor. He must be especially alert when these entrances jump from section to section in the group.

2. *Problems in Intonation.* Bad intonation is usually caused by carelessness. If the inner ear (the imagination) forms the right concept of the sound *before the note is played*, the adjustment of pitch on out of tune notes should take place as a matter of course. Therefore, the instructor must patiently train his players to imagine correctly and then to *hear* what they are doing. No ensemble ever plays any better in tune than its conductor demands.

When the intonation is generally bad throughout a passage take the notes slowly so that the students can form the correct concept of the sounds. Place a fermata over the first note in each measure and skip the rest of the measure.

Hold the fermata until the adjustment of pitch is satisfactory. When this is good, re-play the series of first notes without fermata. This procedure clarifies the harmonic outline and usually produces acceptable results. It can be applied to every beat of the measure if necessary.

Where a single chord bristles with wrong notes or bad intonation, build the chord from the bottom upward starting with the string basses and tubas, adding the cellos, trombones and bassoons, and so on. In this way the newly added section is always sounding the top note of the chord. Mistakes are quickly located and corrected. Once the instruments have entered they continue to sustain, spelling the breath, until the chord is complete.

In the violins, particular attention must be paid to the correct sounding of F natural on the E string (top line of the staff). Too often the fingers are lazy in reaching back far enough and the tendency to sharp becomes habitual. The ear gradually comes to accept the wrong sound as the correct one. It will help if the players think "at the end of the string" when they see this note on the page. The same note, together with the E immediately below, are problems for the young flutists, who tend to flat them.

Half steps must also be stressed in the violins. The neighboring fingers touch each other if both notes of the half step are in tune. Minor sixths and augmented fourths played on neighboring strings also require the two fingers to touch. In general, B natural is under pitch in young orchestras.

In the winds, the spotlighting of pairs of fourths and fifths, as executed by different sections simultaneously, will give helpful results. Profitable dividends also accrue when the conductor pays attention to the natural tendency of the flutes to sharp and the clarinets to flat in the upper registers of these two instruments.

Teaching the players to listen to each other is a great factor in improving the whole ensemble sound. Listening for other instruments which are playing the same part, either in unison or at the octave, will also wake up lazy ears.

Good intonation depends upon the conductor's insistence and upon his persuasiveness in teaching the youngsters to adjust pitch instantly on any note which does not sound correctly. This is particularly true in the strings, but it must also be given intelligent attention in the winds. In the final analysis, the intonation in any organization is only as good as the conductor's ear. If his ear is fine, he will get his players to play in tune eventually. If he accepts poor intonation from his performers, he will gradually ruin his own ear.

3. *Ensemble Factors.* The first concern in ensemble is attack. Attack means not only the perfect starting of the first note in the piece, but it means what goes on on each beat thereafter. The notes must respond exactly to the ictus of the stick. Danger spots here come in several forms. (See pages 199–201 for pertinent information.)

Entrances after sixteenth rests are very difficult. The sharp gesture of syncopation will help, but be sure that you are really performing such a gesture. Young players among the winds usually take the breath too late. String players must have the bow *on* the strings during the sixteenth rest. The time it takes to drop it from the air to the string may be just too late for the speed of the piece. Even in spiccato bowing, the bow would start *on* the strings and come off for the first time right after the first up-bow stroke. The spiccato would continue thereafter.

In fast tempos, sixteenths coming on the heels of a tied sixteenth can cause much trouble in the string sections. Whenever possible, the tied note should be replaced by a sixteenth rest. (See Examples 108 and 109.) The conductor should use a properly executed gesture of syncopation to state the sixteenth rest.

Fragmented melodies, moving quickly from instrument to instrument (as happens so often in modern works), or rhythmic motifs skipping around the orchestra (as in Beethoven's symphonies) should have not only rhythmic continuity but tonal continuity as well. The dynamic and the style of execution should be the same throughout. Players should be taught to listen carefully and to imitate what they hear. Since fortes and pianos are more difficult to produce on some instruments than on others, this does not mean an equal effort for all concerned. The ear alone can judge the dynamic.

Notice all of these possible danger spots as you study score. Have solutions worked out in your mind before you go to the rehearsal. But use the solutions *only if they are needed*.

Preparing the Conducting

When the conductor knows his score thoroughly and has given intelligent attention to the problems which may arise in the rehearsal, it is generally conceded that he is ready to stand in front of the chorus, orchestra, or band and lead the rehearsal. Actually, he is *not* ready. He has not yet thought through the application of his expressive gestures and baton technique to the music itself. For the young conductor, this is a most important phase of his work which should not be neglected. When he has a backlog of many years' experience, he may be casual about this angle, but not at first. It is while the totality of habits is being formed that important things must not be overlooked.

In applying gestures to the score, the following points should be kept in mind:

1. Decide what type of preparatory beat is needed in order to get the piece off to a good start. Practice it! Decide on the pertinent style of time-beating (legato, staccato, etc.). Decide on what type of gestures will be used for the difficult cues, musically and rhythmically. Practice them.

2. Find the landmarks in the score which will warn you that a baton problem is approaching. Thus, your mind will be ready for it when it comes. Practice these spots, with gestures, until your ear tells you securely what is to follow. (This becomes a sort of musical wig-wag system like the lights at a railroad crossing.)

3. Decide whether the down gesture or the up gesture will be most effective in conducting this or that cymbal crash. Practice it, together with measures on either side, until it becomes easy in execution.

4. Now conduct your score through, thinking, "Here the legato is good, here the staccato is needed, here is a place where the tenuto will be most effective," and so on. Apply the gestures directly to the score. In the beginning it takes time, patience, and conscious thought to do all of this. Later on, habit will replace conscious thought until the time finally arrives when the hands will interpret instantly and correctly anything the ear may desire to hear in the music. When this state of proficiency is attained, the baton practice will be necessary only where unusual and original problems (rhythmic and otherwise) need a little brushing up in the stick before the rehearsal. A conductor who simply paints pretty pictures with his gestures, or who swings his arms wildly with no real technique back of the performance, wastes so many years (and so much rehearsal time) gaining the experience that provides the solutions. A little slower progress at first, with more care to detail, could save over half of these precious years.

The young conductor is not ready to be "creative" in his gestures until these gestures are first readably clean and technically accurate. The tools of fine, recognizable technique must be kept sharp by practice. A dull tool never is effective in accomplishing a perfect piece of work. The young conductor must sharpen his tools and then apply them to the work in hand. He who adds this type of *technical* preparation to a thorough knowledge of the score itself reduces to absurdity his competitor who knows *only* his score. No musician has ever realized his greatest potential by neglecting his technique.

Preparing the Players

When the conductor raises his baton to start the rehearsal he should have in mind certain goals which he hopes to accomplish before the time runs out. If there is one criticism in the field of music, applicable to us today, it is that there is too much *wasted time* in the practice rooms. There is too much repetition without conscious thought for improvement. So let us stress here, *purposeful rehearsing.*

READING THE STICK FOR GOOD ENSEMBLE

Rehearsal techniques are geared to one thing only, when they produce good results. That is, to get the finest effects possible in the shortest possible time. In the rehearsing of the amateur group, the first time-saver is to get the players to look at the baton, to "read the stick." They must be trained to glance up frequently and to become habitually conscious of the downbeat in each measure. They must be taught to glance up at the double bars, especially where there is a change of pace, in order to know exactly what is going on. They have to *see* the change of tempo. It is too late after they have *heard* it. *In rehearsal, always get the players safely across the double bar before stopping for corrections.* The crossing of the bar is what needs the rehearsing. Accelerandos and ritards also need the eyes on the stick for good ensemble.

In stringed instrument playing there is often a great correlation between the conductor's downbeat and the players' down bow. In many places good rhythm depends upon this correlation.

In times of stress, the players who are trained to do so will rely greatly upon the conductor's downbeat. Also, if a player becomes confused in sight-reading, he need only glance up and play the first note of the next measure on the next downbeat and he is safely back in the ensemble again. In this way, he is never "lost" for more than one measure. This is an excellent time-saver.

As these initial steps are taken in reading the baton, the fine foundation is laid for seeing more and more in the stick as time goes on. (And, why not substitute the purposeful words, "Watch the tip of the stick," for the meaningless, "Watch ME," so prevalent in the profession at the present time?)

TUNING

A great deal of bad intonation in the amateur ensemble stems from faulty tuning. Insist that players listen to the given tuning note. When they are ineffective in matching it, let them play alone, individually, so that they can train the ear to know what to do. Remember in this connection, the ear hears easiest the highest pitch sounded, and/or the loudest-executed note. It must be trained to recognize which of the pitches is the standard. The other pitch is then adjusted to match.

The tuning of the winds in the amateur group is best accomplished by going right down the line letting each player sound his note in sequence. When one is inaccurate, the conductor's ear (and later the student's ear) can so quickly tell whether the pitch dropped or rose in the offending note. When the tone quality of a group is smooth, good intonation is usually the first cause. When the tone is rough, bad intonation is the first offender. So get the group *in tune*.

The tuning A in orchestra is given out by the oboe. (In band the B♭ is used.) If a piano or other instrument of "fixed" pitch is to be used in the ensemble, then the instruments tune to that.

With very young players it is best to have the flutes tune by playing their first A above the staff. This is the range in which most of their notes lie. Tuning with the lower A causes much difficulty in the beginning stages.

It is a good trick to have the solo chairs in the wind sections tune first, coming to a decision on a common A (or B♭) which all can match. (This is especially true in school groups where the instruments may not be of the best quality.) Each section is then synchronized with its first chair player.

MECHANICS OF THE REHEARSING

If the score and parts are equipped with rehearsal letters or numbers, this is a great help. When it is necessary to have the players mark an additional letter, have it placed directly over the bar line "between measures _____ and _____." Then have the players draw a circle around the letter starting and ending on the top edge of the bar-line. When rehearsal letters are missing, or are too far apart, it helps to remember that the forte mark will be common to all parts for music written in Beethoven's time and before. Usually all instruments are playing at the forte.

When it is necessary to count measures, the conductor will again save valuable time if he will say, "Starting at _____, count backwards one, two, three, etc." Time is wasted when he counts the measures himself first and then has to wait until the players have counted them too. Announce where you are starting and take the group with you on the very first counting.

Where there are transpositions in the wind parts, always specify "Concert _____" or "Written _____," whatever the note is. See page 125 for detailed information on this point.

Insist that the players look at the stick whenever you start after any stop. Help them to form the habit of looking. (To do this, you will have to look also.)

Using the hand signals (page 116) can expedite the rehearsing. The conductor need not stop at the double bar to make a forgotten announcement. Instead he holds up the requisite number of fingers and the music proceeds without interruption. It is also a good way to train players in the habit of glancing up at all double bars.

When a conductor drives hard for a *musical* effect during rehearsal, his own sincerity usually permeates the group. It is ordinarily true that players do not resent working hard if the end result is something they are proud to listen to. What they do resent is endless repetition with no constructive results. *The Music is the thing.*

Summing up the chapter, three things emerge as necessities: (1) a thorough knowledge of the music to be played; (2) a secure and readable conductorial technique, with the hands and baton adequately interpreting the score; and (3) an intelligently and thoroughly rehearsed performing group. Given these three conscientiously prepared entities, the performance cannot go below a certain decent standard. How much above the standard it can climb depends, thereafter, upon the innate talent, the personal magnetism and the musical feeling of the conductor himself. Such things are not teachable.

EXERCISES FOR PRACTICE: RECOGNIZING THE DANGER SIGNALS

1. Study each of the following examples in the light of the material presented in this chapter concerning the stumbling blocks for the amateur player. To guide you: the first one, (a), shows two dangerous things; (b) shows two; (c) shows three; (d) shows three. Intonation problems are to be disregarded in this particular set of answers.

2. In (a) and (b) above, tell which notes are most likely to be played out of tune by the violins. [They are playing the sixteenths in (a).]

3. In (c) and (d) tell what intonation problems might exist if very young players are executing these notes on the violins.

4. The ensemble is playing a chord that sounds badly out of tune. How would you go about clearing it up?

5. Describe your tuning process at the beginning of the rehearsal.

6. You want to start 14 measures before letter *A* in the music. What do you announce?

7. Your French horns do not sound as if they were playing the correct note. You see that the note printed in your score is a G. It should sound a C. (The parts are for horn in F.) What do you say to your players in checking this note?

8. Refer to the pages of *full score* in both the band and orchestra sections of this book and write out the type of preparatory gesture you would use to start each excerpt, if your group was to start on the first note printed in each fragment quoted.

9. Your group is ragged on the first measure after the double bar. There is a change of tempo marked at the bar. What *two* things must you check on?

RECOMMENDED REFERENCE READINGS (SEE APPENDIX G)

Boult, Adrian C., *A Handbook on the Technique of Conducting*, Section VII, pp 20–22, "Preparing the Score;" Section VIII, pp 23–24, "Rehearsal."

Goldbeck, Frederick, *The Perfect Conductor*, Book III, Chapter V, pp 123–127, "On Action of Presence," the personal relationship of conductor and musicians.

Grosbayne, Benjamin, *Techniques of Modern Orchestral Conducting*, Chapters 21–24, pp 192–226. This reference contains fine material on Score Analysis, Editing the Score and Preparing the Rehearsal.

Krueger, Karl, *The Way of the Conductor*, Chapter XII, pp 173–220, "The Conductor's Approach to a Composition." Read this when your mind is fresh and ready to concentrate.

Munch, Charles, *I Am a Conductor*, Chapter V, pp 45–56, "Face to Face with the Score;" Chapter VI, pp 57–67, "Rehearsing."

17

Memorizing
the Score

There is no set rule, universally recognized, for memorizing a score; no sure-fire, cut-and-dried method guaranteeing foolproof results. Charles Munch stated in his book (see Appendix G) that he did not require his students in the conducting classes in Paris to work from memory at the outset of their training. He felt that the security of having the score present helped the young conductor. Hermann Scherchen, on the other hand, required absolute memorization and intense mental concentration before he permitted the student to conduct the work. However, Scherchen may have geared this approach to those who had had some previous experience.

Perhaps the most-often-asked question is, "Just what is meant by 'memorizing the score?" Does the conductor who uses no score at the concert really know every note of every instrument?"

The answer is interesting. It varies with the convictions of the conductor. Many of the greatest conductors do "know every note of every instrument." But in the actual performance there is no time to think of each note any more than there is time think, "My notes in this run are A, C, F, G, A, E, G, B, D, C," and so on, when one is playing a solo from memory in public performance. The player may know these notes and be able to write them out perfectly. He may have assimilated the run completely and absolutely. But to put conscious thought such as "A, C, F, G, etc.," before each played note would slow down the performance unbearably. Music moves too fast for this.

The mind should be actively alerted during the formation of the habit, but once the habit has been perfected it will run itself, thus releasing the mind for a genuinely creative expression. The mind *as a conscious force* works hard during the learning process, namely, during the sight-reading of the music and during the first stages of the practicing. But as the music is gradually assimilated, the mental effort gives way to the habitual action. A certain type of "memorization" has taken place.

The performing from memory might be described as a "free-wheeling" of the mind, the auditory apparatus, and the necessary physical motions. As a musician, one mentally listens for the sounds he wants to produce and these sounds come out of his instrument. The response of the skilled hands is so closely linked to the mental concept of the desired music that they seem to be part of the mind itself. This is an uncanny attribute with which man is endowed. We are, by nature, wonderfully made to be self-contained units of efficiency.

The brain specialists in the medical profession tell us that every repeated action makes a deeper and deeper impression on the brain centers involved until after a while the settling into activity of the motivating force for the certain action will cause the action to take place as a matter of course, an instantaneous and uninhibited "circuit" occurring in the brain.

There are many ways to remember many things. We remember how a loved one *looks* (Visual memory). We remember how the wind sounded in the pine trees during a northern vacation, or we remember the sound of a plane going over on a still night (Auditory memory). We think of a certain fenced field in the country and we immediately remember the dangerous bull that was confined therein (Memory by association of ideas). We do delicate piecework in a factory. At first intense concentration is needed to turn out a perfect unit, for the hands are clumsy in the beginning. Later the mind can go off on other thoughts and the hands will continue to turn out perfect work without conscious effort (Memory by habit-forming, repeated action). We find out that we cannot remember how to make a certain little gadget of folded paper. Someone shows us that this fold comes first, then this one and so on. We find that we now know how to make it perfectly (Memory by stepwise sequence, logical analysis, and synthesis.)

We remember some things by visualizing a geometric design. A child wants to play hop-scotch. He remembers how to draw the correct set of elongated rectangles.

We remember certain things by a principle of contrast. This twin always wears the ring with the blue stone in it while that one wears the red stone. We know which is which by contrasting the one thing that is different.

There is also a memory for timing. The teacher whose life is spent in the fifty-minute classroom, or the radio engineer whose day is divided into half-hour periods, soon acquires the *feeling* that the time has elapsed without looking at the clock. This is a memory for the duration of time.

So when we memorize a score, we have many ways, too, to remember things. If the memory balks at conquering a certain passage, perhaps the wrong approach is being used. We must analyze the difficulty and try to

decide which of our many ways to remember things is needed for that particular spot in the music, which memory ability will unlock it for us.

Let us see how this can work out. It may be a place in the score where
remembering how those two quarter rests look between those two quarter
notes in the middle of the passage will straighten us out (Visual memory).
It may be that we can remember what is going on if we play it several times
very slowly so that the ear can really hear exactly what it should be (Auditory memory). Or perhaps it is a passage where we have to be forewarned.
"When that high C is heard, remember that the fermata on the F comes in
the very next measure" (Association of ideas).

Perhaps the baton balks at performing a certain succession of legato and
staccato gestures. We do them many times slowly and correctly, letting the
mind have time to think each one precisely, and after a while the habit comes,
through repeated action, until finally the baton will move perfectly with
scarcely any thought at all (Habit formation through repeated action).

We come to a long passage with many changes in it. We start to pick it
apart to see what it really does. It is, upon analysis, a sequence, repeated
every four measures. Each repetition is one whole tone higher than the one
before. The fact that it had so many accidentals in it made us overlook
this simple solution until we could go at it systematically with real thought.
So now we have used logical analysis and synthesis. The passage is firmly
fixed in the mind.

We have some cues in a score which come so fast that the mind can scarcely
think "flute, clarinet, bassoon, oboe." So we notice how these instruments
are seated in the orchestra thus (Figure 42).

Almost instantly, through geometric design, we can give a perfect rendition of the cues with the necessary speed of execution. The troublesome spot
is solved by performing a simple clockwise square.

We have a nasty passage: 2/4, 3/4, 1/4, 3/8, one measure of each. The
conducting must show only quarter notes throughout. We acquire a com-

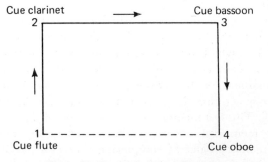

Figure 42. Geometric pattern for cues.

plicated set of memories to handle this one. We set the upper numbers in our mind just as we would a telephone number: two, three, one, one-and-a-half. We practice performing the passage with the baton, repeating it many times until the hand seems to acquire a "feel" for it. We listen to it time and again, until the lopsided rhythm is compensated for by a sort of melodic sound which gradually emerges. And so, by working at it in several ways, we eventually conquer it.

Here is a melody that comes in twice. The first time the low C is followed by D, a quarter note, and the melody goes off into the oboe solo passage. The second time the low C is followed by F, a half note, and this leads directly into the French horn quartet section. Thus, by clarifying the contrast of the changing note (the note that acts like a switch in the track) we can conduct convincingly and securely what is to come (Memory by contrast).

Now we find a clarinet run. Four measures later the same run is played by the flute. We have weighty problems in the intervening measures and cannot concentrate on counting measures, yet we invariably bring the flute in at the right time. The duration of time memory is partly helping us here.

So, in the over-all memorization of the score, many means are employed. Since we are meant to be efficient machines, we have only to replace fear with confidence and to go ahead and work it out. Memory often is just the good result of real mental alertness, of noticing what is going on when it happens.

What Is Meant by a "Memorized Score?"

There are several schools of thought on what is necessary to call a score "memorized." Some say, "One must know every single note of every single part, and be able to write out every part from memory." Others contend that it is sufficient to know "how the melody sounds and the sequence throughout; to know the harmony and what the accompanying instruments do; but not necessarily how each note of each accompanying chord is distributed among the various instruments." This latter definition is akin to memorizing a solo with piano accompaniment. The player knows how the parts fit together and whether they sound right or whether wrong notes are being played by the accompanist, but he has not learned the piano part so that he could perform it alone. There are still other "conductors" who contend that it is "sufficient to know the number of measures and conduct accordingly." Obviously this last definition is the product of the "time-beater" who is doing only that. (One wonders about the emotional appeal of his performances!)

Toscanini, when asked, said that he did not know how he memorized. Chotzinoff (see Appendix G) tells that Toscanini remarked that he had always had a facility for knowing how a score would sound by looking at it. "Sometimes I tell myself a story about a beautiful girl. This melody depicts the forest. This melody is an evil man. . . . ," and so on. One can see why his performances were so often described as having great imagination and great appeal for the audiences. He lived them in his mind.

The author has been told that Guido Cantelli* memorized the part for each instrument *in toto* first, starting with the first flute and working right down through the score. When he finished an individual part he would ask his wife to give him an examination on it. She would ask such questions as, "What note is played by the second clarinet on the first beat of the second measure after A?" After memorizing the several parts Cantelli would group them by families, working with the four or five lines of the family in the score. Then, lastly, he would correlate the whole score.

It is probably safe to say that a score is memorized when one can "think it through" accurately from beginning to end without recourse to the printed page or to audible sound.

Studying the Score in Order to Memorize

So now, let us list the many *approaches* we have to the score which may help in the memorizing. After which, each man for himself! Let him decide what his goals will be and how he will accomplish them.

1. A thorough knowledge of the form of the work.

2. Ability to sing the melody line throughout from memory.

3. The ability to sing each part throughout.

4. The association of the instrumentation with the melodic line, noticing the differences in tone color on the various iterations of the melody.

5. Classification of the rhythmic patterns, the motifs, their development, their use in accompanying passages and in bridge passages.

6. The harmonic analysis of the work with special study on passages of complicated harmony.

7. Locations of the emotional (dramatic) climaxes and what in the score is responsible for their effects.

8. Location of smaller climaxes and of the periods of calm.

9. The counting of measures in certain small sections of the work to understand the length of the segments into which the musical ideas are divided. Checking these in the bridge passages to account for the feeling of formal balance in the score.

10. Charting the work. Writing out, from memory, quickly and without

---

* Guido Cantelli, a protégé of Toscanini, had begun to make a name for himself when he was killed in a plane crash during the nineteen-fifties.

hesitation, a sequential synopsis, singing the melody as you do so. For example: Opening: sustained chord, ff, tutti, fermata. Rhythmic pattern, ♩ ♫.♩♩ ♩, begins in bassoons and clarinets. measure, Fourth enter violins, main theme. (Hum it through quickly.) Link-measure in cellos and basses and theme repeated by doubled clarinets and flute. Theme modulates, two measures after the modulation the big brass enters. . . . etc. In such an analysis, the auditory memory carries the material forward during the measures between the items you write down in your charting. When such a chart can be written rapidly and accurately from memory, the conductor is usually quite safe.

11. Memorizing the part for each individual instrument.

12. Visual memory for the appearance of the music on the page.

13. Contrasting dynamics.

14. Having audible cues within the music itself which, when heard, jog the memory and warn the conductor to be alert for this or that which is to follow.

15. Memorizing the geometric design when cues come very fast. Noticing the changes in this design upon repetition later on in the work.

16. Letting the instrumentation itself be a guide as to what follows next.

17. Recognizing the changing note which acts as the switch in the track, sending the music in this or that direction.

18. Attention to phrasal divisions: noticing interlocking phrases where the new phrase starts in new instruments on the very note whereon the old phrase ends. (Mozart does this so often.)

19. Attention to tutti rests.

20. Using different technical gestures on the repetition of a passage to insure correct continuance of the music.

21. Being conscious of the number of parts actually going on at any given moment in the score. Three-part writing, although seven instruments are playing, etc. How are these three parts distributed among the playing instruments?

22. The storytelling imagery of Toscanini. Letting the themes depict the characters and the story itself as they enter and retire.

While the conductor may not use all of these devices in any one score, still, in his handling of the repertoire, he will find places where each of them will be applicable.

In all of this, let us not forget that the music exists only when it *sounds*, and that fundamentally we are dealing with the memorization of sound as such. Whereas musical talent is the point of departure, ultimate success depends upon whether the price is paid, that price being the unselfish devotion to an ideal where no amount of work or study is too demanding when perfection is the goal.

EXERCISES FOR PRACTICE: MEMORIZATION

1. Memorize a chosen movement (symphony, band score, long chorus). Get it so that you can chart it as given under point 10 above. Be ready to conduct it without benefit of score.

2. During this process decide what your own natural approach to the memorization process is. Are you leaning more on your auditory memory or on your visual memory?

3. Practice the actual conducting of the work, using the gestures you will later on perform before the ensemble. Mark any places which bother you. Give these special attention. Check on your fairness to the composer. Are you yourself enjoying the sound of the performance? Does it inspire you to deliver your very best? (This, incidentally, is a pretty good test of the real musical value of the work and of your own musicianship in relation to it.)

4. *Write out* the short-hand analysis of the work from memory, if you have not already done so. Follow the suggestions given under step 10.

Mastery

18

The Melded Gestures and Psychological Conducting
(*Technical Mastery*)

As the student's baton technique clarifies, he will find it possible to produce from an ensemble, on a static pitch, musical excerpts for which the performers have no music and which they have never seen nor heard before. The baton technique alone is sufficient if a *real technique has been built*. Examples follow.

111. Robert Jager, Class example (seventeen measures). Used by permission.

112. David Bates, Class example (thirteen measures). Used by permission.

When true independence of the hands is gained, it is not impossible to perform a dual rhythm such as that given in Example 113. In this case, the ensemble is divided into two groups, one of which follows the directions given by the conductor's right hand while the other responds to the signals of the left hand.

113. Don Wilcox, Class example (nine measures). Used by permission.

(It might be a good idea to mention that the examples used here were taken from student-performances on final examinations. The examples were written by the students themselves and successfully performed as one phase of the final test.)

In the quoted examples the staccato dot signified the use of the staccato gesture, the long line over a note showed the tenuto gesture in action, unmarked notes were simply performed legato, notes of more than one beat's duration were "melded" (see the section following this discussion), and notes coming after the beat were handled by use of the gesture of syncopation. Rests were indicated by dead gestures. (See Chapter 5 for the complete discussion of these gestures.)

The Melding of Gestures

All time-beating and expressive gestures must be perfected before such "psychological conducting" can be performed successfully. In addition, the conductor's impulse of will must be sturdy. He will have to apply also one more bit of technique which he has not yet learned and which we shall call the "melding" (combining) of gestures. In brief, the term means that *two or more time-beating gestures are combined into one longer gesture which takes up the same amount of time the individual gestures would have taken.* To perform the meld, the ictus of the first of the melded beats is shown. This starts the tone. The baton then follows the general path which those melded gestures would normally have taken in the time-beating pattern, but *no other ictus is shown during the meld.* The next ictus to appear is the one for the beat following the melded beats.

The melded gesture is usually of the tenuto type. Its intensity or tenuousness shows in the unbroken continuation of the sound until the beat following the meld comes along. On the ictus of the beat following the meld the next tone starts. (For the discussion of the tenuto gesture see pages 66 to 68.)

Several examples will serve to clarify the melded gesture. Let us start with time-beating in FOUR. The music is shown in Example 114.

114. Mozart, *Così fan tutte.* Overture (a) (measures 2–3) (b) (measures 6–7).

Since there is only one instrument playing here, the conductor has no ensemble problem. He wishes to show the smooth, unbroken line of the half-note. He therefore melds the first and second beats of the measure into one longer gesture which *does not show the ictus of the second beat of the measure.* The pattern would resemble that given in Figure 43.

The time of beats One and Two is consumed as the baton moves from the

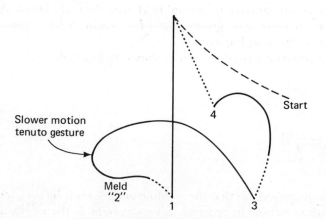

Figure 43. Melding the first two beats.

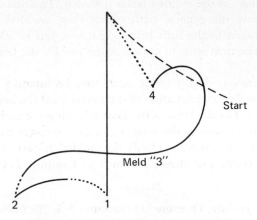

Figure 44. Melding "Two-Three" in 4/4.

ictus of One to the ictus of Three. When the ictus of Three is shown, the soloist performs the second note of the measure (the first of the two quarter notes shown in Example 114) and the last quarter note is played on the ictus of Four. Regular time-beating in Four resumes on the next measure. NOTE: this passage need not necessarily be conducted in this manner. It is used here for illustration only.

Melded gestures must not delete anything from the time values of the beats melded.

Let us take another example. Suppose the class is told to sing "La" whenever the baton says to do so. The baton shows the ictus of One with a good strong impulse of will. The group sings La. The baton shows the ictus of Two. The group again responds with La. Now the baton moves through Three without showing any ictus, but showing only a tenuto, continuous sound. The group sustains its second-beat tone through Three. An ictus is now shown on Four. The group sings "La" again. Such a pattern would look like that shown in Figure 44.

It would produce a rhythm such as shown in Example 115.

115.

La, La,   La,

Again let us emphasize that the melding gesture must be very tenuous and very smooth in outline in order to leave no doubt in the minds of the performers that they are to sustain the sound. The conductor must likewise have the feeling of continuous tone, not interrupting it with rhythmic pulsations in the baton.

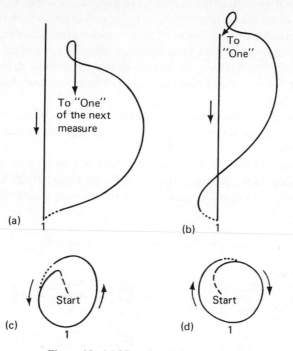

Figure 45. Melding the whole measure.

To show the presence of a whole note, the ictus of One is shown and then all of the remaining beats of the measure are melded into one long gesture. The pattern might look like any of those given in Figure 45.

As shown in (c) of Figure 45, the meld of the full measure is sometimes performed as a circular motion. The ictus of One is the lowest point of the circle. The second measure of Example 116 might be conducted as shown in Figure 45(a).

116. Mozart, *Don Giovanni.* Overture (measures 17–19).

The melded gesture is the very soul of *phrasal conducting*. Once the reader has become accustomed to recognizing it, he will begin to understand motions made in performance by many of the world's great conductors—motions which previously made but little sense to him. When changing to phrasal conducting, the conductor must be sure that the rhythmic drive of the music is such that the musicians can carry on perfectly without his time-beating gestures at that point.

Before going into the detailed discussion of the Psychological Conducting, let us examine two more examples from the repertoire where phrasal or melded gestures may be successfully used.

In Example 117 the first two beats of measures 2 and 4 may be melded, the baton showing One, then moving toward the right where the third beat is performed as a cut-off gesture. The baton would stand still during this

117. Mozart, *La Clemenza di Tito*. Overture (measures 3–6).

tutti fermata-rest. A sudden, sharp, upward gesture of syncopation would then state Four, precipitating the triplet entrance at the end of the measure.

118. Schubert, *Symphony No. 8* (*"Unfinished"*) *in B minor*, Op. posth. First movement (measures 1–8).

The familiar passage in Example 118 lends itself well to the use of the melded gestures. The first measure is beaten out fully, thus setting the tempo securely. Measure 2 melds the first and second beats, but shows the ictus for Three. Measure 3 shows One and then melds the remainder of the measure. The fourth measure is beaten out in full, indicating each of the quarter notes. Measure 5 is like measure 2. In measure 6 the first beat is shown. This is followed by a gesture of great sustaining power, in double piano, and this last gesture sustains for three measures showing only the slightest dip as the first beat of measures 7 and 8 passes. The entrance of the sixteenth notes in the ninth measure is prepared by a rhythmic, legato gesture on Three of the eighth measure. This gesture would be similar to the preparatory beat at the very beginning of any piece. Once the violins enter in measure 9, normal time-beating takes over.

Psychological Conducting

This thing which we have termed the "psychological conducting" is a sort of final test of the young conductor's over-all proficiency. It tests his technique, his control of the group and his musical imagination.

Psychological conducting we now define as the process of getting a group of singers or players to respond, on a single pitch throughout, to the messages it receives from the conductor's hands and baton alone. The group has no music to read and the conductor announces nothing. The terminology implies a transfer of ideas from the conductor's mind to the performer's mind through the medium of correct and precise conductorial technique without the use of verbal directions or written notation.

For success in this endeavor, the time-beating gestures and the several styles of expressive gestures must be clean-cut and identifiable. The melded gesture has to be usable whenever long notes require it and the dead gesture must leave no doubt that there is a request for silence in its passivity. One thing more must be mentioned. That is the important use of the gesture of cutting off the sound. In the psychological conducting, since no written score is being read by the performers, this last-named gesture must replace the time-beating gesture on the last note preceding a rest (at the end of a series of continuous time-beating gestures) if the tempo is moderato or faster. Unless this is done, the group will usually sing an extra note.

119.

In the second measure of Example 119 the second beat is a quarter note. This is followed by a rest on the third beat. The tempo is allegro moderato. The second beat of this second measure will, therefore, be conducted with a *cut-off gesture instead of a time-beating gesture.* This cut-off occurs on the ictus of the time-beating gesture. If the regular time-beating gesture is made, followed by a cut-off, the latter comes too late and the group sings a note on the rest. This brings out the important fact that every conductorial gesture must be made in sufficient time for the group to react properly to it. When the gesture of cutting off replaces correctly the time-beating gesture, in cases such as that quoted, the group will sing the given quarter note and will be silent on the rest. Continuing with the example, beat Three may be conducted either as a dead gesture or simply as a preparatory gesture for the entrance on Four. The first beat, One, of the next measure will again have to be an active gesture of cutting-off. (The underlying rhythmic pulse should be steady and exact throughout.)

In the slower tempos it is quite safe to show the beat itself and follow it with the cut-off. There is time to show both adequately before the singers can respond on the next following beat.

In psychological control of all entrances *after* the beat (the eighth rest followed by the eighth note in all of the foregoing examples), the gesture of syncopation is used. Remember, the stick must stand perfectly still momentarily before this gesture and the sudden, sharp motion of the gesture must coincide exactly with the moment of the takt of the beat after which the note is to be sounded. This gesture is seen too late for the group to respond *on* the beat, and it therefore sings *after* the beat.

Writing Examples for Psychological Conducting

In all musical examples used for psychological conducting, the notation must be limited to notes requiring *one or more* beats for their performance, or to *single-note entrances after the beat*. This is true throughout unless the beat is so slow that it can be adequately subdivided to show the "And" and, therefore, the presence of two eighths for that beat. (Example 111 shows this.)

The dotted quarter with eighth is usable since the conductor can control the eighth by making a gesture of syncopation on the second beat of the quarter note. When he does this, however, he will have to "drive" for the next beat following the eighth note. Unless this following beat has great impulse of will, and is made precipitously, the singers will not sing a new note on it.

The student should now write his own exercises for psychological conducting. Two copies should be made. One is used on the conductor's stand and the other is given to the instructor in order that the latter may see whether the young conductor is producing from the group what he intended. There is no better way to develop the "impulse of will" than practice in "psychological conducting."

The following list of possibilities will serve as a guide in the writing and conducting of the original examples.

1. Write one note per beat, or notes requiring more than one beat per note.

2. Notes requiring more than one beat per note may be performed by use of the melded gestures.

3. Any number of beats of rest may be written and conducted by use of the dead gestures. All tutti rests are to be so shown during these drill studies.

4. The last note before a rest must be beaten as a cut-off gesture in moderato and faster tempi. The cut-off replaces the time-beating ictus.

5. The eighth note followed by the eighth rest is usable if a *very short* staccato gesture is made to indicate it, or if each beat so written is performed as a very demanding and very short cut-off gesture.

6. The eighth rest followed by the eighth note is usable and may be produced by the gesture of syncopation on the rest.

7. The eighth following the dotted quarter will be forthcoming if the gesture of syncopation replaces the time-beating gesture on the dot of the quarter note.

8. Fermatas are always usable and good.

9. All dynamics may be used and should be carefully marked in the written example.

10. All of the expressive gestures may be used and should be indicated in the manuscript as follows: a dot over or under a note indicates the staccato gesture; a long line signifies tenuto; no marking for notes of the simple legato character.

11. Accelerandos and ritards are usable and good.

12. Crescendos and diminuendos are usable and good.

13. Changes of meter are excellent.

14. The left hand may bring in or cut out some of the singers independently of the right hand.

15. Accents of individual notes may be shown by enlarging the preparatory gesture leading into the accent.

The young conductor who can produce what he wants in the foregoing categories from the musicians, who have no music and to whom he gives no verbal instructions, need have no worries about his control of the situation when he is working with his future orchestra, band or chorus. His technique is a true technique of the stick. He is no longer cheer-leading but he is turning into a Conductor.

Since this is the last chapter of a technical nature, the reader will now find added here a section requested by my fine student-critics who have read this manuscript in its pre-publication form. Their feeling that the following unit would be of value to them when they themselves were out in the field has persuaded the author to add it here. It amounts to a quick checklist to avoid backsliding.

First may we say, however, that it is the undying conviction of the writer that *positive* thinking is of far greater value than negative thinking. Correct results come when the mind concentrates on *what to do* rather than what *not* to do. The following list, then, may be of value in stating the problems, but the student is urged to think "Do this" and *not* "Don't do that."

Common Technical Errors and Their Negative Effect on the Performing Group

1. The unrhythmic preparatory beat causing ragged performance of the first measure.

2. Indecision on the part of the conductor. This results in uncertain and timid response from the group.

3. Stiffness or undue tension in the shoulder (shrugging) or arm, resulting in unrhythmic time-beating and harshness of tone quality in the group.

4. A crookedly curved wrist, wrist toward the left and hand toward the right, in the effort to get the stick straight in front of the conductor. The line should be straight from elbow to knuckles of fingers. Adjustment for straightness in the baton can be made by sliding the point of contact of the heel of the stick more under the base of the thumb. When the right wrist (not hand) curves to the left, it interferes with good flexibility in the wrist and produces whole-arm conducting. This makes for a lack of definiteness in the beat-points as shown by the tip of the stick.

5. Too much impulse of will in cut-off gestures. Results in an unpleasant accent at the end of the note.

6. Reaching toward the group with the baton in general or with the left hand in making cues. Tends to push the music away from the conductor and audience. The purpose of the performance is to get the music out into the auditorium. Pull it from the players. Do not cram it back into their throats. Also, reaching toward the musicians often brings with it a bending of the torso which is anything but graceful in the view presented to the audience. It is entirely unnecessary.

7. A general tendency to make soft (p and pp) gestures much too large. This results in a lack of dynamic control and dynamic variety in the performance and a monotonous rendition.

8. Too high a rebound (reflex) in the stick after the downbeat. This results in an unreadable time-beating. It springs, usually, from too much emphasis on the rhythmic pulse and not enough attention to the forward-flowing line of the music. There is too much vertical motion and not enough horizontal distance between the beat-points.

9. Carelessness in the straight-line motion of the stick, especially in the vertical plane. When too much of the natural curve is permitted, the ictus

of the beat is often out of sight. The tip of the stick may even flick back over the conductor's right shoulder at the top of the rebound, or drop below the music stand. In the horizontal line the second beat in *FOUR* is dangerous, curving too far leftward and thereby becoming invisible for the players on the conductor's far right.

10. Too much accenting of the rhythmic pulse. This produces a strident tone from the group. It is cheer-leading, not conducting.

11. Thinking ahead too late to show a good declaration of intent, thus handicapping the group's response.

12. Fear of subtle tempo changes and variations when the music itself is fairly crying for relief from monotony. This results in static performances and mechanistic renditions.

13. Poor indications of coming tempo changes in crossing double bars. This results in ragged setting of the new tempo and poor ensemble for a measure or two. (After the last beat in the old tempo, the baton must make its preparatory beat in the new tempo.)

14. A jitter in the stick (not nervousness, but lack of real control) when it should be standing still before the gesture of syncopation. Instead of a confident entrance after the beat, the group responds with indecision and raggedness.

15. Lack of a good preparatory gesture after rests or fermatas. This results in indecisive attack.

16. Too large time-beating gestures when the group is silent or static on a sustained tone. This is annoying to the audience.

17. Lastly and most important of all, lack of flexibility in the baton wrist (it should "give" on each ictus). This results in a lack of definition in the *tip* of the stick itself. The motion is poured over the whole stick instead of being centered neatly and clearly in the tip of the stick. It eliminates any chance for the tip to describe the music—which is its function. The horizontal line between ictus-points should be well arched.

A little psychological conducting in front of your band, orchestra, or chorus once a week or so will soon tell you whether you are slipping. It is a good drill for the players, too. They watch, understand, and become flexible when these drills are used often. Conductor and conducted benefit mutually. Don't be afraid to use them!

EXERCISES FOR PRACTICE: DEVELOPING THE PSYCHOLOGICAL CONDUCTING

1. Produce the following studies by conducting someone who has no music to read from. (The conducted person can be a singing or playing musician, or a non-musician who hums a monotone in response to the gestures.)

Staccato = •
Tenuto = —
Legato, no marking

JOAN GASSAWAY

Used by permission

(More exercises are to be found in the Appendix on page 277.)

2. Use the same studies and add the staccato, legato, tenuto gestures at will, trying to get the group to respond to your indications. Do it by gesture. *Dont' talk about it.*

3. Check the example sheets in Appendix F. Then write several examples of your own for performance in class. They should be limited to the things outlined on page 233 of this chapter.

RECOMMENDED REFERENCE READINGS (SEE APPENDIX G)

Goldbeck, Frederick, *The Perfect Conductor*, pp 123–127. This reference deals with the conductor's impulse of will.

Malko, Nicolai, *The Conductor and His Baton*, Section on "Agogics," pp 213–220.

19

Public

Performance

(Musical Mastery)

After a while comes the public performance. The scores have been studied diligently, the musicians have been rehearsed to the utmost, the audience has come to the concert hall (some for love of music, others from a certain loyalty to the amateur group). The lights are dimmed and the conductor walks to the podium.

How does he walk? With confidence, with authority, and like a young man with a purpose in life. He is dignified, but friendly. He is sincere in his desire to make beautiful music and the audience, therefore, respects him. Applause which is cordial greets him and he acknowledges this with a courteous bow when he arrives at stage front. The formal bow is his only way of saying a polite "Thank you for your kindness," and later on in the program, "for your attention."

Is there something to say about this bow? Yes, there is. Heels together, arms at the sides or one arm hanging freely and the other resting on the belt; when the bow is performed, the eyes glance downward; and in the most formal of stage bows the artist holds the bowed position until he counts, not too slowly, to ten, gradually resuming the upright position as he hears the end of the count. (In opera houses on the curtain calls, often the bowed position is retained for the entire ten counts, especially if the applause is thunderous.)

The conductor steps onto the podium. He raises the baton and his left hand. The musicians are ready, but they know he is not going to start immediately. This first raising of the hands will wait for the audience to become quiet. If the audience does not respond immediately, the tip of the stick may turn sharply downward, and even rest momentarily on the music stand.

When the attention is finally centered on the stage and the hall is silent, a second quick raising of the stick alerts the musicians. "Here it comes," they say to themselves, and the downbeat follows.

Before that last quick, alerting gesture the conductor has set his tempo in his mind and has thought the sound of those opening notes. (It is his occupation while the audience is quieting.) He has also thought (especially if he is young and inexperienced) how he will make that important opening gesture. He does not alert the players until he himself is fully ready. (After all, they cannot start without him, and he is in command of the situation.) He does not begin until that wonderful moment when he, the audience, and the musicians all are ready.

In the event the audience does not come to attention as it should, he turns toward them, shoulders back, not scowling, not smiling, but looking as pleasant as possible and signifies by his conduct that he will wait until the hall is ready. A moment seems long under these circumstances, but remember, people came to listen to the concert, and (so help you!) they are going to do it. Almost any audience will quiet itself eventually if the conductor waits for it to do so. This is all part of the show. If it takes too long, he can raise his left hand (as he faces the audience), palm toward them, and just wait for silence. When it comes he proceeds with the performance as scheduled.

Conducting the Performance

Now comes the question, "What is different in the conducting of the performance as distinguished from the rehearsal-room techniques?" Two answers clamor for attention here. First, and of foremost importance, in the performance the great magnetic quality of the theater comes into being. For a while, the audience is to lay aside the cares and burdens of the daily routine and to spend a little time in another world. Everything else may be momentarily forgotten. The performance is the thing. As the absorption grows, subtle new things will creep into the music. Beauties which began to reveal themselves in the rehearsal room will suddenly take on an added luster. The music speaks in its own right.

Second, the conductor and the musicians realize that the performance must now move from beginning to end without stops for repairs. The concept of the entire work as such must be realized. And the conductor's technique, if it has been of good quality in the rehearsal, should be adequate for the performance. He will remember, however, that showmanship has its place in the public performance, and he will bear in mind the fact that he is now *"taking the audience with him,"* so that his gestures, at times, will be as much for their guidance as for that of the musicians.

In the public performance, the conductor lives his music in a way relatively impossible in the rehearsal room. In performance, he does not impose conscious control over his hands and his gestures, but rather becomes unmindful of the technical aspect and lets the music speak freely through his hands. If he has practiced conscientiously and his interpretive gestures have become habitual, he has nothing to worry about. If he has not done so, his innate instincts for cheer-leading will take over, and heaven help him!

Ending the Performance

The last note comes. It is time for the cut-off; a crucial moment! How this is done has a tremendous impact on the consequent applause. In loud endings, if the last note is permitted to peter out, the applause will be weakened. During that important last note one must not heave a sigh and think, "Good. It's over." It is *not* over until *after* the applause has started. Many endings are spoiled because this thought has been permitted to intrude itself before the last note was finished.

A fast, loud number should end brilliantly with some bravura in the cut-off, which will demand a thunder of applause. If, on the other hand, the number is meant to end softly, hold out the diminuendo and do not release the audience from its absorption in the sound until a moment of complete silence has occurred at the end. Keep the hands poised an instant after the final cut-off. Then lay the stick down slowly. If there is a delay in the applause after such an ending, it is a distinct compliment to the music itself. It is best to choose music with a bravura ending for the final number on the program.

Applause is acknowledged by the conductor at the end of each piece. In a formal concert where applause between the movements of a symphony occurs, it is generally quieted rather than accepted. However, when a furor comes and the audience demands the right to express in no uncertain terms its approval of the performance, then the applause has to be accepted, even between movements of the symphony.

The last piece is finished. The program is over. The conductor has shaken hands with the concertmaster—his way of thanking the entire orchestra for their cooperation and fine work—and he has left the stage. The applause continues. He returns *immediately* to the stage, goes to the front, bows again and leaves once more. Remember, in professional circles, *this first return to the stage is made immediately*. If not, the applause may die. Applause is money in the pockets of the performers and as such it must be encouraged. So the conductor does not dally back stage on his first exit. On the second and later exits, he may be a little more leisurely, but he is smart if he does not let the applause die for lack of interest in it. Modesty at this time is not good showmanship. And it is a false modesty, for courtesy to the audience demands a "Thank you" for their support and kind approbation.

Regarding the Soloist

What does the conductor do about all of this when there is a soloist to share in the applause? If the soloist played an important part in the music, but remained seated in his place in the orchestra, the conductor motions to him to stand and acknowledge the plaudits. If the soloist is out in front of the orchestra (a stand-up solo, as it is called), then the soloist occupies the lime-light for the nonce (*not* the conductor). At the end of the performance, the soloist turns to the conductor and shakes hands with him, thereby including conductor and orchestra in the applause. The conductor does *not* force himself into the picture by extending his hand to congratulate the soloist *before* the soloist acknowledges the presence of conductor and orchestra by turning to them to thank them. The soloist is the center of attraction at the moment, and what he does with the applause is his own business. The *appreciative* soloist always shares it with the conductor and the musicians of the ensemble.

The soloist, also, often shakes hands with the concertmaster (who is the official representative for the members of the orchestra) and thereby expresses special appreciation to the players themselves. The concertmaster should *stand* to acknowledge the handshake, either of the soloist or of the conductor. He resumes his seat immediately afterward unless a signal is given to the members of the orchestra also to stand. This sign is given by the conductor, *not* by the soloist. The musicians resume their seats when the conductor leaves the stage, sitting down when the concertmaster (or the first chair at the conductor's left when he faces the band) resumes his seat.

When there is a special soloist in front of the group, or a quartet of soloists, they precede the conductor as they enter and leave the stage. The conductor invariably goes last. If they do not include him in the applause, he simply stands quietly on the podium until the soloists are ready to leave and follows them out.

Building the Program

A word or two should be included in this chapter about the importance of the choice of program for the concert. Most formal concerts seek to achieve a climax at or near the end which will enthuse the audience to return for the next performance. "Send them home happy," is a good slogan.

Programs often open with some number that is not too long, so that late-comers may be seated during the break between the first and second selections. This is succeeded by the "big" number—the symphony, or the largest work on a band program. Usually the first half of any concert is devoted to the heavier works—while the audience is fresh. Then, as the program progresses, the lighter numbers which do not require so much concentration from the listeners follow along in sequence.

Theodore Thomas, the great founder-conductor of the Chicago Symphony Orchestra, said something to the effect that he gave the people what they wanted to hear, but he also gave them something to "chew on" at every concert. By this he meant that, in training his audiences to appreciate great music, he made sure that he got them to the concert by playing something they wanted to hear, but he also served up something they *ought* to hear and come to know and love. He remembered the audience—and he did not neglect to educate them, by exposing them to the finest in music.

In program building, the most fatal enemy is monotony. The music should be arranged so that the audience is interested throughout. This is true whether the playing organization is a grade school group or a professional symphony. And even on the grade level a good choice of variety in the music will carry the audience interest with it. Action is not to be overlooked in providing interest on this level of achievement. Let the little clarinet players stand in this piece. Let three "musicians" play this part of the piece alone. Change the lighting on the stage for one number. And there is no law against an off-stage trumpet call even if the orchestra is not playing the *Leonore No. 3*. Variety can be thousand-fold in the concerts by the younger players, and if the audience is entertained—and amused—they will love it.

CAUTION: In any public performance to be conducted with the baton, be sure it is on the conductor's music rack before the performance begins. If you are conducting without music, be sure you have the stick in your own hand as you start out on the stage.

The public performance is a necessary adjunct to the training of the student-musician. Such a performance requires the group to accept the responsibility for turning out as nearly perfect a job as possible. One very fine professional conductor who had a great knack with the good amateur orchestra used to challenge them to still better efforts with, "No. We can't sell that."

When the young conductor works with the amateur group he must have confidence in himself through a thorough knowledge of the scores, and equal confidence in his musicians, which he has gained in knowing that the rehearsing has been both sufficient and complete. Only then can he walk on the stage at concert time with the necessary assurance to inspire his players to achieve their finest performance.

RECOMMENDED REFERENCE READINGS (SEE APPENDIX G)

Boult, Adrian C., *A Handbook on the Technique of Conducting*, Section IX, p 25, "Performance."

Braithwaite, Warwick, *The Conductor's Art*, Chapter XI, pp 77–79, "Performance."

Munch, Charles, *I Am a Conductor*, Chapter IV, pp 37–44, "Making the Program;" Chapter VII, pp 68–76, "Concerts."

Prescott, Gerald R., and Lawrence W. Chidester, *Getting Results with School Bands*, Part V, "Performing for the Public;" Chapter XIX, pp 227–246, "Concert Program Building;" pp 247–258, "Contests and Festivals."

20

Creative
Conducting
(*Ultimate Mastery*)

When the student can handle successfully, neatly, and with ease, the material given in Chapter 18, he may feel that he has arrived at the place of genuine accomplishment in the performance of the basic techniques of the baton. His mind, obviously, is working; the Impulse of Will has been strengthened; and the hands are giving instant response to the directives sent out by the mind. If, in addition to this, he is *making music* as a conductor, the indications are that he is ready to branch out into the field of *creative* conducting.

But creative conducting is safe only when a state of genuine poise and confidence has arrived. It should not be unskillfully attempted before this, nor should it be made an excuse for a lack of genuine conductorial technique.

Creative conducting centers on the leader's own individual personality. Its most necessary attribute is an active imagination which will catch the spirit of the music and will play with a goodly number of ideas for variety in the baton work—never sacrificing clarity, however, for caprice.

Creativity must be approached intelligently. It has two checkreins in the form of positive answers to the following questions:

1. "Does the created gesture interpret the music better than the standard gesture?"

2. "Does it speak to the players with no attendant confusion and with added color?"

Affirmative answers speak well for the gesture. If either answer is negative, dismiss the gesture summarily from your mind.

How is the creative process carried out in relation to the conducting technique? A certain series of gestures is used to present a certain musical idea. Then a new series of motions is thought through which will describe differently, but just as accurately and just as musically, the same sequence of measures. The basic purpose is to avoid monotony. There is nothing more deadly to the musicians, the audience and the music itself than a static time-beating pattern repeated into infinity.

Time-beating gestures may be varied by size, by melding, by intensity, by the lilt and the tilt of the stick, by the speed of the motion from one point to another (a slow motion going a short distance will take as long as a faster gesture moving a greater distance), by a reshaping of the curves between the beat-points in order to describe the contour of the melody itself, and by changing the level in space of the various gestures. In all of this, the clarity of the first beat of the measure must be preserved. Its rebound should not go more than half the height of the main line of descent; but once the rebound has taken place, it is possible to raise the ictus-point for the ensuing beat.

The conductor should always work to describe, with the tip of the stick, the music in hand and the spirit underlying it. In this way the conducting can become as varied as Music itself.

And so the final words arrive . . .

Feel the texture of the tone as you call it forth. Sense that the hands and baton are molding, shaping, sculpturing a living thing, for Music is an Art that exists and breathes only while it is being performed.

Remember that certain gestures in conducting are for the purpose of guiding the listeners to what you want them to hear. The audience itself is the ultimate reason for your public performance. Respond to their intensity as they respond to yours. Listen to the music yourself and be not unmindful that *it* is speaking to *you*.

Finally, above all, be sincere and honest in your approach to the creative element in conducting. Keep modest, work hard, and do not forget the composer. "After all," as Zimbalist, the magnificent violinist, so beautifully remarked on one occasion, "the greater genius is the one who put the notes on paper in the first place. All we, as interpretive artists, can do, is do the best we can."

Appendixes

Figure A-1. This arrangement is good when the tenors and basses are strong and the sopranos and altos fully adequate.

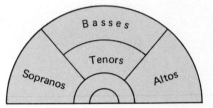

Figure A-2. A highly recommended setup is given here. Unified strength is given to the sopranos and altos in their joining behind the men's voices. This setup is also good when boys' voices are timid in school groups. The centering of tenors and basses together in front gives them confidence through proximity to the conductor.

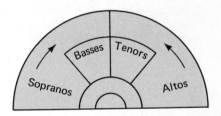

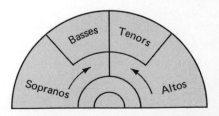

Figure A-3. A good arrangement or unity between sopranos and altos, since their voices are not split by the intervention of the men's voices.

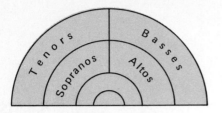

Figure A-4. This is good when tenors and basses are strong. Note that it shows the tenors on the same side as the sopranos, which is preferred by some conductors. This placement of the tenors is feasible in the preceding chart, also, if desired.

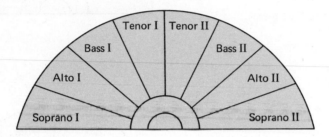

Figure A-5. The large double choir is shown here in one of the standard setups. This formation is often used in large auditoriums where the strength of the soprano sound needs to come from both sides of the stage. Otherwise, the setups of Figures A-1 through A-4 may be used with each section split into first and second parts.

NOTE: *In all of the foregoing arrangements the sopranos are located at the conductor's left, comparable in position to the first violins in the orchestra or to the leading clarinets in the band. Customarily, the lead melodies come from the conductor's left. However, there are instances in which conductors have experimented with the sopranos on the right, and a few prefer that setup.*

Special Choral Groups

Figure A-6. Three Women's Voices. *This is the standard setup for this type of vocal ensemble, owing to the usual close correlation between the first and second sopranos in vocal composition. The other choice would be with the altos in the middle.*

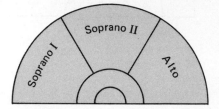

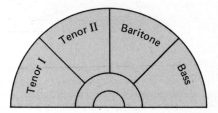

Figure A-7. Men's Chorus. *The most common arrangement is given here.*

Figure A-8. Men's Chorus. *This formation is also standard and may be used if desired or whenever it is necessary for acoustical purposes.*

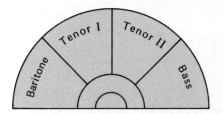

Orchestra

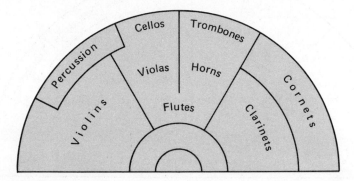

Figure A-9. Grade School Ensemble. *The present trend is to use only one violin part in the young orchestra, that is, "first" violins only. It is not wise to split a weak section into two parts. When all children play first violin, strength is confidently adequate. Most grade school orchestras have a surplus of clarinets and cornets. These should be seated at the right, blowing toward the strings. This helps to soften their tone for the audience and to hold the group together. The location of the percussion behind the strings also helps to produce good rhythm in the ensemble. Furthermore, when the percussion is too close to the young brass section, the latter usually plays much too loudly. The violins must* always *be seated at the conductor's left so that their ff-holes face the audience for maximum sound.*

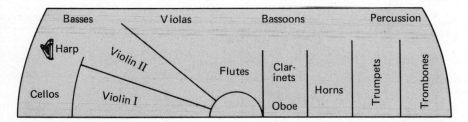

Figure A-10. Pit Orchestra. *Customarily, the pit orchestra also groups the strings on the conductor's left with the winds in the center and on the right, blowing toward the strings. This helps the balance against the stage voices. The shape of the pit has to be considered in any setup of this type. In school performances, if the pit is shallow (from audience to stage) and very extended (left and right), it helps to seat the trumpets near the front on the conductor's right. Their strength holds the group together.*

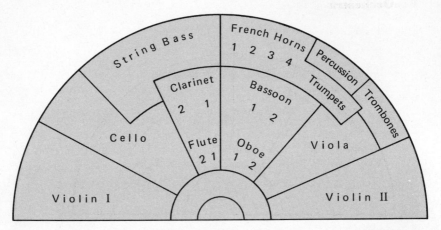

Figure A-11. Traditional Symphony Arrangement. *The difference between traditional and modern arrangements for symphony orchestras lies in the positions of the second violins, the cellos, and the basses. Compare this setup with that in Figure A-12. Four things must be observed in all orchestral setups: (1) The first violins must be on the conductor's left; (2) The first chairs in the woodwinds are grouped in the center with the sections spreading outward from them; this is for efficiency when only solo winds are called for in the score. (3) The trumpets are usually seated so that they blow somewhat across the orchestra, not directly toward the audience. (4) The basses should stand behind the cellos, since they double the cello line an octave lower almost constantly. A unified bass line results.*

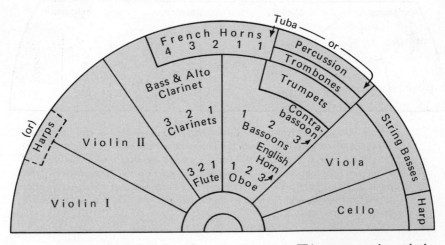

Figure A-12. Modern Symphony Arrangement. *This arrangement has evolved largely during the twentieth century, and many orchestras use it as standard now. Sometimes violas are on the outside.*

Band

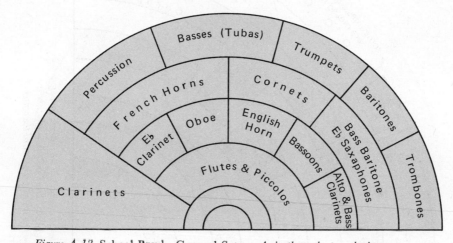

Figure A-13. School Bands, General Setup. *As in the orchestra, the instruments that play the lead melody line (the clarinets) are placed on the conductor's left as he faces the band. The trumpets and cornets are generally located so that they do not blow directly toward the audience. Sometimes two rows of clarinets replace the flutes at the conductor's right. In this case the flutes and piccolos are grouped in the center, the alto and bass clarinets are moved back a row, and the saxophones slide to their own right or are placed behind the English horn. When there are too many trombones, the baritones may be moved ahead a row, between the saxophones and the cornets. Within the clarinet section, the first clarinets are grouped near the front with the seconds and thirds filling the back part of the section—a decided difference from the seating of the second violin section in the orchestra.*

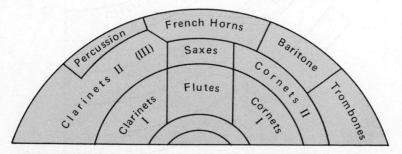

Figure A-14. Young Band, Incomplete Instrumentation. *This is a typical adaptation of the larger band setup for a grade school band.*

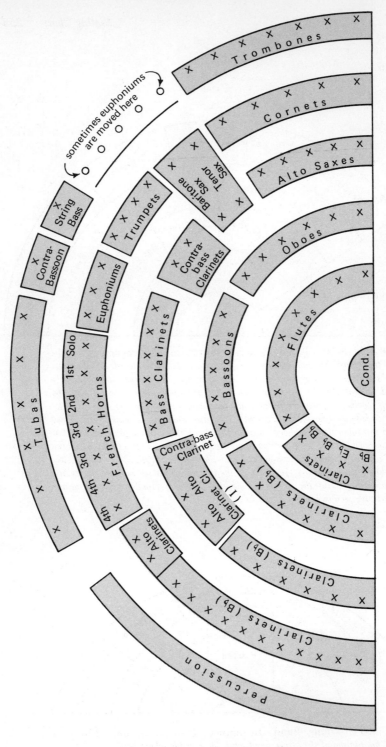

Figure A-15. Symphony Band. The setup given here is subject to variations, among which are: bassoons move from row two, center, to row three, outside right; bass clarinets and saxophones move to row four, outside right; cornets move toward the center; baritones move to back row as indicated in the figure.

B Instrumentation

Order of Instruments in the Score

ORCHESTRA

Piccolo
Flutes 1, 2
Flute 3 (sometimes plus Piccolo)
Oboes 1, 2
English horn
Clarinets 1, 2
Alto Clarinet
Bass Clarinet
Bassoons 1, 2
Contrabassoon
French horns 1, 2
French horns 3, 4
Trumpets 1, 2, 3
(Cornets)
Trombones 1, 2
Trombone 3 and Tuba
Timpani
Percussion
Harp
Violins 1
Violins 2
Violas
Cellos
Basses
To balance such an orchestra the strings would number, from violins to basses, respectively, approximately 20, 18, 12, 10, 8.

BAND

Piccolo in C(and/or D♭)
Flutes I, II
Oboes I, II
E♭ Clarinet
Clarinets I
Clarinets II
Clarinets III
E♭ Alto Clarinet
B♭ Bass Clarinet
E♭ Alto Saxophones I, II
B♭ Tenor Saxophone
E♭ Baritone Saxophone
Bassoons I, II
Cornets I
Cornets II, III
Trumpets I, II
French horns I, III
French horns II, IV
Trombones I, II
Trombones III
B♭ Baritone horns (treble clef)
Euphoniums (bass clef)
Basses
String Basses
Timpani
Percussion

Language Chart: General Terms

ENGLISH	GERMAN	FRENCH	ITALIAN
Major	Dur	Majeur	Maggiore
Minor	Moll	Mineur	Minore
B sharp	Bis, His (Kreuz)	si dièse	si diesis
B natural (ti)	H	si	si
B flat	B (Be)	si bémol	si bemolle
A sharp	Ais	la dièse	la diesis
A natural	A	la	la
A flat	As	la bémol	la bemolle
G sharp	Gis	sol dièse	sol diesis
G natural	G	sol	sol
G flat	Ges	sol bémol	sol bemolle
F sharp	Fis	fa dièse	fa diesis
F natural	F	fa	fa
F flat	Fes	fa bémol	fa bemolle
E sharp	Eis	mi dièse	mi diesis
E natural	E	mi	mi
E flat	Es	mi bémol	mi bemolle
D sharp	Dis	re dièse	re diesis
D natural	D	re	re
D flat	Des	re bémol	re bemolle
C sharp	Cis	ut dièse	do diesis
C natural	C	ut	do
C flat	Ces	ut bémol	do bemolle

Notation Terminology

UNITED STATES	BRITISH
double whole note (eight counts)	breve
whole note	semi-breve
half note	minim
quarter note	crotchet
eighth note	quaver
sixteenth note	semi-quaver
thirty-second note	demi-semi-quaver
sixty-fourth note	hemi-demi-semi-quaver

Language Chart Orchestral Instruments

ABBREVIATION	ENGLISH	GERMAN
Fl.	Flute (s)	Flöte, Flöten
Ob., Hb.	Oboe(s)	(H) oboe, (H) oboen
E. H.	English horn	Englisch Horn
Cl., Kl.	Clarinet(s)	Klarinette(n)
B. Cl., Bkl.	Bass clarinet	Bassklarinette
Bn., Fg.	Bassoon(s)	Fagott(e)
C. Bssn., Con. Bn.,	Contrabassoon	Kontrafagott(e)
C. Fag., C. Bon.		
Hn., Cor.	French horn(s)	Horn, Hörner
Tr., Tbe. (pl.)	Trumpet(s)	Trompete(n)
Crnt., Kor.	Cornet(s)	Kornett(e)
Trb., Tbn., Tbni. (pl.)	Trombone(s)	Posaune(n)
Pos.		
Tuba, Btb.	Bass Tuba(s)	Basstuba
Timp., Pk.	Timpani (pl.)	Pauke(n)
*Sn. Dr., Tr., C. C.,	Snare (side) Drum	Trommel
B. Dr., Gr. Tr.,	Bass Drum	Grosse Trommel
C., Gr. Cassa		
Cymb., Bck., Ptti.	Cymbals (pl.)	Becken (pl.)
Trgl.	Triangle	Triangel
Tmbn., Tamb.	Tambourine	Tamburin, Schellentrommel
Ch., Glk., Cloch., Camp.	Chimes	Glocken
Harp, Hpe., Arp.	Harp(s)	Harfe(n)
Vl., Vn.	Violin(s)	Violine(n)
Vla., Va., Br.	Viola(s)	Bratsche(n)
Vlc., Vc.	Cello(s)	Violoncello(-e)
Cb., Kb.	Double bass(es)	Kontrabass(-bässe)

The following instruments are seldom used in the orchestra:

Sax.	Saxophone(s)	Saxophon(e)
Bar., Eph.	Baritone horn(s) Euphonium(s)	Euphonion Baryton
Xyl.	Xylophone	Strohfiedel (Holz und Strohinstrument)

* The term tamburo is a general term meaning *drum;* tabor, small drum. For complete and detailed percussion information the Reader is referred to: *Modern School for Snare Drum,* Morris Goldenberg, Chappell & Co., New York, 1955 ©

FRENCH	ITALIAN
Flûte(s)	Flauto(-i)
Hautbois	Oboe, Oboi
Cor anglais	Corno Inglese
Clarinette(s)	Clarinetto(-i)
Clarinette-basse	Clarione, Clarinetto basso
Basson(s)	Fagotto(-i)
Contre-basson(s)	Contrafagotto(-i)
Cor(s)	Corno(-i)
Trompette(s)	Tromba, Trombe
Cornet(s)	Cornetto(-i)
Trombone(s)	Trombone(-i)
Tuba basse	Tuba di basso
Timbale(s)	Timpano(-i)
Caisse claire	Piccolo Cassa
Grosse caisse	Gran cassa
	Tamburone
Cymbales (pl.)	Piatti (pl.)
Triangle	Triangolo
Tambour de Basque	Tamburino
	Tambourine
Cloches	Campani
Harpe(s)	Arpa, Arpe
Violon(s)	Violino(-i)
Alto(s)	Viola, Viole
Violoncelle(s)	Violoncello(-i)
Contrebasse(s)	Contrabasso(-i)
Saxophone(s)	Sassofono(-i)
Baryton	Bombarda
Claquebois	Gigelira(Silofono)

Name of Bowing	Section of Bow Used	How Performed	Notation	Typical Use
ON-THE-STRING BOWINGS—STACCATO				
Martelé	Any section of the bow is practical from whole bow to half an inch of bow. ⊓ V	The bow applies pressure to the string while standing still before moving. The pressure is sufficiently released, at the instant the bow starts to move, to produce a good sound. The bow stops still at the end of the stroke, and again sets pressure preparatory to the next stroke. This bowing is the underlying foundation on which ultimate clarity of style is built.	*(musical notation)* Sometimes: *(musical notation)* Sometimes: *(musical notation)*	This bowing cannot be used in fast passage work. The tempo must be slow enough to provide time for the stopping and the setting of the bow between notes. It is used for all types of on-the-string staccatos from *pp* to *ff*. Used wherever heavy ictus is needed in the sound. Also for accents.
Slurred Staccatos	Any section of the bow is good. ⊓ and V. Most often V.	A series of martelé strokes moving in one direction of the bow. The bow does not leave the strings between notes.	*(musical notation)*	Most often written, when written, on long runs. *(musical notation)* is practical. in Moderato or slower, and *f* or heavy.
"Staccatos"	Any section of the bow. ⊓ and V	Any note with a stop at the end of it may fall under the generic term "staccato" on the stringed instruments.	Invariably printed with a dot above or below the note, but not all dots mean on-the-string staccatos. See Spiccato, Sautillé, Staccato volante, Ricochet below.	Anywhere a stop is desired after a note. The note may be long or short, but if followed by a momentary stop it is some variety of Staccato.

Whole bow Smoothly	Entire length of bow from frog to point ⊓ ∨	Bow must remain parallel with the bridge throughout its length of stroke. Requires bow-arm to reach forward as bow moves from middle to tip, and pull inward as motion goes from tip to middle.	*(Adagio notation)* — Any slow passages where breadth or length of tone is important.
Slurs	May be performed in any section of the bow. ⊓ and ∨	The bow moves smoothly in one direction while the fingers change the notes on the string or strings.	*(notation)* — Used wherever the slur-line indicates in the music. Used in legato melodic passages, in short motifs, and in scales and arpeggios where indicated.
Détaché	Middle or middle to point ⊓ ∨	Short separate bows played smoothly: *not* slurred, *not* staccato.	*(fast tempo notation)* — In passage work where the notes are of equal length and are *not* marked with staccato dots. Also used in broad figures of this type on the eighth-notes *(notation)*. Used in fast *fortes* for notes with staccato dots among slurred notes.
Louré	Any section of the bow is feasible ⊓ and ∨	The bow *continues its motion* as in any slur, but releases pressure slightly between notes so that the notes become somewhat articulated.	*(notation)* — Used for expressiveness in slurs where the notes need emotional individuality and in slurred bowings on the *same pitch* to distinguish rhythm.
Tremolo (Bowed)	Middle and middle to point ⊓ ∨	Very short separate bows, very fast. Actually a speeded-up détaché bowing. Motion centers in flexibility of the wrist. Not necessary to count the number of notes per beat. Usually indefinite.	*(Adagio notation — trem.)* — For the excitement of a fast shimmering effect in chordal accompaniments or in melodic playing. Softer effects are played near the point of the bow. Louder at the middle. If very loud, inside players on each stand broaden to détaché instead of tremolo.
Tremolo (Fingered)	Any section of the bow is practical ⊓ and ∨	The bow plays smoothly as in a slurred bowing. Fingers alternate rapidly on a pair of notes on *one string* —as rapidly as a trill.	*(notation)* — Wherever a trill-effect is desired on notes more than the interval of a second apart.

OFF-THE-STRING BOWINGS

Spiccato (Controlled)	Anywhere between frog and middle including middle ⊓ ∨	The bow is dropped on the strings and rebounds of its own accord. Must be held very lightly by hand and allowed to recoil of its own volition.	*(musical notation)*	From *pp* to *f* in passage-work where lightness and sparkling character is desired.
"Chopped"	At the frog ⊓ ∨	Similar to Spiccato, but heavier, with less finesse.	Fairly fast tempo with staccato dots on the notes. *Molto allegro* *(musical notation)*	When a spiccato effect is called for but the dynamic is too loud for a real spiccato.
Sautillé (Uncontrolled Spiccato)	Middle, and very slightly above and below the middle ⊓ ∨	A very fast détaché which is so rapid that it flies off the string each time the bow changes its direction from ⊓ to ∨, and ∨ to ⊓. The hand moves in a more perpendicular swing in the wrist joint than for tremolo.	Moderato tempi and loud dynamics. *(musical notation)* $\hat{f\!f}$ Presto *(musical notation)* and Prestissimo *(musical notation)*	In very fast, continuous passage work where lightness and speed are the requisite.
Staccato volante (Flying staccato)	A series of spiccatos in one direction of bow, ∨ -bow only	The bow is dropped on the strings, rebounds, and drops again without changing its direction, continuing in this manner.	(volante) *(musical notation)* Presto *(musical notation)*	For lightness on scale passages usually. For the two-note -bow slurred-staccato in very fast passages.
Ricochet	A series of spiccatos in one direction of the bow, ⊓ -bow only	The bow is dropped on the strings going down-bow and allowed to bounce the requisite number of times.	*(musical notation)*	Short, light, sputtering runs and "galloping" rhythms as in the William Tell Overture.
Ricochet tremolo	Middle ⊓ ∨	Two down-bow bounces followed by 2 up-bow bounces. (spiccato).	Presto *(musical notation)*	To replace the single spiccato on repeated notes, especially in fast tremolos of long duration.

From Orchestral Bowings and Routines by Elizabeth A. H. Green. Used by permission. (See Appendix G.)

D Synopsis of Musical Form

Musical Form deals with the patterns underlying the construction of our many types of musical composition. A composer, desiring to write a simple Minuet, will use a small two-part song-form. If his Minuet is to have an added Trio, he will build around the pattern of the three-part song-form. If his aim is to write the first movement of a symphony, the form adopted will usually be the Large Sonata Form. Such forms are subject to variation just as patterns for clothing are subject to variation. There is, therefore, a certain amount of flexibility to be found in the application of these forms to individual compositions.

The experienced conductor knows that one of his greatest aids to score memorization is a thorough acquaintance with the form of the particular composition being studied. Many conductors make this a point of departure. Since Musical Form is quickest grasped through the medium of the worked-out example, the following very simple development may be of assistance to the student who has not yet had formalized instruction in this branch of music theory.

The GERM of the musical thought is a basic rhythmic figure or a simple grouping of several notes:

(a) Monometer: one major accent

(b) Bimeter: two major accents

Perhaps the best-known Germ in all of music is the opening notes of Beethoven's Fifth Symphony:

The Germ may be *developed* in many ways to lend variety and interest, while preserving the feeling of unity within the work. The conductor should be alert to recognize the composer's cleverness in the handling of his motifs. Development may take place through the following means:

1. Transposition of the notes:

2. Expansion of the intervals between the notes:

3. Contraction of the intervals between the notes:

4. Diminution of the note time-values:

5. Repetition of the members of the motif:

6. Omission of members of the motif:

7. Irregular changes in the order of the notes, rhythm unchanged:

8. Retrograde motion, rhythm unchanged:

9. Combinations of members of the Germ:

10. Inversion: turning the intervals upside-down:

11. Various combinations of the foregoing, used simultaneously; as Inversion and Repetition:

The development of the Germ often results in the MOTIF, the basic thought of the composition. In the case of our example, it might be stated as follows:

The next example presents (1) the Motif (first two measures), (2) the Phrase (second two measures), (3) the Period, ending on the eighth measure, (4) the second theme of a Two-part Song-form, ending on the sixteenth measure. This simple form may be enlarged greatly by the composer by doubling the length of each section as given here in the small form:

The Two-Part Song-Form

When the second theme of a Two-part Song-form is followed by the first theme again, then the Three-part Song-form results. This is shown in the next example:

The Completed Three-Part Song-Form

In a real musical composition, the length could be doubled by marking repeat dots at the double bars. The composition may further be lengthened by the addition of Introduction and Coda, each of which may assume quite some proportion in the larger compositions.

The gradual expansion of Form proceeds as follows: (Refer to the preceding examples.)

The PHRASE: four or eight measures ending with a cadence or a half cadence.

The PERIOD: eight or sixteen measures. If it is eight measures, it is then four plus four, with a cadence separating it from the next section; or if sixteen, then eight measures ending on the Dominant, plus another eight measures ending on the Tonic. (The shorter form was used in the tune developed herein.)

The TWO-PART SONG-FORM (A–B): eight measures ending on the Dominant (Section A) and eight measures ending on the Tonic (Section B). In the long form, each section is sixteen measures instead of eight.

The THREE-PART SONG-FORM (A–B–A): Short form, eight measures (A), eight measures (B), eight measures of (A) used as a D.C. Long form, sixteen measures each.

The RONDO forms: A Rondo is like a layer cake where the cake is always the same but the filling between each layer is different. Technical names are Theme and Episode. The Theme, either in its original form or embellished, occurs more than twice in the Rondo form. For specialized details, the reader is referred to one of the books on Musical Form in Appendix G.

The THEME AND VARIATIONS: the theme usually consists of four or more measures. It can be followed by any number of variations the composer may wish to write. These variations may take the form of embellishments of the melody, changing meters and rhythms, changes in mode, developments of germs drawn from the principal theme, and clever adaptations of the various devices numbered 1 to 11 in the fore-part of this discussion. In the classical period, these transformations adhered rather closely to the original harmonic structure, but this is not true in the subsequent writings. Classed as types of Theme and Variation are the often-encountered CHACONNE and PASSACAGLIA.

The FUGUE concerns itself with a principal theme called the subject. As each instrument enters, it plays the subject, previously stated in another instrument. Once having stated the subject the instrument continues with counterpoint to the subject, which counterpoint may be called the countersubject when it has an individual character of its own and recurs repeatedly. The first instrument states the subject in the Tonic key; the second instrument renders the subject either a fifth higher or a fourth lower than the original instrument. Such a statement is called the *answer*. The third instrument usually states the theme an octave higher or lower than the original instrument, and it, in turn, is followed by a fourth instrument on the subject—this in the case of a four-voice fugue. The conductor's job is to see that each statement of the theme is clearly heard as such. When the third voice enters, balance requires the two voices already playing to be toned down. Most fugues have a stretto section where the subject and answer are brought as close together as possible. Many fugues include a coda.

The (early) CLASSICAL SONATA FORM: Part I is usually somewhat in excess of a sixteen-measure unit. It starts in the Tonic key and modulates to the Dominant, in which key the first part ends at the double bar. Part II starts again with the first theme, but this time in the key of the Dominant and gradually moves back into the Tonic for the ending of the movement. If the first part is in a minor key, then the modulation before the double bar may go to the Major with the section following the bar in the Major.

The LARGE SONATA FORM is used almost invariably for the first movement of the multiple-movement works such as symphonies, quartets, solo sonatas of the romantic and post-romantic periods, and solo concertos after the early classic period. (In the latter, a lengthy orchestral exposition precedes that of the solo instrument.) Part I of this form is called the *Exposition*. It is comprised of two themes of contrasting character, the first in the Tonic key, the second in the Dominant. Part II, the *Development*, is to be found after the double bar in the classic and romantic symphonies. This concerns itself with the rather exhaustive treatment or "development" of motifs drawn from the first two themes. Part III is called the *Recapitulation*. It brings in the material of the Exposition once again. In the classical use of this form, the second theme is in the Tonic key in the Recapitulation. This form is often expanded by a lengthy introduction (usually slow) and a closing theme or codetta which is present (if not of major importance) in Mozart and Haydn symphonies and sometimes assumes the proportions of another major theme in the works of the romantic period (Brahms symphonies, for example).

The MODERN SONATA FORM in use today is far freer than its predecessors in its motion, in its key relationships, and its general structure. The double bar, which is an almost ever-present adjunct of the Large Sonata Form, is most often missing in the modern version.

Let us emphasize again that this short summary gives only the obvious and most generalized structures. In actual composition, each work has its own idiosyncrasies and the work states its form rather than the form stating the work.

Any of the forms discussed herein, except the Fugue and the Modern Sonata Form, may be found lengthened by the composer through the addition of repeat dots at the double bars.

The reader is now referred to Arnold Schoenberg's "*Models for Beginners in Composition*," New York, G. Schirmer, 1942–43, and to "*The Symphony and the Symphonic Poem (Analytical and Descriptive Charts)*" by Earl V. Moore and Theodore E. Heger, Edwards Brothers (Ann Arbor), 1949.

E Terminology
for the Conductor

The following list of one hundred terms is comprised of foreign language designations which the young conductor should know. Common words such as legato, allegro, etc., are not included in the list. It is taken for granted that the college student in music will know such customary markings. The terms given here are frequently encountered in conducting the standard repertoire and the school music of a training nature. A lack of knowledge of these words can cause the conductor to make bad mistakes, rhythmically, musically, and in handling the instrumentation and routines generally. Since the lists are limited to the more common terms, the student will have to resort to the large musical dictionary for further help when needed.

Classification is made alphabetically under three headings: (1) Terms of a general nature, (2) Terms affecting the tempo and time-beating, (3) Terms affecting the handling of the instruments themselves.

Terms of a General Nature

A DUE (*a 2*). To be played by both, as by first and second flute.

COLLA PARTE. With the other part; often refers to accommodating the soloist at that place in the score.

COME PRIMA. Like the first time.

COME STA. Exactly as written; do not change anything.

CON. With; seen in other forms as a contraction with the article in Italian, thus: *col, coi, colle, cogli, colla* (depending upon the gender and number).

EN DEHORS. Out in front of; means the part so marked should be projected through the ensemble; it must be heard.

ERSTES MAL. The first time.

FORTE POSSIBILE. As loud as possible.

FRAPPÉ; FRAPPER. The downbeat; to beat time.

GLISSEZ; GLISSER. Slide; to slide.

IMMER. Always

L'ISTESSO (LO STESSO). The same; used usually with the word *tempo*, meaning that the new part should be in the same tempo as the preceding part.

MARCATO. Marked, accented.

MENO. Less.

MEZZO. Half; usually *mezza voce*, softly, as if whispered.

MODO. Style, manner.

MORENDO. Dying away.

MOTO. Motion.

MURKEY BASS. Broken octaves, lower note coming first.

MUTA. Change; usually reads *muta in* _____, meaning change the instrument to the pitch designated. Most often seen in timpani and French horn parts.

OHNE. Without; usually *ohne Dämpfer*, without mute.

OSSIA. Otherwise; often refers to a simplified part—otherwise do it so.

PARTITUR. The score.

PETIT. Little.

PEU. A little.

PIACERE, A PIACERE. At pleasure.

PIENO. Full.

PIU. *More;* most often seen with *mosso*, meaning more motion, slightly quicken the tempo. Also, plus.

PULT. Desk, a music stand. Usually refers to number of stands which are to play the part.

RIPIENO. similar to *tutti*, It distinguishes the accompanying instruments from the soloist.

RUHIG. Tranquil.

SCHNELL. Quick, rapid, *presto*.

SCIOLTO. Fluently.

SCORDATURA. Tuning contrary to the normal, addressed to the strings.

SEC, SECCO. Dry, very short, no after-ring.

SEGUE. Follow, continue in the same manner.

SEHR. Very.

SENZA. Without; usually *senza sordini*, without mutes.

SMORZANDO. Suddenly dying away.

SOTTO VOCE. In an undertone, soft voice.

SPIANAR LA VOCE. With smooth voice.

STENTATO. Labored.

STIMME. A single voice or part in the score.

STREPITOSO. Noisily.

STRISCIANDO, STRISCIATO. Legato motion, smooth.

SUBITO. Suddenly; usually with a *piano* marking.

TROPPO. Too much.

TUTTI. The whole ensemble, everybody.

UNISONI. In unison; as *violini unisoni*, all violins in unison.

VIDE. A cut; VI is printed where the cut starts and DE is shown at the end of the cut, thus: VI . . . DE.

VIRGULA. The old terminology for the baton.

VOCI PARI. Equal voices.

Terms Affecting the Tempo and Time-Beating

A PUNTO. Exactly in rhythm.

ACCELERANDO. Gradually increasing the tempo.

AD LIBITUM. At liberty; take time, permit liberties here.

AFFRETTANDO. Excitedly, increasing the tempo.

CON ALCUNA LICENZA. With some license; not perfectly rhythmic.

ETWAS LANGSAMER. Somewhat slower.

IM TAKT. In tempo.

LANGSAM, LANGSAMER. Slow, slower.

MÄSSIG. Moderato.

PRESSANDO. Hurrying, pressing forward.

RHYTHMÉ. Rhythmic feeling emphasized.

RUBATO. Varying the note values within the rhythm, not strictly as written.

STRETTO. Condensing, accelerating the tempo. (Do not confuse with the stretto of the fugue form, which is only a condensing of the distance between subject and answer.)

STRINGENDO. Accelerating the tempo.

SUIVEZ. Follow; usually refers to following the soloist who may take some liberties with the tempo for expression.

TACET. Silent; usually means the particular instrument does not play in that movement of the work.

TAGLIO. A cut.

TAKT. The time, the measure, rhythmically; sometimes, an accenting of the first beat in the measure.

TEMPO PERDITO. Unsteady tempo.

TEMPO REGGIATO. Regulate the tempo, usually to accommodate the soloist.

TEMPO RUBATO. Not strictly on the beat.

ZURÜCKHALTEN. Ritard.

NOTE: the term *Agogic* is a general classification for the modifying of the tempo in favor of the expression.

Terms Affecting the Handling of the Instruments Themselves

A PUNTO D'ARCO. At the point of the bow.

AM STEG. Played with a light bow stroke very close to the bridge so that the quality of the tone is shimmering, sounding the component harmonics of the fundamental tone (*Ponticello*).

ARCO. Bow, with the bow.

ARCHET. Bow, with the bow.

COL LEGNO. With the stick of the bow; usually performed by striking the strings with the stick of the bow.

CON SORDINI. With mutes.

DÄMPFER. Mute; usually *mit Dämpfer*, with mute, or *ohne Dämpfer*, without mute. Often seen as *gedämpft* (stopped) in horn parts.

FIRST TREBLE; SECOND TREBLE. First soprano; second soprano.

LEGNO. Wood (of the bow).

OTEZ. Remove (the mute).

PAUKENSCHLAGEL—the timpani stick.

PONTICELLO. Light tone near the bridge so upper partials sound in the tone.

SORDINO. Mute; also *sourdine*.

SPITZE. Point of the bow.

STEG. Bridge.

STIMMUNG. The tuning.

SULLA TASTIERA; SUL TASTO. On the fingerboard; a command to bow the string just over the end of the fingerboard for a light, flute-like tone.

SUR LE CHEVALET. Literally, "on the little (wooden) horse," bowed very close to the bridge, *ponticello*.

SUR LA TOUCHE. On the fingerboard, same as *sulla tastiera*.

SUR UNE CORDE. On one string; the melody to be played entirely on one string. The German word for string is *Saite*.

TON BOUCHÉ. Stopped tone in French horn playing.

+. Refers to plucking the string with the *left* hand when used in string music, and to playing the notes so marked as stopped tones on the French horns when given in their parts.

F Additional Practice Problems, Written Examination Forms

Practice Problems

PROBLEMS IN CHANGING METER, CHANGING STYLE,
AND NUMBER OF MEASURES

Each example should be repeated without pause, until easy.
1. Two measures in TWO, legato; one measure in THREE, staccato.
2. Two measures in FOUR, staccato; one measure in THREE, tenuto.
3. Two measures in TWO, tenuto; one measure in FOUR, staccato.
4. Two measures in THREE, staccato; one measure in FOUR, legato.
5. One measure in ONE, legato; two measures in TWO, staccato.
6. Three measures in ONE, staccato; one measure in SIX, legato.
7. Three measures in TWO, tenuto; one measure in FOUR, staccato.
8. Two measures in THREE, legato; one measure "dead" gesture.
9. Two measures in TWO, tenuto; one measure in ONE, dead gesture: the length of the measures remains the same throughout.
10. Two measures in TWO, staccato; one measure in FOUR, legato, with a gesture of syncopation on Four.
11. Two measures in THREE, legato; one measure in FOUR, tenuto, with a cue in the left hand on the third beat of the four-beat measure.
12. Three measures in TWO, legato; one measure in FOUR, dead gestures,

with a cue in the *left hand only* on the third beat of the dead-gesture measure.

13. Two measures in FOUR, legato; one measure in THREE, gesture of syncopation on each beat. (Think the sound of the after-beat articulations.)

14. One measure in fast THREE, legato; two measures in ONE; length of the *measures* remains the same throughout.

MORE DIFFICULT PROBLEMS

The following problems are more difficult to execute because more is demanded of the mind. *Four* factors change in each problem instead of three as in the preceding exercises. Here the number of measures changes, the meter, the style and the dynamic. This requires smaller gestures and some control with the left hand for the indication of *piano*. Do not attempt these until the mind works easily on the first set of studies. Each study is to be repeated many times without a break between repeats.

1. Two measures in TWO, legato-piano; one measure in THREE, tenuto-forte. Practice also with reversed dynamics.

2. Two measures in TWO, staccato-forte; one measure in THREE, legato-piano. Practice with reversed dynamics.

3. Two measures in TWO, tenuto-forte; three measures in THREE, staccato-piano. Use also reversed dynamics.

4. Two measures in TWO, legato-forte; one measure in THREE, gesture of syncopation, piano. Reverse the dynamics.

5. One measure in FOUR, tenuto-forte; two measures in TWO, gesture of syncopation, piano. Reverse the dynamics.

6. Two measures in FOUR, legato-piano; one measure in THREE, gesture of syncopation, forte. Reverse the dynamics.

7. One measure in FIVE (3 + 2) using legato on the "3" and staccato on the "2." Follow this with one measure in a very broadly accented FOUR.

8. Two measures in FIVE, (2 + 3), each measure moving from *piano* to *forte* during its five beats, followed by three measures in TWO, staccato-piano.

PROBLEMS IN THE FERMATA

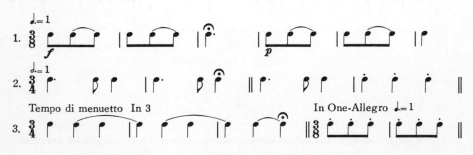

continued

Compose melodies to fit the stated rhythms and sing them as these examples are practiced.

PROBLEMS FOR PSYCHOLOGICAL CONDUCTING

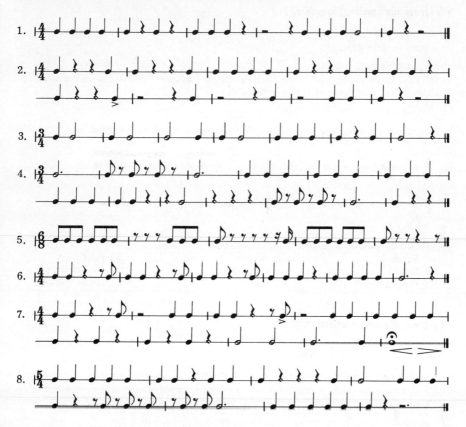

Written Examination No. 1

A FEW FUNDAMENTALS

1. Diagram the following beats:
    (a) Four beats per measure   (b) Three beats per measure   (c) Nine beats per measure
2. Diagram the four varieties of time-beating in two:
    (a)   (b)   (c)   (d)

3. Diagram the preparatory beat and one full measure for each of the following:

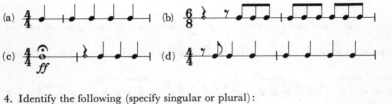

4. Identify the following (specify singular or plural):
    (a) hautbois   (d) Becken   (g) piatti
    (b) fagotti   (e) Bratsche   (h) cor anglais
    (c) Posaune   (f) corni   (i) corno Inglese

Written Examination No. 2

THE EXPRESSIVE GESTURES

1. Every conducting gesture has three parts. They are
    (1) _____
    (2) _____
    (3) _____
2. Conducting gestures are divided into two main categories, which are:
    The_____gestures.   The_____gestures.
    These are characterized by the presence of   These are characterized by the absence of
    _____   _____
    These require_____from   These require_____from
    the players.   the players.
3. Under this heading are to be found the   Under this heading are to be found the
    following gestures: following gestures:
    (1) _____   (5) _____
    (2) _____   which are used in the following places:
    (3) _____   (1) _____
    (4) _____   (2) _____
                                             (3) _____
4. Each of the gestures above is performed in the following manner:
    (1) _____
    (2) _____
    (3) _____
    (4) _____
    (5) _____
5. Time-beating in 1-to-the-bar differs from all other types of time-beating in that_____
    _____
6. Diagram 12/8 time in twelve.

Written Examination No. 3

APPLICATION OF THEORY

1. What type of gesture should be used at the places indicated in the example given below?
   (20)

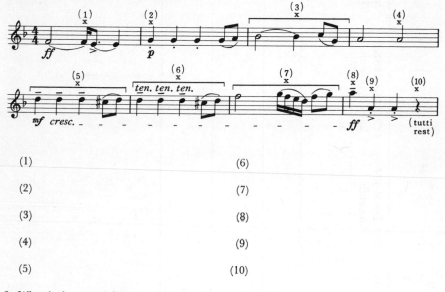

(1)   (6)

(2)   (7)

(3)   (8)

(4)   (9)

(5)   (10)

2. What is the *general* direction of the preparatory beat? (1)
3. What is the *specific* direction of a preparatory beat? (1)
4. What things should a good preparatory beat show? (2)
5. Define the word fermata. (2)
6. Discuss the use of the left hand in (1) dynamics, (2) cues, (3) time-beating, (4) phrasing, (5) the preparatory beat, (6) the cut-off. (24)

Written Examination No. 4

General Topic	BACH-HANDEL Early Classic	MOZART-HAYDN Later Classic	BEETHOVEN Romantic	TCHAIKOWSKI Later Romantic	MODERN CLASSICAL
Style in general for the period					
Harmonic structure					
Use of Dynamic Markings					
Style in use of the Staccato					
Rhythmic Structure					

Written Examination No. 5

SCORE STUDY

Study the sheet of score from Mendelssohn's Third Symphony, Op. 56 on page 282.
1. Write the harmonic analysis for the chords.
2. Figure out your transpositions, converting the written notes to concert pitches, on the lines given immediately below.

In A   In D   In B♭

3. Name each instrument in the score, specifying whether one or more is indicated.
   1.   7.
   2.   8.
   3.   9.
   4.   10.
   5.   11.
   6.   12.
4. List some of the motifs, or germs of motifs, used on this page of score:

5. Describe the gestures you would use in performing this music. (Measures are numbered above the timpani line.)

Mendelssohn, *Symphony No. 3* ("*Scotch*") *in A major*, Op. 56. First movement (measures 37–42).

Written Examination No. 6

TRANSPOSITIONS

Trombone I+II

Trombones

Violas

Trumpet in D

Trombones I+II

Trombone 3

Tubas

Horn in G

Horn in D

SOUNDS

Horn in E

Horn in C

SOUNDS

Piccolo in C

SOUNDS

Alto Flute in G

Eng. Horn

Oboe II

SOUNDS

Horn in E♭

SOUNDS

Horn in G

SOUNDS

Cornets in B♭

SOUNDS

G Bibliography

The following books are specifically mentioned in the Recommended Reference Readings.

Bakaleinikoff, Vladimir, *Elementary Rules of Conducting*. New York: Belwin, Inc., 1938.

Bamberger, Carl, *The Conductor's Art*. New York: McGraw-Hill Book Company, 1965.

Berry, Wallace, *Form in Music*. Englewood Cliffs, New Jersey: Prentice-Hall, Inc., 1966.

Blackman, Charles, *Behind the Baton*. New York: Charos Enterprises, Inc., 1964 (Carl Fischer, Inc., sole selling agents).

Blaukopf, Kurt, *Great Conductors*. Trans. Miriam Blaukopf. London: Arco Publishers, 1955.

Boult, Adrian C., *A Handbook on the Technique of Conducting*. Oxford: Hall the Printer, Ltd., 1936.

Braithwaite, Warwick, *The Conductor's Art*. London: Williams and Norgate, Ltd., 1952.

Chotzinoff, Samuel, *Toscanini, An Intimate Portrait*. New York: Alfred A. Knopf, Inc., 1956.

Christiani, Adolf F., *Principles of Expression in Pianoforte Playing*. New York: Harper Brothers, 1886 (Broude).

Coward, Henry, *Choral Technique and Interpretation*. London: Novello & Co., Ltd. N.D. (Also, New York: H. W. Gray Co.)

Crist, Bainbridge, *The Art of Setting Words to Music*. New York: Carl Fischer, Inc., 1944.

Crocker, Richard L., *A History of Musical Style*. New York: McGraw-Hill Book Company, 1966.

Davison, Archibald T., *Choral Conducting*. Cambridge: Harvard University Press, 1940.

————, *The Technique of Choral Composition*. Cambridge: Harvard University Press, 1945.

Earhart, Will, *The Eloquent Baton*. New York: M. Witmark and Sons, 1931.

Finn, William Joseph, *The Conductor Raises His Baton*. New York: Harper Brothers, 1944.

Gal, Hans, *Directions for Score Reading*. Vienna: Wiener Philharmonischer Verlag, No. 439, 1924.

Goldbeck, Frederick, *The Perfect Conductor*. Pellegrini and Cudahy, 1951 (by Frederick Goldbeck).

Goldman, Edwin Franko, *Band Betterment*. New York: Carl Fischer, 1934.

Goldman, Richard Franko, *The Concert Band*. New York: Rinehart and Co., Inc., 1946.

Green, Elizabeth A. H., *Orchestral Bowings and Routines*. Second Edition. Ann Arbor: Ann Arbor Publishers, 1957 (by Elizabeth A. H. Green).

Grosbayne, Benjamin, *Techniques of Modern Orchestral Conducting*. Cambridge: Harvard University Press, 1956.

Howerton, George, *Technique and Style in Choral Singing*. New York: Carl Fischer, Inc., 1957.

Jacob, Gordon, *How to Read a Score*. London: Hawkes and Son, 1944. (Boosey & Hawkes in the United States.)

Jones, Archie M., *Techniques of Choral Conducting*. New York: Carl Fischer, Inc., 1948.

Kahn, Emil, *Conducting*. New York: The Macmillan Company, 1965.

Kennan, Kent, *The Technique of Orchestration*. New York: Prentice-Hall, Inc., 1952.

Krueger, Karl, *The Way of the Conductor*. New York: Charles Scribner's Sons, 1958 (by Karl Krueger).

Lang, Philip J., *Scoring for the Band*. New York: Mills Music, Inc., 1950.

Leidzén, Erik, *An Invitation to Band Arranging*. Philadelphia: Oliver Ditson Co., 1950

Malko, Nicolai, *The Conductor and His Baton*. Copenhagen: Wilhelm Hansen, 1950.

Marshall, Madeleine, *The Singer's Manual of English Diction*. New York: G. Schirmer, 1956, 1957, 1951, 1953.

Matthay, Tobias, *Musical Interpretation*. Boston: Boston Music Co., 1913.

McElheran, Brock, *Conducting Technique, for Beginners and Professionals*. New York: Oxford University Press, 1966.

Moore, Earl V. and Theodore E. Heger, *The Symphony and Symphonic Poem*. Ann Arbor: Edwards Brothers, Inc., 1949.

Mozart, Leopold, "A Treatise on the Fundamental Principles of Violin Playing." Trans., Edith Knocker. London: Oxford University Press (1856), 1948.

Munch, Charles, *I Am a Conductor*, New York: Oxford University Press, 1955.

Pietzsch, Hermann, *Die Trompete. The Trumpet*, ed. by Clifford Lillya and Renold Schilke. Ann Arbor: University Music Press, Inc., N.D.

Piston, Walter, *Orchestration*. New York: W. W. Norton Co., 1955.

Prescott, Gerald R. and Lawrence W. Chidester, *Getting Results with School Bands*. Minneapolis: Paul A. Schmitt, 1938. Third printing with Carl Fischer, Inc., 1939.

Read, Gardiner, *Thesaurus of Orchestral Devices*. New York: Pitman Publishing Co., 1953.

Rimsky-Korsakoff, Nicolai, *Principles of Orchestration*. Vol. 1. London: Russian Music Agency, N.D.

Rogers, Bernard, *The Art of Orchestration*. New York: Appleton, Century, Crofts, Inc., 1951.

Rood, Louise, *How to Read a Score*. New York: Edwin F. Kalmus, Inc., 1948.

Rudolf, Max, *The Grammar of Conducting*. New York: G. Schirmer, Inc., 1950.

Scherchen, Hermann, *Handbook of Conducting*. London: Oxford University Press, 1933.

Schoenberg, Arnold, *Models for Beginners in Composition*. New York: G. Schirmer, Inc., 1942.

Schonberg, Harold C., *The Great Conductors*. New York: Simon and Schuster, 1967.

Schwartz, Harry W., *Bands of America*. New York: Doubleday and Co., Inc., 1957.

Thomas, Theodore and Frederick Stock, *Talks About Beethoven's Symphonies*. Boston: Oliver Ditson Co., 1930.

Wagner, Joseph, *Band Scoring*. New York: McGraw-Hill Book Co., Inc., 1960.

————, *Orchestration, A Practical Handbook*. New York: McGraw-Hill Book Co., Inc., 1959.

Wagner, Richard, *On Conducting*. London: William Reeves, 1897.

Weingartner, Felix, *On Conducting the Beethoven Symphonies*. London: Breitkopf and Haertel, 1907 (trans. Jessie Crosland). (Also, New York: Kalmus.)

Wodell, Frederick W., *Choir and Chorus Conducting*. Philadelphia: Theodore Presser Co., 1931.

Worrell, J. W., "*Music by the Masters*," The Instrumentalist, XIV, No. 3 (1959), pp. 46–47. 92.

The following books are closely related to this field of endeavor and are also highly recommended for reference reading. They are, however, not mentioned specifically in the main part of the book.

Andrews, Frances M. and Joseph A. Leeder, *Guiding Junior High School Pupils in Music Experiences*. New York: Prentice-Hall, Inc., 1953.

Berlioz, Hector, *A Critical Study of Beethoven's Nine Symphonies*. Trans. Edwin Evans. London: William Reeves, N.D.

Brindle, Reginald Smith, *Serial Composition*. London: Oxford University Press, 1966.

Bussler, Ludwig, *The Theory and Practice of Musical Form*. Ed. by J. H. Cornell. New York: G. Schirmer, 1883.

Carse, Adam, *The Orchestra in the XVIIIth Century*. Cambridge: W. Heffer and Sons, Ltd., 1940.

Davis, Ennis, *More than a Pitch Pipe*. Boston: C. C. Birchard and Co., 1941.

Dykema, Peter and Hannah M. Cundiff, *School Music Handbook*. Boston: C. C. Birchard and Co., 1955.

Ewen, David, *The Man with the Baton*. New York: Thomas Y. Crowell Co., 1936.

Finn, William J., *The Art of the Choral Conductor*. Boston: C. C. Birchard and Co., 1939, 1960 (Second Edition, two volumes).

Forsyth, Cecil, *Orchestration*. New York: The Macmillan Co., 1914, 1935, 1941 (Second Edition).

Gallo, Stanislao, *The Modern Band*. Boston: C. C. Birchard and Co., 1935.

Garland, Wallace Graydon, *Popular Songwriting Methods*. New York: American Music Guild, Inc., 1942.

Gardner, Maurice, *The Orchestrator's Handbook:* Great Neck: Staff Music Publishing Co., 1948.

Holmes, Malcolm, *Conducting an Amateur Orchestra*. Cambridge: Harvard University Press, 1951.

Jacob, Gordon, *Orchestral Technique*. London: Oxford University Press, 1931.

Kagen, Sergius, *On Studying Singing*. New York: Dover Press, 1950.

Kufferath, Maurice, *L'art de diriger l'orchestre*. Paris: Librarie Fischbacher, 1890.

Leeder, Joseph A. and William S. Haynie, *Music Education in the High School*. Englewood Cliffs: Prentice-Hall, Inc., 1958.

Nallin, Walter E., *The Musical Idea*. New York: The Macmillan Co., 1968.

Otterstein, Adolph W., *The Baton in Motion*. New York: Carl Fischer, Inc., 1940, 1942.

Prout, Ebenezer, *Musical Form*. London: Augener and Co., 1893 (fourth edition). (Theodore Presser Co., U.S.A.).

Schoenberg, Arnold, *Style and Idea*. New York: Philosophical Library, Inc., 1950.

Van Bodegraven, Paul and Harry Robert Wilson, *The School Music Conductor*. Chicago: Hall and McCreary Co., 1942.

Van Hoesen, Karl, *Handbook of Conducting*. New York: F.S. Crofts and Co., 1944.

Topical Index

Index to Figures
and Musical Examples

Italic type refers to number of Figure or Musical Example.